REREADING LITERATURE

W. H. Auden

REREADING LITERATURE
General Editor: Terry Eagleton

W. H. Auden

Stan Smith

Basil Blackwell

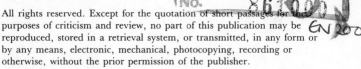
© Stan Smith 1985

First published 1985

Basil Blackwell Ltd
108 Cowley Road, Oxford OX4 1JF, UK

Basil Blackwell Inc.
432 Park Avenue South, Suite 1505,
New York, NY 10016, USA

British Library Cataloguing in Publication Data

Smith, Stan, *1943–*
    W. H. Auden. –(Rereading literature)
    1. Auden, W. H. –Criticism and interpretation
    I. Title   II. Series
    821'.912   PR6001.UAZ/

    ISBN 0–631–13381–X
    ISBN 0–631–13515–4 Pbk

Library of Congress Cataloging in Publication Data

Smith, Stan, 1943–
    W. H. Auden.
    (Re-reading literature)
    Bibliography: p.
    Includes index.
    1. Auden, W. H. (Wystan Hugh), 1907–1973 – Criticism and interpretation.   I. Title.   II. Series.
PR6001.U4Z826 1985   811'.52   85–5990
ISBN 0–631–13381–X
ISBN 0–631–13515–4 (pbk.)

Typeset by System 4 Associates, Gerrards Cross, Buckinghamshire
Printed in Great Britain by Whitstable Litho Ltd, Kent

Contents

To those who live in Warrington or Wigan,
or who lived there when Auden wrote the line.

Editor's Preface

Literary criticism has constructed a whole range of W. H. Audens, each one with some claim to being the genuine article. There is the precocious public-school Marxist of the early poetry, slick, clinical and too clever by half, the intellectual flirt or brainy exhibitionist peddling portentous scraps of psychoanalysis in a verse so arrogantly obscurantist that it is sometimes hard to say whether it urges Fascism or communism. In one narrative, this emotionally retarded adolescent matures into the civilized Christian liberal of the later work, full of social charm, transcendental mystery and dazzling technical virtuosity. In an alternative reading, the later Auden is an overbred coterie versifier whose fussily inbred craft, garrulous and emptily versatile, contrasts poorly with the lean economy and political urgency of the younger poet. One can speak, then, of two different Audens, praising one and up-braiding the other; or one can reject this duality and assert the underlying continuity of the poet's persona, for either good or bad, all the way from angry socialism to Anglican serenity.

In a challengingly original move, Stan Smith's study settles for neither two Audens nor one. It aligns itself neither with those critics who have applauded Auden for abandoning politics, nor with those who have reproved him for it – not because it seeks to occupy some barren middle ground, but because it dismisses the whole notion that Auden simply 'abandoned politics' as absurdly simplistic. Power, authority, subjugation, liberation, 'deviant' sexuality, the just society: these concerns, as Smith intricately demonstrates, remain just as pressing in the later as in the earlier Auden, though cast in a quite different idiom. In this perspective, the playfulness and multiple ironies of the later poet can be read not as a defeatist political withdrawal, but as an instance of that 'carnivalesque' spirit, subverting the solemnities of bourgeois authority with the iconoclasm of humour and the body, which connects with the 'anarcho-communism' of Auden's Blakean youth.

Yet this is not to claim, on the other hand, that Auden's work manifests an essential unity. For what 'unites' the poetry all the way through, as Smith eloquently shows, is paradoxically nothing less than the themes of doubleness, multiplicity and division – the drama of the deconstructed self, which knows itself to be lived by powers beyond its own making, the product of historical antagonisms, the infinite plurality of language and the warring forces of the unconscious. It is in this refusal of closure, and of a 'natural', singular identity and absolute truth that Smith locates the persistent radicalism of W. H. Auden – that provisional assemblage of forms, idioms and personae which never mistook itself for anything like a genuine article, and which in refusing the allure of authenticity bore constant witness to the realm of struggle and division which is history itself.

Terry Eagleton

Acknowledgements

I should like to thank Terry Eagleton for asking me to write on Auden just when I was thinking of doing so; Penny Wilson, Heather Glen, Kiernan Ryan and the fellows of New Hall, Cambridge, for many kindnesses during a sabbatical's reading; Catherine Drucker and Francesco Binni for advice and comments on Auden; and R. J. C. Watt for reading the various drafts with enthusiasm and glee. Special thanks go, as ever, to Jennifer Birkett, for her tireless and at times ruthless reading and rereading of the text, and her many splendid suggestions, some of them literary. I am also grateful to Philip Carpenter for his kindness and encouragement, and to Stephan Chambers and Claire Andrews for their astute editing – the kindest cuts of all. Finally, I must record once more my gratitude to the librarians of Cambridge University Library, and, at a time when education cuts are eating deeply into already scant resources, to those of Dundee University Library, for their helpfulness and advice.

Grateful acknowledgement is made to Random House, Inc. for permission to quote from the copyrighted works of W. H. Auden; and to Faber and Faber for permission to quote from Auden's *Collected Poems* and *The English Auden*, both edited by Edward Mendelson.

Author's Note

Sections of this book, in particular, chapters on the plays and on the critical reception of Auden, have had to be cut for reasons of space; it is hoped that they will appear elsewhere in due course. For the same reasons, the bibliography has been largely restricted to primary sources in Auden's own work. Abbreviated titles are used throughout the text to refer to volumes by Auden (or to those with a contribution by him) and to the most frequently cited critical editions of his work. Full titles and their abbreviations are given in the bibliography.

1   The Folded Lie:
Auden and Ideology

There is a story, a moral fable called 'W. H. Auden' which goes something like this. Once upon a time there was a good little boy from a solid middle-class background, who went to public school and Oxford, fell into bad company, and became a Marxist and a Freudian. Then he went to Spain during a civil war and saw that Marxists were a bad thing because they closed down all the churches. So he ran away to America and became a Christian. After this he was a lot happier and became a grand old man of letters. Then in his old age he came home to Europe and Oxford, and died peacefully in his bed. He lived happily ever after in his poems.

There is another story, which bears a superficial resemblance to this, and is also a moral tale. It says: once upon a time there was a petty-bourgeois intellectual born into the dying culture of a declining empire. The after-shock of a world war caused by inter-imperialist rivalries, the rise of Fascism and the growing threat of a second world war, brought about by social and economic collapse, drove many from his background briefly to identify with the international working-class struggle. Having discovered that you can't make an omelette without cracking eggs, however, this sensitive young man soon defected, returning to the Christian pietism of his origins, emigrating to an America which was now the ascendant imperialist power. As the Cold War brought a shift into global confrontation between capitalism and socialism, he became increasingly strident in his denunciations of the creed he had once espoused. Elements of this kind are always politically unreliable and such renegade activity is to be expected. During his brief flirtation with Marxism he wrote some powerful political poems, most of which he subsequently disowned. Thereafter he wrote much insipid verse which was lauded for the wrong reasons. Though this poetry proclaimed his reconciliation with the status quo it could not conceal the great unhappiness of his wasted talent. Such is the fate of all who turn their back on the movement of history.

There are many different versions of these stories, and not all are told with such partisan fervour. Some emphasize the superficiality of one or the other belief. Some affirm the superficiality of both, seeing them simply as ways of providing metaphors for his poetry. A few even presume the equal seriousness of both. Each version has a comic or tragic inflection, or the two modes can be reconciled by the device of irony. A fable of redemption can be rewritten as a saga of betrayal, a journey of self-discovery re-presented as a flight into self-delusion. We can read Auden's life as a chronicle of ignorance overcome or truth denied, as warning or example, poetry or pity. What all the accounts share, however, is the structure of the traditional Aristotelian narrative, with a beginning, a middle and an end. A character who knows but does not know himself progresses to a crisis of recognition which is also a reversal of fortune. This reversal both makes and breaks him; thereafter he will never be the same.

Strictly speaking, of course, a poet is simply a bundle of texts. Unfortunately for the purists, at least one of those texts is a biography, whether written or inferred. Auden himself made it clear on many occasions that he thought 'most genuine artists would prefer that no biography be written', and that 'The one thing a writer . . . hopes for, is attentive readers of his writings. . . . And he hopes they will read with patience and intelligence so as to extract as much meaning from the text as possible' ('Shakespeare's Sonnets', *FA*, p. 90). His elegy for Yeats spoke of how, at his death, the poet 'became his admirers' and of how 'The words of a dead man/Are modified in the guts of the living.' In the essay just quoted he speaks of the ghost of Shakespeare possibly puzzled by William Empson's famous reading of Sonnet 94, but none the less grateful for his 'loving care'. In 'Making, Knowing and Judging' (*DH*, pp. 47–8), he goes as far as to nominate his own ideal reader, and also outlines the two questions he would ask of any poem:

> The first is technical: 'Here is a verbal contraption. How does it work?' The second is, in the broadest sense, moral: 'What kind of guy inhabits this poem? What is his notion of the good life or the good place? His notion of the Evil One? What does he conceal from the reader? What does he conceal even from himself?' (*DH*, pp. 50–1)

The play between 'technical' and 'moral' places the emphasis on the constructed 'I' of the poem, which in turn constructs a reader to decipher this 'I' from the workings of what, after all, is no more than a 'verbal contraption'. Both 'guy' and 'reader' are effects of the text.

In 'The Virgin and the Dynamo' (*DH*, pp. 61–71) Auden speaks of the poem as a 'pseudo-person', but he omits from his description the analogy with the mirror-image in the first version of this essay, 'Nature, History and Poetry'.

> In a poem as distinct from many other verbal societies, meaning and being are identical. Like an image in the mirror, a poem might be called a pseudo-person, i.e., it has uniqueness and addresses the reader as person to person, but like all natural beings, and unlike historical persons, it cannot lie.[1]

The mirror is a complex image in Auden's writings, and the idea that a poem cannot lie seems to belie Auden's disownings of some of his own thirties poems for their 'dishonesty'. But the mirror here seeks to define that peculiar effect of a text: it is in reality all surface, merely the play of language – what the essay 'Squares and Oblongs' calls 'a game of knowledge', which at the same time gives the illusion of depth, of concealing and revealing – 'a bringing to consciousness, by naming them, of emotions and their hidden relationships' (*PAW*, p. 173).

What Auden is trying to negotiate here is the doubleness of the text, which is both a historical product, subject to all the pressures on language of its originating moment, and yet a discourse that floats free of its origins, finding as many moments of meaning as it has readers, in a perpetually open-ended play of history and signification. Poetry, in the frequently cited words of the Yeats elegy, 'makes nothing happen'. And yet it does re-enter history, in the much less commonly cited words of the same poem, as 'A way of happening, a mouth'.

This strange, dehumanizing metonymy, insisting on the act of speech while simultaneously detaching it from any human hinterland in a speaking subject, catches the paradox of this double historicity. A poem can be read at any time, and, in reading, it enters into a precise historical moment, the moment of the reader quite distinct from that of the originating author. Perhaps Auden dropped the mirror analogy because it opened up too radical a volatility in the idea of the text. For of course what the mirror always offers us, when we look into it, is *our own image* as a 'pseudo-person'. But if each moment of reading this same poem can be exchanged for any other moment of reading, none is privileged, including the author's.

In 'The Virgin and the Dynamo' Auden writes that, as a condition of its existence, 'Every poem must presuppose . . . that the history of the language is at an end' (*DH*, p. 67). At the same time, it is not created *ex nihilo* but has a past, 'requires pre-existing occasions of feeling and a pre-existing language out of which to create'. It therefore carries with it, as its freight, the baggage of a 'historical . . . fallen world', a world 'full of unfreedom and disorder'. However, he goes on, 'Of a recollected feeling it cannot be said that it is appropriate or inappropriate because the historical situation in which it arose no longer exists.' Poetry outlives its historical occasion, to become an infinite series of its own self-generating occasions: 'Every poem, therefore, is an attempt to present an analogy to that paradisal state in which Freedom and Law, System and Order are united in harmony. Every good poem is very nearly a Utopia. Again, an analogy, not an imitation; the harmony is possible and verbal only.'

As a verbal contraption, a poem reconciles the historical anxiety of its genesis with the utopian bliss of its reading, which offers us the assurance that 'The historical world is a redeemable world.' The false conclusion would be to assume that, 'since all is well in the work of art, all is well in history. But all is not well there' (*DH*, pp. 70–1).

Central to all these observations of Auden's on the relation between the delights of the text and the strains of a fallen world is the idea of *discourse*. The poem is a 'pseudo-person', in fact no more than a play of language, a 'game' or 'contraption'. Thus every text is a double field, and its doubleness is compounded by the fact that it is *my* experience – an experience of pleasure, satisfaction, delight – at the moment that *I* impute its contents to the subjectivity of *another* – the pseudo-'I' who supposedly speaks. This other who addresses me, 'person to person', is my own reflection, as reader, speaking back to me out of the mirror of another man's words.

The Auden we perceive as a historical figure is also the product of discourses which run through and beyond him. There was (no doubt about it) a poet called W. H. Auden. There is a general consensus that he did certain things, lived in certain places, and wrote certain texts. But the meaning of those events, like the meanings of those texts, is not perpetually fixed in history, unchangeably inscribed in the record. When we come to read Auden, we must be alert to the fact that we can, in reality, only *re*read him. The poems he produced have been rewritten by the historical process, as he himself acknowledged when he sought, with hindsight, to modify, censor and repress some of them. But Auden the historical subject has been rewritten too. 'We shan't, not since Stalin and Hitler,/trust ourselves ever again: we know that, subjectively,/all is possible', he wrote in 'The Cave of Making'. There is no original meaning that we can recover, only the play of language in our own moment of history, interlocking with the play of language of texts which have a certain antiquity, but are nevertheless our contemporaries, waiting for their ideal reader – a perpetually deferred and imaginary subject.

Joseph Warren Beach's *The Making of the Auden Canon*[2] is the *locus classicus* of the assault on Auden the turncoat. It is also the starting-point for most of the American apologists for Auden, providing the dilemma they have to resolve. In examining how Auden transformed his 'canon' after 1941 to bring it into line with a 'radically altered pattern of philosophical attitudes', Beach noted 'the surprising adjustability of Auden's work written from the point of view of a given ideology to the requirements of a quite different ideology involving a different point of view'. For Beach, the 'integrity' of a work of art arises from the 'integrality of the artistic conception. And this in turn involves the integrity of the poet's mental process.'[3] The making of a canon, then, is the construction of a homogeneous poetic personality:

> Through the man's work we are reaching out to the man.
> And if it is true that the style is the man, we feel...that
> we are making contact with at least as much of the man
> as shows in his work; and that we know sufficiently with
> whom we are dealing. With Auden we are not sure of
> this....
>   It is, in the last analysis, a question of identity,
> and...our fullest admiration goes to the poet who on
> this point never leaves us in doubt.[4]

Most subsequent critics have worked on the same assumption and, even where Auden does not seem to fit, their project has been to force him into the mould of a unitary personality. John G. Blair,[5] for example, while conceding that Auden's work seems 'bewilderingly diverse at first', is 'convinced that there is a fundamental wholeness and consistency in his poetry – considered as poetry', even if this means imitating Auden and excising some of the early work from the record.[6] This retrospective healing over of rupture is a frequent feature of Auden criticism. A particularly crafty example is that of Herbert Greenberg, who makes duality itself, and the struggle against it, 'the continuity underlying his intellectual develop-ment', the 'unvarying problem' in all his work. For Greenberg, 'it is clear in retrospect that his conversion to Christianity climaxed a movement of thought heading in a single direc-tion.'[7] Gerald Nelson comes to terms with a contradictory Auden by positing that the early and late poems seem to be 'written by what amounts to two different men', the later Auden seeing the agonies of the thirties as 'mere nonsense, just a kind of joke'.[8] George W. Bahlke rejects Beach's 'convic-tion that Auden's work does not form an organic unity', and finds 'a consistent vision of the meaning of human experience' in 'an awareness of the comic contradictions underlying human experience', and an 'acceptance...rather than satirical con-demnation...directed toward reform'.[9] Indeed, the need to affirm 'organic unity' seems intimately related to the heading-off of reform.

Frederick Buell, writing in the aftermath of that 'modern cult of youth and revolution' which swept American campuses in the 1960s, feels compelled to find even in Auden's early work 'a poetry of moral balance and social integration, one in which an acutely ironic consciousness does not negate appreciation or enjoyment of the limited human goods still available to us in a time of historical crisis'. The danger is that such 'unreal, consciously fantastic' rebellion may align itself with 'something far more earnestly revolutionary than itself, for example a Marxist ideology', and 'thus become a small but heady weapon in a genuine struggle'.[10] Such a prospect suddenly breaks through the academic calm of François Duchêne's 1972 study, to launch him in his epilogue into a long, intemperate spat at the 'infantilism' of 'dionysiac youth' in 'an orgasmic culture', pursuing, in a 'society freed from scarcity', the 'limits of romantic limitlessness'.

The tirade helps to explain Duchêne's hostility to the 'political distemper' of the early Auden as the perversion of a 'voyeur obsessed but irremediably alien'. Auden's mercurial career, 'a bewildering succession of apparently absolute "truths" which he has been the first to discard when they had served their turn', finds its unity, he argues, in this spiritual sickness.

For Duchêne there can be no revolutionary change of place: 'Deep transformation can only be brought about by men's slow efforts to improve themselves individually.'[11] For Richard Johnson too, in *Man's Place*, it is the 'underlying humanistic impulses' which can unify the verse in 'a single large enterprise, that of defining the uniquely human and of opposing those forces that have reduced our sense of our place in the world'.[12] Not surprisingly, that place turns out to be midway between extremes.

American liberals are never more aggressively certain of themselves than when they are humanistically affirming our human uncertainty. 'Every double-meaning phrase restates the certain uncertainty of the human position', says Johnson, for 'our skepticism and knowledge are the basis of, not escapes from, building well, acting, becoming fully human'.[13] In Johnson's extended definition of politics, the most political thing we can do is to sit around all day puzzling about what is to be done. In this he agrees with Edward Callan's *Carnival of Intellect* which argues that 'Auden's conception of man's responsibility for Nature's freedom...sets him apart from those poets...more immediately concerned with social and political ideologies',[14] as well as with Blair in 1965, who finds even in the earliest Auden a hostility to dogma, whether Freudian, Marxist or Christian, and a belief that 'some composite or reconciliation of extreme positions is needed. Only wholeness and integration can lead to satisfactory human living.'[15] The critical consensus that lies behind all these accounts of Auden, with their insistent attempts to dispose of the political, the revolutionary, the irruptive, the contradictory and the extreme, is still that formulated most authoritatively as recently as 1981 by Auden's literary executor, Edward Mendelson, in the concluding remarks of *Early Auden*: reconciliation, responsibility and the quest for 'wholeness'.[16] And Auden will be shaken down until he fits.[17]

One of the best of Auden's early critics, Monroe K. Spears, admits to some puzzlement in this quarter. Describing *The Orators*, for example, as 'curiously tantalizing', he adds that 'one feels constantly on the verge of discovering the key that will make the whole thing clear. Since thirty years have failed to reveal anything of the sort, one must conclude that the feeling is illusory.' Likewise he finds in the drama 'a radical incoherence', where Freud and Marx 'don't jell'.[18] When he is most puzzled, however, Spears departs from the assumption that he has to make sense of a biographical subject (who must be, of course, in some way a unitary being), into the recognition that Auden is a *text*, a badly wrapped parcel of discourses. It is when the text is most problematic that the illusion dissolves for a moment, to disclose that it is 'A way of happening, a mouth', not the utterance of a speaking subject. There is another hiccup in Spears's study, when, in his chapter on the thirties, he feels compelled to quote anachronistically from Auden's commencement address at Smith college in June 1940, 'at some cost to logical continuity', he says, 'because it exemplifies so perfectly the ambiguity of Auden's thought at this transitional stage, the mixture of cultural and religious terms'.[19] Auden, analysing the origins of the present war, tells his audience, 'Jung hardly went far enough when he said, "Hitler is the unconscious of every German"; he comes uncomfortably near being the unconscious of most of us.' He continues 'The shock of discovering through Freud and Marx that when we thought we were being perfectly responsible, logical, and loving we were nothing of the kind, has led us to believe that responsibility and logic and love are meaningless words; instead of bringing us to repentance, it has brought us to a nihilistic despair.' Such a realization is a shock to self-satisfied subjects, revealing that 'In the last analysis we do not live our lives, but are lived. What we call I, our little conscious ego, is an instrument of power outside itself. But it is a conscious instrument. To reason and obey logical necessity are its functions.' As Auden had written a year before in his elegy for Ernst Toller, the German expressionist dramatist who had committed suicide in New York:

We are lived by powers we pretend to
    understand:

They arrange our loves; it is they who direct at the
    end
The enemy bullet, the sickness, or even our hand.

It is their tomorrow hangs over the earth of the living
And all that we wish for our friends: but existence is
    believing
We know for whom we mourn and who is grieving.

The passive voice subverts the insistent 'we', which itself
shifts precariously from subject-position to subject-position.
For the 'we' who are lived are not the same as the 'we' who
pretend to understand, neither is the 'we' that knows – or,
rather, believes it knows – the same as the 'we' who mourns,
and none of these are the same as the speaker of the poem,
nowhere named as 'I', for *he* is able to take a sceptically believing distance both from knowing and from believing we know.
Doubleness is inscribed everywhere here, not only in the difference between the conscious subject and the 'powers', but
between us and our own hand, the enemy and his own hand.
Finally, it is there in that dissolution of 'we' in the last line
into 'who' and 'whom', in which a momentary community of
grief is itself dispersed into subject and object who are not
interchangeable, for the mourned cannot mourn the mourner.
Yet at the same time, in language, a community of believing
is reaffirmed: we *believe* we *know* who we *are* who *grieve*; we
believe we *know* the lost subjectivity it *is* we *grieve* for. We give
that subjectivity a name, in the third stanza, and address him
throughout, summoning a ghost to hear our faith in his reality.
Thus, even though it is the tomorrow of those powers which
'hangs over the earth of the living', what can transform this
tomorrow is 'all that we wish for our friends'. The wishing
brings into existence a dimension for which we alone are
responsible. Wishing ourselves to reason and to obey logical
necessity, believing in what we wish and will, is the way in
which this perpetually disappearing subject can refix itself in
the always sliding subject-position where it can speak and be
spoken to, know for whom it mourns and who is grieving.

The neutral summer has no voice, but the mourning subject does.

Auden here resolves all the contradictory definitions of his work in critic after critic, for he suggests that the debate about 'divided consciousness', 'change of heart', 'consistency' and 'integrality' are all based on a false assumption: that there is a single, unitary self who either remains the same or goes through a transformation. What we have instead is a subject who is always double, in that he is both a consciously self-defining ego and at the same time a mass of unspoken meanings which invest every line of that which is spoken.

Beach came close to the truth when in some fury he protested about the way in which texts such as the ode 'To My Pupils' and the Vicar's Speech from *Dogskin* are transformed by being taken from their original contexts and published separately. This, he said,

> implies such a curious notion of the creative process, not as something organic involving living tissues with their appropriate functions, but rather as the arrangement of words in patterns, which may at one moment signify one thing and at the next mean something quite different.
> . . . Stephen Spender has remarked on the way Auden had 'of tacking lines from a rejected poem onto a new one – as though a poem were not a single experience but a mosaic'.[20]

Such ignoring of 'the piece as it was originally conceived' may drive Beach to apoplexy, but he has unwittingly put his finger on the key issue. For of course a text *is* 'the arrangement of words in patterns', and it is only the most wilful ideological blindness which can take the humanist metaphor of a unitary subject presented in the full-blooded organic tissue of the poem as a literal transcription of reality. And if texts are mosaics of words, then since those words (as Auden repeatedly insisted) belong to a public discourse and are not created *ex nihilo* by the poet, they are subject to the shifting significations of the context in which they are read. Auden's play *The Ascent of F6* was for years a nearly unreadable text, stodgy, old-fashioned, dealing with dead issues. A performance at the Edinburgh Festival in 1983, in the wake of the Falklands War, electrified it as a critique of jingoistic platitudes stirred up by the gutter press to con a gullible public into support for an unpopular government and to send people euphorically to their deaths. The text, as in the Yeats elegy, 'is scattered among a hundred cities/And wholly given over to unfamiliar affections'; the words have no unique original meaning authenticated by the authority of the author.

But Auden, in his stance at Smith and in these various elegies, goes further than this. He speaks implicitly of the subject itself as an ideological nexus, a point where various discourses intersect to generate the ego which is then required to take responsibility for itself. Auden's thirties plays all explore the extent to which consciousness is constructed by the ideologies of the family and the state, and the way in which the media of communication, newspapers and radio, help to construct of an image of what it is to be a self-directing individual, appropriating the individual to the discourses of society at the very moment of his or her formation. That this was not an 'extreme' opinion of his youth is revealed in the sly reply in 1967 to a question about the Vietnam war, cited by Dennis Davison:

> But what do I, or any other writer in the West, know about Vietnam, except what we can glean from the newspapers and a few hurriedly written books? . . . I believe a negotiated peace, to which the Viet Cong will have to be a party, to be possible, but not yet, and that, therefore, American troops, alas, must stay in Vietnam until it is. But it would be absurd to call this answer mine. It simply means that I am an American citizen who reads *The New York Times*.[21]

Throughout his life, Auden was preoccupied with the implications of a revelation he first had at school. In 1934 he contributed an essay to Graham Greene's collection, *The Old School*. In manuscript the essay was called 'The Liberal Fascist'. In a significant act of censorship, its published title was

'Honour'. The suppressed title remains the sub-text of the whole piece, and the play between the two explains what Auden meant in 1940 by saying that Hitler 'comes uncomfortably near being the unconscious of most of us'.

The essay concedes that 'As what one sees depends on what one is' he must first identify the already-formed subject, the creature of class and family, that went up to Gresham's in 1920. The school was a liberal institution, but 'it is impossible to see how any school . . . where boys and staff are both drawn from the monied classes, can hope to see the world picture of that class objectively.' For the *raison-d'être* of such an institution is the 'mass production of gentlemen'. A prime instrument for effecting this was 'the honour system', in which every child was put on his honour not to swear, smoke, say or do anything indecent, and to report any breach of these rules. The system worked, producing 'the clean and healthy school' masters and parents wanted: 'From a boy's point of view on the other hand, I feel compelled to say that I believe no more potent engine for turning them into neurotic innocents, for perpetuating those very faults of character which it was intended to cure, was ever devised.' Everyone knows, he says, 'that the only emotion that is fully developed in a boy of fourteen is the emotion of loyalty and honour'. This is why it is so dangerous, for by appealing to it you can do anything you choose: 'like a modern dictator you can defeat almost any opposition from other parts of the psyche', but, if you deny these emotions expression they will never grow up, will go backward, and go bad on you.

The injunction to inform on one's neighbour 'meant that the whole of our moral life was based on fear, on fear of the community, not to mention the temptation it offered to the natural informer', making one 'furtive and dishonest and unadventurous'. Imprinting the unformed consciousness by 'utilising the sense of community' can achieve almost anything, but once that pressure is removed 'your unfortunate pupils are left defenceless. Either the print has taken so deeply that they remain frozen and undeveloped, or else, their infantile instinct suddenly released, they plunge into foolish and damaging dissipation.' 'The best reason I have for opposing Fascism', Auden suggests, 'is that at school I lived in a Fascist state' (*EA*, pp. 321–6).

It is clear that this revelation of how ideology constructs not only the conscious but the unconscious was profoundly educative. It lies behind Auden's conviction that we are all 'double' creatures, and it explains how we can endlessly engage in the kind of anti-social and auto-destructive impulses represented by Fascism. The Hitler in our unconscious is an unholy alliance of repressed libido and internalized authority – an authority which is not ours but that of some parental imago printed too deep to be eradicated. The peculiar combination, in Fascism, of libidinal release and authoritarian violence, has its roots here, not in the particular apparatus of a particular educational institution, but in what it reveals about the whole basis of socialization throughout our society.

In *The Dyer's Hand*, Auden was to write of Kafka's great insight, 'that our habitual conceptions of reality are not the true conception' (p. 167); in his essay on Stravinsky he observes that 'We are all actors; we frequently have to hide our real feelings for others and, alone with ourselves, we are constantly the victims of self-deception' (p. 480); and it is precisely the deliberate repression of this knowledge for which Auden indicted liberal democracy in his obituary for Yeats in *Partisan Review* in 1939.

In 'The Public v. the Late Mr. William Butler Yeats' the Counsel for the Defense justifies Yeats's illiberal thinking as a necessary reaction to liberal ideology, which constantly occludes the realities of power under a rhetoric of virtue and knowledge:

> The most obvious social fact of the last forty years is the failure of liberal capitalist democracy, based on the premises that every individual is born free and equal, each an absolute entity independent of all others; and that a formal political equality, the right to vote, the right to a fair trial, the right of free speech, is enough to guarantee his freedom of action in his relations with his

fellow men. The results are only too familiar to us all. By denying the social nature of personality, and by ignoring the social power of money, it has created the most impersonal, the most mechanical and the most unequal civilisation the world has ever seen, a civilisation in which the only emotion common to all classes is a feeling of individual isolation from everyone else, a civilisation torn apart by the opposing emotions born of economic injustice, the just envy of the poor and the selfish terror of the rich. (*EA*, pp. 389–93)

The 'personality' is socially constructed out of these unequal discourses, and what it 'knows' depends upon what is offered to it, not only at the level of consciousness, but subliminally, by what it takes for granted as the normal experience of its class. Thus, at Gresham's, what was propagated and confirmed quite unconsciously in every exchange was the world-picture of the monied classes – something taken for granted as the way reality was constructed by those who shared in it. If Auden found himself at odds with this view, what had opened up this area of ambiguous freedom was not an *acte gratuit* of cognitive transcendence, but quite simply a clash between the ideological discourses he brought with him as the 'son of book-loving, Anglo-Catholic parents of the professional class' and the discourses he entered as a pupil. This gave him the critical distance which, in his 1934 contribution to Richard Crossman's *Oxford and the Groups*, he had seen as essential for an honest appraisal of our condition: 'Today the light which has been shed by Freud and Marx on the motivation of thought makes it criminal to be uncritical, and no movement, secular or religious, which is afraid to examine dispassionately and acknowledge openly what self-interest would make it want to believe is worthy of anything but contempt.'[22] Freud and Marx, like Kierkegaard, he was to write in *The New Republic* in 1944, approach the human being as 'a *subject*...a being in *need*, an *interested* being whose existence is at stake'.

It is the unmasking of ideology, then, not just at the conscious level but in the very formation of the subject, that Auden attributes to Freud and Marx, as he wrote in a review of the Freud-Fliess correspondence, in *The Griffin* in 1954, making possible 'real knowledge of the psyche by regarding mental events, not as natural events, but as historical events' to be interpreted by the methods of the historian. In 'the natural order what is real must necessarily be true', but 'in history, a deliberate lie, a mistaken notion, are as real and important as the truth', for such lies actually make something happen. But perhaps Auden's most perspicacious account of this process, the more significant for its late date, is his review of Erik Erikson's Freudian reading of *Young Man Luther* in 1960 (*FA*, pp. 79–87).

Here Auden returns to the theme which had dominated his own work in the thirties: the power of ideology to recruit new subjects, to reproduce the given order of things by reproducing the subjects who produce it as willing, co-operative agents. 'Subject' here takes on a double sense, for the individual who feels himself a free agent is at the same time, and in the very illusion of that free agency, *subjected to* the power of the social formation, a willing subject of its sovereign authority. Auden quotes with approval Erikson's extended definition of ideology as, not just consciously held beliefs and convictions, or the propaganda which sustains them, but as 'an unconscious tendency underlying religious and scientific as well as political thought: the tendency at a given time to make facts amenable to ideas, and ideas to facts, in order to create a world image convincing enough to support the collective and the individual sense of identity'.

Auden further quotes Erikson's observation that in some periods of history, 'and in some phases of his life cycle, man needs a new ideological orientation as surely and as sorely as he must have light and air.' Such a moment of dislocation, in which individual and historic crises coincided, produced the young Luther. (Clearly, Auden sees some analogy here to what happened to his own generation.) Auden speaks of Luther's Protestant era as the era of the Rebellious Son, replacing 'the collective external voice of tradition by the internal voice of the individual conscience, which, since it is internal to the subject, is his contemporary'. But for Auden, this era of 'the interiorization of the paternal conscience' is now at an end. The new crisis that has to be resolved requires the rediscovery of an authentically collective solution, reconciling 'lutheran individual' and 'catholic community', the '*We are* of society' with the '*I am*' of each of its members. What Auden calls 'the grisly success of various totalitarian movements' is that they offered 'bogus solutions' to these 'real needs' – 'one of which is the need for personal authority both to obey and to command'. This last is a clear echo of what Auden had written in a review of Bertrand Russell's *Education and the Social Order* in 1932:

> The trouble is that Mr Russell refuses to admit that man's nature is dual, and that each part of him has its own conception of justice and morality. In his passionate nature man wants lordship, to live in a relation of power with others, to obey and to command, to strut and to swagger. He desires mystery and glory. In his cerebral nature he cares for none of these things. He wants to know and be gentle; he feels his other passionate nature is frightening and cruel.

The success of Fascism lay in its power to mobilize these passional impulses, to awaken the Hitler in all our unconsciousnesses. In his 1960 review, Auden is still concerned with this duality, which he now defines in terms of a distinction between 'impersonal behaviour' and 'personal deeds'. The role of psychoanalysis, he says, is to free us from the 'slavery' of behaviour, to disclose that 'frequently, when we imagine we are acting as ourselves, we are really only exhibiting behaviour.'

In the lectures collected as *Secondary Worlds* (1968) Auden returned to this distinction, to give his most comprehensive definition of that 'primary world' in which ideology is presented to us as our own reified past, including the forms of discourse we inherit:

> The Primary World contains everything that has not
> been made by man, including himself, and, also, what-
> ever of man's historical past is still on hand as reified
> in a humanly fabricated world of languages, mythologies,
> legends, creeds, tools, works of art, etc. Though made
> by man, his past is no longer in his power to alter . . .
>
> [A]ny history is already a secondary world in that it
> can only be written or told in words, and the only
> elements in the primary world which language can
> exactly reproduce are the words that people speak there.
> It cannot describe all the physical properties of an object
> or all the temporal sequence of a motion or event.
> Language must abstract and select. (*SW*, pp. 49–50)

Behind all particular words and deeds, therefore, lies what
might be called the discursive unconscious, the hinterland of
meanings implicit in any act or utterance, repressed as
signification in the very act of selecting. Repression is built
into the act of speaking and writing, for 'If all the infinite
variety of actual beings and events in the primary world,
because equally actual, seemed equally significant to us, no
history could be written at all' (*SW*, p. 51). Yet those repressed
discourses of the primary world continue to invest the meanings we carry forward as our own chosen significances, as
Auden suggests later, returning to think on the way individual
subjects are implicated in the whole web of discourses which
constitute them both as unique individuals and as species-
beings (*SW*, pp. 118–26).

The human condition is further complicated by the fact that
'man is a history and culture making creature, who by his
own efforts has been able to change himself after his biological
evolution was complete.' This has endowed each of us with
a 'second nature', 'created by the particular society and culture
into which we happen to have been born . . . not by our free
choice, but by the accident of birth and economic necessity'.
As individuals, 'we are countable, comparable, replaceable.'
This dimension of the subject corresponds to the collective
and personal unconscious Auden explores in his earlier work,

that realm which the demagogue touches to fury and a liberal society presumes upon to remain inert.

But there is another dimension to the subject, that of the freely willing and choosing 'person', the speaker who says 'I'; and this subject is called into being by language, by that community of discourse which constitutes the person as one who can be the subject as well as the object of a sentence, as one who can mourn as well as be mourned, and whose existence is believing 'We know for whom we mourn and who is grieving': 'As persons, who can, now and again, truthfully say *I*, we are called into being...not by any biological process but by other persons, our parents, our siblings, our friends.' It is in dialogue that we are constituted as persons:

> To understand the nature of speech, we must begin, not with statements in the third person...but with proper names, the first and second personal pronouns, and words of summons and command, response and obedience. Adam, where art thou? Lord, I am here. Follow me. Be it unto me according to thy word. (*SW* pp. 120–2)

Language, nevertheless, in a remark Auden was fond of quoting from Rosenstock-Huessy (but whose ambiguity for his argument here he does not fully appreciate) has a power which transcends the personal: '"Living language always overpowers the thinking of the individual man. It is wiser than the thinker who assumes that he thinks whereas he only speaks and in so doing faithfully trust the material of language; it guides his concepts unconsciously towards an unknown future."' For it is here, of course, that the repressed returns, in this guidance from the unconscious which overpowers the speaking subject.

It is at this point that we can begin to pull together Auden as text and the biographical Auden. For what the late Auden is saying here is that both the literary text and the human subject are constructed in discourse:

> Parents give each child a name...Hearing himself called by his name, he becomes aware of himself as a unique

person. As uttered by his parents, his name is prenominally the second person singular *Thou*. In responding, his name is prenominally the first person singular *I*. The second person precedes the first: we respond and obey before we can summon and command. (*SW*, p. 122)

This constitution of the subject in discourse the French Marxist Louis Althusser has called 'interpellation'.[23]

Of the literary text Auden says something very similar: 'its meaning is the outcome of a dialogue between the words of the poem and the response of whoever is listening to them. Not only is every poem unique, but its significance is unique for each person who responds to it.' The 'knowledge' it conveys is the kind 'implied by the Biblical phrase – *Then Adam knew Eve his wife* – knowing is inseparable from being known' (*SW*, pp. 130–1). In this the poem is to be distinguished from the 'Black Magic' of the propagandist, who uses language as 'a way of securing domination over others and compelling them to do his will. He does not ask for a free response to his spell; he demands a tautological echo'; for 'Propaganda, like the sword, attempts to eliminate consent or dissent and, in our age, magical language has to a great extent replaced the sword' (p. 129). But in this, propaganda simply reproduces the inauthentic relation between subjects that obtains in lying. If 'Every dialogue is a feat of translation', lies 'undermine . . . faith in all men and all speech. It is with good reason that the devil is called the Father of Lies' (p. 126).

If this lying Father, the patriarch of ideology, is to be resisted in the primary realm of history as in the secondary world of the poem, then the relation of the individual subject with his or her past has to be dissolved and reconstructed in a dialogue of reader and text which takes each beyond self-interest. Poetry can do this because it is not 'an act of self expression', but 'gratuitous utterance'. It tries to embody 'an experience of reality common to all men', and the poem is only an expression of the *poet's* experience 'in that this reality is perceived from a perspective which nobody but he can occupy' (pp. 130–1).

The experience of reading a text, then, is of an exchange of subject-positions (this is what Auden means by 'translation').

In one of his last poems, 'A Thanksgiving', Auden looked back on some of the interruptions of his personal narrative in terms of the literary discourse through which they were mediated and finally understood. Falling in love produced one abrupt alteration of discourse:

> Then, without warning, the whole
> Economy suddenly crumbled:
> there, to instruct me, was Brecht.
>
> Finally, hair-raising things
> that Hitler and Stalin were doing
> forced me to think about God.

What is striking is that each of these occasions is seen as a conjunction of external necessity and a circumscribed personal response. For although the discourse which explains each moment of crisis seems to be chosen freely, it is clear that it is also dictated by circumstance: it emerges only at its proper time. Indeed, in the case of Brecht it seems to be waiting for the moment of catastrophe that will allow it to be visible – it has always been there, in fact, but the subject, confined within a different 'common sense', was unable to see it. Similarly, the change to religion is not just a disinterested intellectual conversion, but something 'forced' on the subject by the contradictions of a pressing necessity. Old age, with its own forms of necessity, in turn shifts his attention to other 'tutors'.

Auden's admission that without these mentors 'I couldn't have managed/even my weakest of lines' sets up a disturbing ambiguity. It dethrones the master before the patriarchs of the discursive tradition he has just so masterfully summoned into existence. This 'weakest of lines' is also the weakest of lineages; it stutters and jumps, and cannot be held down to linear continuity. Even more pointedly, there is a sense in which he has not appropriated the lineage, but been appropriated by it: the lines he couldn't manage, like a ham actor, are lines which have been written for him by the authorial voices to whom he defers. The brilliant pasticheur never talks alone. He had 'sat at the feet' of his first mentors, but even now, in the competence of age, he is still looking for 'tutors'. The masterful subject, in what is almost a last will and testament, hands on a lineage of which he is not the master but merely the bearer, realizing that those other voices are inscribed everywhere in what are supposed to be his 'own' lines. Repeatedly orphaned by biographical or historical circumstance, the poetic subject prepares for the final dislocation of his line in an act of homage to his various adopted fathers.

For Auden, then, changes of heart and changes of hat are primarily questions of adopting, and being adopted by, a new paternal line. In *The Orators*, his Airman had speculated that 'The true ancestral line is not necessarily a straight or continuous one', but leaps over generations so that 'the true ancestor' may be uncle or grandfather (*EA*, pp. 75–6). 'In Memory of Sigmund Freud' is concerned with the breaking of an inheritance, all those 'plausible young futures' transformed, in the space of a stanza, into 'problems like relatives gathered/puzzled and jealous about our dying'. If the poem opens with a faltering of the line – faced by so many deaths 'of whom shall we speak?' – it ends with a recognition that, while 'One rational voice is dumb', the succession continues in all its contradictoriness, calling up as mourners that divine 'household of Impulse' in which mother and son, Aphrodite and Eros, destroyer and builder, are reconciled.

What Freud offered was a new discourse in which to describe and inscribe ourselves, that 'new ideological orientation' of which Erikson was to speak. We live, now, 'different lives' because of that change of climate Freud brought about; but this was no smooth transition, but an abrupt rupture with old ways of seeing and interpreting:

> he merely told
> the unhappy Present to recite the Past
> like a poetry lesson till sooner
> or later it faltered at the line where

> long ago the accusations had begun,
> and suddenly knew by whom it had been judged,
>> how rich life had been and how silly,
>> and was life-forgiven and more humble.

Without this faltering of the line, in its double sense, such a change of readings would not have been possible.

'In Memory of W. B. Yeats' is centrally concerned with the idea of a ruptured succession at the very moment that it tries to heal it by an appeal, to the dead father-figure, to 'Sing of human unsuccess/In a rapture of distress'. Rapture and rupture are here intimately linked , in this time of the breaking of nations (1939), when as the Freud elegy says, 'grief has been made so public, and exposed /to the critique of a whole epoch/ the frailty of our conscience and anguish.' Auden's elegy for Yeats ends with an appeal to the 'unconstraining voice' of a dead man to 'persuade us to rejoice'. In its last words it begs the voice of the text to pass on its inheritance and, 'In the prison of his days/Teach the free man how to praise'. In the primary world of reified discourses, the voice of 'praise' has to break with a language that is everywhere founded in 'curse'. Language becomes a dual inheritance, which has to be farmed to make a vineyard out of a desert. There is a peculiar doubling back of reader and writer here, for it is Auden the writer who, appealing to the texts he reads, pleads with them to 'persuade' their readers to rejoice. Yet this is the same writer who has earlier said 'Poetry makes nothing happen.'

The description of poetry as 'A way of happening, a mouth' shares in this doubleness. For 'mouth' is a radically ambiguous image. It is, as I have suggested earlier, the figure of an utterance without a subject in a world where the snow, disfiguring the public statues, represents a larger crisis both for the human figures and for the figurations of language. It links, thus, with the mercury sinking 'in the mouth of the dying day', and the figure of Yeats disappearing into the mouth of the grave. But in context it also comes as the culmination of a river image that has run through a whole paragraph, starting with the madness and weather of Ireland (notoriously rainy), passing through the 'valley of its saying', and flowing south to debouch as the mouth of an estuary, emptying into the sea of public discourse. The metaphor thus recalls the image of the peasant river and the mourning tongues of the first section, and points towards the locked and frozen seas of pity and the healing fountain in the desert at the end of the poem.

This ambiguity highlights another one. For it is language itself which is the basis of this duplicity. Time, we may notice, 'Worships language and forgives/Everyone by whom it lives'. It is easy to miss the actual meaning here. The poem does not say 'everyone who lives by it', the more normal and expected meaning. It insists instead on the primacy of the language, which uses the human subject as its carrier and 'vessel', and empties it like a cup or a river at the moment that it frees each from the 'cell of himself', capriciously using a 'strange excuse' to pardon and dismiss. For the dying subject, then, language is a matter of 'nurses and rumours', subversively decentring all his imperiously centralized sovereignty, the provinces of his body revolting against the capital, silence invading the suburbs. Language gathers together to construct a subject by whom it lives. But it then disperses again, leaving the vessel empty of its poetry. The sovereign subject is an illusory unity, an Irish vessel which, in a double sense, *lies*, as later the seas of pity '*lie*/Locked and frozen in each eye'.

It's quite remarkable how many alternative ideas of language occur in this poem, from the reading of instruments which all 'agree', through the 'mourning tongues', 'rumours' and 'codes of conscience', the 'roaring' of brokers on the floor of the Bourse, to the honouring, worshipping, persuading, rejoicing, singing, praising and teaching, set against the pardoning, forgiving, excusing and cursing of the last section. It is not Yeats in the end who is mourned and addressed, but discourse itself. All that the individual subject can know is that moment of failure and distress, when 'The current of his feeling failed.' Yet it is out of this very failure and unsuccess that the succession of discourse is passed on: 'he became his admirers.' As an 'unconstraining voice', the father becomes the child of his own children, for 'The death of the poet [is] kept from his poems'; he becomes, that is, merely an effect of the text. Language had moved from an original fullness of meaning to scattered rumours and then to silence, for the individual subject. In the end, even his personal death is taken up into discourse and becomes simply, for a few thousand, the thought of 'a day when one did something slightly unusual'. By the same token, we see that the poet invited to follow, persuade, sing and teach in the final section *may* not be Yeats at all, but his successor, perhaps even Auden himself, who in this elegy has in fact followed his mentor in an act of honouring and praise.

The visual immediacy of 'mouth' gives a peculiar shock of strangeness to the idea of poetry in 'In Memory of W. B. Yeats'. By comparison, the more abstract 'voice' is an acceptable and traditional usage. It is a central metaphor in that ideology of the speaking subject that lies behind all our perceptions of poetry, leading Beach, for example, to believe that a poem is 'something organic involving living tissues', rather than 'the arrangement of words in patterns'. Substituting 'mouth' for 'voice' reveals the grotesqueness of such an assumption, the shock of its concretion exposing the ideological blindness implicit in our casual thinking. In 'September 1, 1939', however, Auden deconstructs the concept of 'voice' itself. It is not surprising that he fiddled several times with this poem before finally suppressing it, for in its mixture of lyric plangency and attitudinizing rhetoric it says much more than the guy inhabiting the poem knows about his historical posture and posturing. For the shifts of tone and register reveal the illusoriness of the unitary subject it struggles to affirm, the failure of the succession it tries to call into being, and the irreducible plurality of the discourses it strives to fuse into a single self-possessing 'voice'.

There is a counterpoint of assurance and unsettledness in the poem's opening which sets the scene for the ambivalent passages to come. On the one hand, the opening words place the subject at the centre of his experience, foregrounding the 'I' and organizing the environment around him in all its massed plenitude. On the other hand, the specificity of Fifty-Second Street and of the date (Hitler's invasion of Poland and the annexation of Danzig) is undercut by the indeterminacy of place (merely 'one of the dives') and the fear and uncertainty of this expatriate who has been made into a displaced person by the events in Europe. Yet the uncertainty and fear in turn restore him to a public discourse, dethroning him from his lofty stool by disclosing that he is only one more carrier of those impersonal waves that now circulate the globe, 'Obsessing our private lives'. The immediate reaction of the threatened subject is an act of censorship, pushing into silence 'The unmentionable odour of death' which 'offends' the night; yet the very mention of the unmentionable draws it into discourse. The next mode of verbal resistance is an attempt to contain the crisis in the cool abstractions of 'Accurate scholarship', but the 'offence' returns at once to transform the scholar's archaeology into the unearthing of a corpse, disclosing 'the whole offence' that has driven a culture mad.

To this madness our obsessions are a party. The 'private' cannot be divorced from the public. The personal scarring that ocurred at Linz (Hitler's birthplace) is only one more moment in the offence that stretches 'From Luther until now' which Auden, in his review of Erikson, attributes to the era of the Rebellious Son. Totalitarianism is successful, Auden notes there, because of the threat to our 'sense of identity' which comes from 'our current lack of belief in and acceptance of the existence of others' (*FA*, p. 87). It was not only Jung's 'huge imago' of the internalized sadistic father as 'psychopathic god' that deformed Hitler and his culture. There were more immediate causes, one of which, as the Left proclaimed throughout the twenties and thirties, was the huge burden of reparations imposed upon the Weimar Republic by the victorious allies. In a sense, then, we require neither psychoanalysis nor history to reveal the causes of this madness. It is common knowledge already:

I and the public know
What all schoolchildren learn,

> Those to whom evil is done
> Do evil in return.

Knowing is revealed in its doubleness throughout the poem. All that scholarship unearths is what we knew all along, in our bones: that we had it coming to us; that underneath the 'clever hopes' lay 'a low dishonest decade' that deceived itself about its own iniquity, and now seeks to evade the consequence of its own acts. Knowledge is always two-faced, revealing and concealing, imposing its own ideological closure as it discloses. Explaining something is not the same as defeating it. In the public world it is the rubbish of rhetoric that rules, and because we did not act but merely talked and analysed, we must now suffer. Discourse is now simply the 'vain/Competitive excuse' each language pours into the air of this metropolis – 'vain' in that, locked in its vanity, each tries vainly to excuse itself rather than understand and change what has happened.

Most of our knowledge is ideology of one form or another. It may be the public propaganda of the air-waves, or that embodied in the skyscrapers, which 'proclaim/The strength of Collective Man'. It may be the 'euphoric dream' in which we conceal to ourselves our own condition, the 'conventions' which 'conspire' to make the bar 'assume' the false identity of fort and home. Ideology is a collective conspiracy in which we connive 'Lest we should see where we are,/Lost . . .' Yet by clinging to this 'average day' we exacerbate our condition. It is the delusion that informs our catastrophe. If the faces along the bar would look at their images in the mirror clearly they would see that –

> Out of the mirror they stare,
> Imperialism's face
> And the international wrong.

For Auden here, the acknowledgement of complicity is the beginning of wisdom. Until we know this, we know nothing, for all our scholarship.

It is in speech that such delusions grow, and it is here too that the individual is continually pinned down to his or her subject-position. The 'dense commuters', for example, emerge into the ethical life each morning repeating the vows that reinscribe them in their families and jobs. Auden now repeats that reinscription for himself, in answer to three questions: who can release them, who can reach the deaf, who can speak for the dumb?

The answer seems to be: I can, with my little voice. But the pressure of the sentence in this stanza forces its meaning against the grain. In an earlier stanza he had noted that Thucydides knew 'All that a speech can say/About Democracy'. The implication was that there is more than this to be said. The speech, that is, fails to define its object, misses the point. Now in this stanza the poet concedes his powerlessness at the very moment he seems to be prepared to assume the mantle of vatic hero. By foregrounding the voice he achieves the sudden estrangement of what is usually an accustomed metonymy. And this exposes the real inadequacy of the bourgeois subject:

> All I have is a voice
> To undo the folded lie,
> The romantic lie in the brain
> Of the sensual man-in-the-street
> And the lie of Authority
> Whose buildings grope the sky:
> There is no such thing as the State
> And no one exists alone;
> Hunger allows no choice
> To the citizen or the police;
> We must love one another or die.

If you want to undo something that is folded, a disembodied voice is the last thing you need. What you need is *hands*. But the characteristic definition of the bourgeois subject, in poetry as in democracy, is that of the freely self-articulating voice. Exiled Thucydides and mad Nijinsky, though outcasts, at least had hands because they managed to write. The accurate scholar must have had hands because you cannot 'unearth' anything without them. Even the builders of these skyscrapers had hands in order to make their proclamations. How do those 'Faces along the bar' manage to 'Cling to their average day' without hands? The only way you can 'release', or 'reach' the deaf, is with hands. The only way the dumb can 'speak' is with their hands. But 'All I have is a voice.'

Absorbed in narcissistic self-consideration, the citizens of the bourgeois democracies have brought their doom upon themselves by refusing to take their hands out of their pockets and get them dirty. The whole metaphoric infrastructure of the poem undoes the 'folded lie' of an ideology that positions the subject – whether as poet or citizen – as voyeur and voice, an abstracted and passive *consumer*. The 'common sense' of *l'homme moyen sensuel* is most frequently a refusal of the evidence of his senses. In the course of the poem, every sense is negated, from the 'unmentionable odour' to the 'blind skyscrapers', from the deaf and the dumb to the failure of the tactile and kinetic here. The sensuality of the average man is really no more than a 'romantic lie in the brain', an ideologically distorted, cerebral misreading of what his senses try to tell him.

Authority, however, has hands, and is prepared to use them. Its buildings 'grope the sky' with a lust for power not loth to expose itself. An authentic democracy would not set up a clash of interests between the man-in-the-street and Authority, the citizen and the police. In the Just City, it would be the necessity not of hunger but of reason that left no choice but to love one another or die. But everywhere in this fallen city the supposedly unitary human subject is dissolved into innumerable roles and functions, filling different subject-positions in different discourses. In each, all are simultaneously deaf and dumb. Everyone of these 'free' persons is also the carrier of systems of power. And this doubleness (figured in the contrast between what one sees in the bar mirror and what one *knows* oneself to be) is then reproduced in the profoundest ambiguity of the whole poem.

What is not clear in these ostensibly confident assertions is whether the two statements, 'There is no such thing as the state/And no one exists alone', are the words of the poet, or the lies of man-in-the-street and Authority. A case can be made for either, because both versions, though contradictory, are equally true. This is why it is a 'folded' lie. In the ideology of the anarchic, selfish individual, 'There is no such thing as the State' is a desperately self-gratifying lie, for there clearly *is* a state, to which the man-in-the-street owes duties as a citizen. Likewise, in the ideology of Authority, 'no one exists alone' becomes a self-justifying lie excusing every inroad made into the rights of the citizen. At the same time, the words could also be those of the powerless but truth-telling voice, insisting that the State is merely a a reified abstraction from human acts and choices, and the delusions of splendid isolation imagined by the man-in-the-street romantic fantasies, masking his real dependence on the whole body politic, like the spurious separation of the 'private lives' of individual consumers from a 'public' bodied over against them. Language folds back on itself, revealing the ideological lie contained even within the affirmations of truth.

The only way to elude this power of positive lying, in which every text is subverted by its negation, is to speak with the irony and indirection that is linked to justice in the last stanza. But even here the lie suborns affirmative speech, creeping in through that possible Shakespearian pun which may not be intentional but can't be resisted (and rarely is in Auden's verse) because it has provided the main motif of the preceding stanza. For if the world lies defencelessly open in its drunken stupor, through the hazy rhetoric it is possible to see that this is the product of an indefensible lying, resistible only by an irony in which language subverts its own attitudinizing in the moment of utterance, and flashes out innuendos which acknowledge, at one and the same time, that I am being deadly serious but am also dead drunk.

The self that is 'composed' at the end of this sequence is, then, a legless as well as handless voice, who can only get it together by turning himself into a written text, 'composed', with all the composure that implies, and beleaguered simultaneously. What the poem affirms, in effect, is its own desperate sense of failure, its yearning for a community and a succession, at the moment that it realizes this is no more than one grand rhetorical gesture before falling on the floor.

One can understand Auden's embarrassment in the grey light of dawn. But it is precisely its honesty in catching the duplicity and bad faith that makes it a fine and powerful poem, revealing more than the guy at the bar will ever know. The poem undoes the folded lie of the ideologically composed subject, to reveal what he is actually made of – Eros and dust, negation and despair, the desire to be deceived and the desire to know, and to speak that knowledge.

2 Dissolving the Mask: The Early Poems

'We must suffer them all again.' Twenty-five centuries ago Thucydides had already diagnosed it all. A low dishonest decade had confirmed the diagnosis. Is progress, then, a delusion? Is nothing ever permanently won by enlightenment from the eternal return of the repressed? Is knowledge simply our own false consciousness, pretensions to understanding which only deceive the more? Toller had died by his own hand. The Europe which had taken refuge in his head, maybe, was already too injured to get well, and the charm of 'the big and friendly death outside' too powerful to resist. But why did this death-wish have such a hold? How do these 'powers' come to have such authority, to become the authors of our deeds? The Toller elegy had spoken of what his 'shadow unwittingly said', and of Toller, dead, lying 'shadowless at last', as well as of mourners and enemies alike chased by their own shadows away from the grave. These shadows, in Jungian psycho-analysis, are precisely all those elements of the self repressed in the process of its formation, that other side of the double man which, in crisis and trauma, can return to claim its birth-right. The shadow is the unwitting discourse implicit in every positive utterance, and it is through its offices that those huge imagos seize power in our unconscious. But if we can listen to what it says, we may reach a true understanding, capable not only of interpreting but of changing the world. It was this promise that Freud offered, unsettling 'the ancient cultures of conceit' with a technique which simply asks us to look back with no false regrets, to remember like the old and be honest like children. Such a technique, Auden wrote in 'In Memory of Sigmund Freud', would dissolve the 'lucrative patterns of frustration' out of which the monolith of the State was constructed, in all its positive power.

In 'The Protestant Mystics' (*FA*, pp. 49ff.) Auden speaks of the human creature as one uniquely 'born with no behavior-directing instincts', having to learn by prejudice and custom even the simplest things. Human society 'can only endure by conscious effort, the passing on of a tradition from the older generation to the younger'; it is 'always institutionalized, governed not by instinct or force, but by authority.' The prime source of this authority is language, which comes with a paternal imprimatur: a father, Auden says, points to an animal and commands his son: '"Look. A fox."' It may well be a badger, but we cannot begin by doubting: 'unless his son has faith in his father and believes that he knows the right names for all the animals. . .he will never learn to speak.' This act of naming is also an interpellation of the looking subject. Most of our assurances about the nature of the universe, the just form of society, our own identity, 'we hold not by faith but by habit – they are what we are used to and we cannot imagine them otherwise.' When something disrupts this confidence, we suffer a crisis in which self and world are alike called into question. Such a crisis in the handing on of tradition and authority is that evoked in 'Our hunting fathers' (1934).

The story these fathers told 'Of the sadness of the creatures' is no longer believed. It stands revealed as ideology in the anthropomorphic metaphors it employs: the lion's 'intolerant look', the quarry's 'dying glare', 'Love raging for the personal glory', 'liberal appetite and power'. In 'The Protestant Mystics' Auden distinguishes between our species-being, where we are all identically subject to the same laws, and 'the pronoun *We* is singular not plural, for the pronoun *I* has no meaning', and that existence as 'a unique person who can say *I*, with a unique perspective on the universe'. The crisis 'Our hunting fathers' records is a faltering of the old 'We' of a collective story, and the seeking of an alternative 'We' in the dedication 'To think no thought but ours'. This break requires illegality and anonymity – a refusal of the name and the law of the fathers. The refusal calls the subject itself into doubt. If I refuse the being called into existence by the voice of the father, if, instead, I regard it as an imposture, imposed upon me by my culture and language, where is authentic selfhood to be found? This is the crisis of the subject in Auden's early poems, which constantly dissolves the problematic self back into the nexus of language, social being and history that generated it.

The Freudian concept of 'repression' is a key to this process. In the essay 'The Good Life', which he contributed to the volume *Christianity and Social Revolution* in 1935 (*EA*, pp. 342–54), Auden wrote of the role of the 'incest motive' (Oedipus complex) in generating the subject. It is not, he says, something 'pristine and anterior to mentality' but, on the contrary, 'It is in itself the mind's ulterior motive.' The conscious mind is formed in the very process of repressing the 'incest motive', and the two are integrally related and mutually constitutive: 'the incest motive is propagated in the pristine unconscious by the mind itself, and in its origin is not a pristine impulse but a logical extension of the existent idea of sex and love.' The fall into knowledge, that is, generates at once the text of consciousness and the sub-text of the unconscious, which relates to the conscious subject as the reverse of a page relates to the page. A 1933 sonnet (*EA*, p. 146) uses an analogy from script to explain how thought is formed in the very moment of repression, speaking of the urge 'To cancel off from the forgotten score/The foiled caresses from which thought was born'. Poem IX from *Look Stranger* describes the world of consciousness as one where power everywhere imposes itself as order and authority:

> The total state where all must wear your badges,
> Keep order perfect as a naval school:
> Noble emotions organised and massed
> Line the straight flood-lit tracks of memory
> To cheer your image as it flashes by;
> All lust at once informed on and suppressed.

'The Good Life' speaks of Fascism as a 'defeatist' view which regards reality as unchangeable and progress a 'delusion'. Its very dynamism derives from this fatalism, for 'Oppressed classes, without hope, desire vengeance, and may easily adopt a blind eschatology.' It is such a return of the oppressed that 'They', a poem in *Another Time*, sees happening on a global scale in 1939. All Europe is threatened by a shadow that falls 'on our dearest location'. The pond reflects back to the famous not their own loved images but 'Terrible Presences'. These bring to us 'The resentment of outcasts'; 'they wear our weeping/ As the disgraceful badge of their exile', for it is because we banished 'their anarchist vivid abandon' that they now return to occupy our narrow spaces. 'We conjured them here like a lying map' – suddenly we realize that we are the map, we the lies. The unconscious is not a realm of pure vital possibility. It is already structured by all the forces that shaped consciousness, and its creatures come 'already adroit, having learned/ Restraint at the table of a father's rage;/In a mother's distorting mirror/They discovered the Meaning of Knowing.' Thus 'They' come 'equipped /To reply to terror with terror,/With lies to unmask the least deception'. Having refused an authentic liberation – that offered by Freud and Marx – we are now forced to suffer the destruction of error by violence. The 'bridegroom' will now be a violator; barren, we will conceive in punishment, not blessing; 'the crooked that dreads to be straight' will be reformed by 'a horrible rector' – Fascism. Now, in the last words of the poem, 'even our armies/Have to express our need of forgiveness.'

'The Well of Narcissus' (*DH*, pp. 93–167) considers that process by which the self is estranged in an ideology which 'composes' an identity 'obvious' to itself:

But it is impossible for me not to feel that my body is other than I, that I inhabit it like a house, and that my face is a mask which, with or without my consent, conceals my real nature from others. It is impossible consciously to approach a mirror without composing or 'making' a special face, and if we catch sight of our reflection unawares we rarely recognize ourselves. I cannot read my face in the mirror because I am already obvious to myself.

If this obviousness is to be dissolved, it must be confronted in the movement of its formation. And this means, in the words of 'The Good Life', 'unmasking hidden conflicts', allowing the subject to 'escape from his image' through 'the exercise of *eros paidogogos*', through 'confession...drawing attention to unnoticed parts of the field of experience'. Such an examination will reveal 'thought and knowledge not as something spontaneous and self-sufficient, but as purposive and determined by the conflict between instinctive needs and a limited environment'. It will reveal, in fact, 'the importance of social structure in influencing character formation', and 'the reality of the class struggle' (*EA*, pp. 352–3). Dissolving what the Freud elegy calls 'the set mask of rectitude' is the political task psychoanalysis makes possible for the early Auden.

Writing about Edgar Allan Poe's stories in 1950 (*FA*, pp. 210–12) Auden offered a formula which could be applied to his own early writings. 'There is', he wrote, 'no place in any of them for the human individual as he actually exists in space and time, that is, as simultaneously a natural creature subject in his feelings to the influences and limitations of the natural order, and an historical person, creating novelty and relations by his free choice and modified in unforeseen ways by the choices of others.' Instead, Poe offers a series of stories whose heroes exist not as changing, developing subjects and agents but only as 'unitary states'. In one kind of tale, the 'hero has no history because he refuses to change with time'; in the other, he 'has none because he cannot change, he can only experience', and he is 'as purely passive as the I in dreams; nothing that happens is the result of his personal choice, everything happens *to* him.' In this latter kind, 'What the subject feels – interest, excitement, terror – are caused by events over which he has no control whatsoever.' But in the other kind of story there is a different stasis, in those 'states of wilful being' which express 'the destructive passion of the lonely ego to merge with the ego of another, the passion of the conscious ego to be objective, to discover by pure reason the true relationships which sensory experiences and emotions would conceal...self-destructive states in which the ego and the self are passionately hostile...even the state of chimerical passion, that is, the passionate unrest of a self that lacks all passion'. It could almost be a programme note for the states of anxiety, restlessness and hysterical stasis we find in the three volumes of poems from 1928 to 1933.

Auden links 'the development of such a fiction in which the historical individual is missing' with the 'development of history as a science' and a social world where 'the individual seems more and more the creation of historical forces' and 'less and less capable of directing his life by any historical choice of his own'. The remark helps explain the title 'Missing' first given at about this time to the 1929 poem, 'From scars where kestrels hover'. The ambiguity of that word 'subject' in Auden's remarks above – the subject who 'feels' but is powerless, and who is 'subject to' the natural order but unable to choose and act – indicates precisely what is 'missing' from this poem: 'the historical individual' capable of directing his own life.

This poem turns repeatedly on the moment of repression. In the very moment of 'looking over/Into the happy valley' the leader has to 'turn away' to separation, austerity: 'The slow fastidious line/That disciplines the fell'. Consciousness means renouncing that unproblematic unity of being, and the 'line' of the hill draws the seeing self into a paternal lineage, founded not in union but in exile. In the same way, the opening 'scars' suggest both escarpment and cicatrix, both in their different ways recording a breach now partially healed over. Yet this leader seems to be 'unwounded', though his companions are 'doomed' – indeed, before the sentence is finished they have been reduced to 'voices in the rock' who have already 'died beyond the border'. What has reduced them to mere traces is the same act of repression out of which the apparently authoritative leader emerges as the surveying ego.

The second section of the poem then turns back on this

commanding gaze, warning of the deaths of heroes who did not believe in death, redefining bravery as 'resisting the temptations/To skyline operations', refusing the expectations of those visitors who come expecting to find that nothing has changed, 'Choosing their spots to view/The prize competitors'. Whatever might be obscure in this elliptical and evasive poem, one thing is clear: the dubious association of power and the commanding look. Instead of affirming this connection, the poem closes with an even more acute sundering of leader (who 'must migrate') and 'host' (who passes 'Alive into the house'). In these contrary movements the 'historical individual' disappears into those gaps in the text, across those borders of meaning where we suspect an explanation may reside.

Like the disappointed visitors, the reader too can find no confident point of view in which to take up position, and is also compelled to migrate. If the hero goes missing in these early poems, so does the speaker/reader as subject. We are left instead with a kind of new objectivity where the subject seems no more than the shifting linkage of a succession of sentences, passively suffered perceptions, images, metonymies, feelings, that pass across the poem like clouds in a mirror. 'Between Adventure' speaks of a meeting in which 'Calling of each other by name' appears to guarantee the mutual 'good nature/Obvious in each agreeable feature'. But this obviousness deceives, concealing hate and fear:

> On narrowness stand, for sunlight is
> Brightest only on surfaces.

It is only in this play of the linguistic surface that the bourgeois ego of 'A Free One' can maintain his conqueror's 'erect carriage', which is really a 'balancing subterfuge'. The reader too is implicated in this difficult balancing act, and reading the poem involves a perpetual unsettling.

'Do not imagine you can abdicate;/Before you reach the frontier you are caught', advises the poem later called 'Venus Will Now Say a Few Words'. In the untitled original both speaker and addressee only slowly come into focus, the accumulating information grudgingly allocating them their positions. The 'you' addressed in the opening line is defined first of all by his 'part'. He is primarily a generic individual, not a unique person, but the details of his various activities give him a more specific identity as a privileged and loved being, relaxing in his darling's arms – the simile is disturbing – 'like a stone', making the most of 'hours of fuss'. Just as he emerges to this central place in the narrative, however, he is decentred by the speaker's coming clean. She is the life-force, and his supposed 'joy is mine not yours'. It is not, despite the ambiguous syntax, he who has 'come so far,/Whose cleverest invention was lately fur', for the next line makes it clear that it is Venus who sees both him and fur as *her* inventions: 'Lizards my best once who took years to breed'. The poem proceeds contemptuously to dethrone this self-satisfied subject from his assumption of mastery:

> To reach that shape for your face to assume,
> Pleasure to many and despair to some,
> I shifted ranges, lived epochs handicapped
> By climate, wars, or what the young men kept,
> Modified theories on the types of dross,
> Altered desire and history of dress.

The deepest impulses of the self, its despair, its sense of famine and anguish, its pious escapism, are not, Venus says, 'your own', but merely mean 'that I wish to leave and to pass on', selecting another carrier for her favours. That carrier will in turn be 'signed for, made to answer, topped'. The analogy with discourse, infiltrating the whole poem, presents the subject as no more than one inflexion of a general grammar, not the articulating subject of language but merely its vehicle. Just as it is Venus who summons this respondent into being by inviting him to consider what he does, so the subject is interpellated by history, signed for and made to answer. Yet precisely by entering into discourse the subject also accepts the fact of supersession, and the poem itself now abruptly terminates him, just as it first called him into being. The reader has come to share the role of addressee. As the poem ends, it is we who find ourselves arbitrarily dismissed, locked into our subject-positions at the very moment that the discourse which has constituted us snatches that position away from us, leaving us belatedly to realize that we too have been 'Holders of one position, wrong for years'.

This unsettling of the reader is a repeated way of subverting the subject in the early poems. Poems such as 'This Loved One', with their insistent depersonalizing generality, restore us as readers to that volatile abyss before the self was formed, before 'this loved one/Was that one and that one', entering into a particular history and family, acquiring a 'pleasing name', neighbours and ghosts, learning to greet and exchange language. At the same time, this entry into language is seen as an 'old loss'; we enter on 'mortgaged lands'. Living only in the endless crossing of frontiers, changing of houses, the subject seems to exist only as an abstract item of exchange, like money, or language, real only in the transaction of 'coins to pass/In a cheaper house'.

Many of the early poems re-enact, as if in some compulsive repetition, the processes by which the subject is formed, taking us again and again through the crises first mapped out in the poem which opens Auden's publishing career, in *Poems* (1928), where the moment of separation which 'brought knowledge, you', brings too a 'two-faced dream' in which knowledge is lost in ideology. Some of the most powerful narratives of threat and betrayal arise from this sense of a suborned subject, who, like the lying mouth of another poem, will 'murder or betray/For either party equally'. All utterance in these poems has a double function, speaking not only *for* the self-articulating subject but also *through* him, betraying him to the power of the patriarch. This is the point of that shift from the fantasy of masterful selfhood, in 'On Sunday Walks', to the reality of subversion revealed in dream and 'waking fright', whose handsome conquerors 'Say what they say/Know what they know', but whose knowing and speaking are delusions. All that 'father's son' really knows is 'what they said/And what they did', taken in by a discourse that dispossesses as it claims: 'All glory and all story/Solemn and not so good'.

The child, Auden was to write in 'Criticism in a Mass Society' in 1941, 'is born as a closed system of reflex responses' and the aim of education is to enable it to grow into an adult 'who is open to the degree to which he ceases to be merely accessory to his position and becomes aware of who he is and what he really wants'. He 'could be different if he chose. The necessity that can make him free is no longer his position as such, but the necessity of choosing to accept or reject it.'[1] The role of *eros paidogogos* in these early poems is to render the reader/subject's own position precarious, to dislocate the reader into a new perception of the subject's role in the construction of meanings.

Three poems of 1936 all begin with the same formula, interpellating a 'who' whose relation with its landscape is then rendered problematic: 'O who can ever praise enough/The world of his belief?'; '"O who can ever gaze his fill",/Farmer and fisherman say, "On native shore and local hill"...', and 'Detective Story'. The last opens with the question 'For who is ever quite without his landscape?' only to plant, in the middle of that landscape, a corpse which renders it enigmatic and requires, in the end, a total revaluation of subject and landscape alike, by calling into question the very 'story' within which both are inscribed. The reader reproduces the crisis of the poem's subject. In the Blakean terms of 'O who can ever praise', the reader too is compelled to 'deny' father's love, 'be lost' to mother's womb, become 'Bride and victim to a ghost', and be thrown into 'the pit of terror' to 'bear the wrath alone'. This bearing, though, changes from the passivity of the victim to the child-bearing of the bride, at the moment that the subject chooses to bring itself into being, as anger and rejection. The reader too, first produced by the text, then learns to become its producer, and in the process effects a self-transformation.

Auden's essay on the detective story 'The Guilty Vicarage' (*DH*, pp. 146–58), elucidates this point. Caught throughout the story in a 'dialectic of innocence and guilt', the reader, Auden suggests, is an accessory to a series of positions and knowledges, for if he shares in the ignorance of the affronted community, he can participate too in the detective's search for the clues that will finally reveal the culprit:

> The magic formula is an innocence which is discovered
> to contain guilt; then a suspicion of being the guilty one;
> and finally a real innocence from which the guilty other
> has been expelled, a cure effected, not by me or my
> neighbors, but by the miraculous intervention of a genius
> from outside who removes guilt by giving knowledge of
> guilt.

Having parenthetically remarked that 'the best victim is the
negative Father or Mother Image', Auden then concludes on
the role of fantasy as 'an attempt to avoid one's own suffering':

> The fantasy, then, which the detective story addict
> indulges is the fantasy of being restored to the Garden
> of Eden, to a state of innocence, where he may know
> love as love and not as the law. The driving force behind
> this daydream is the feeling of guilt, the cause of which
> is unknown to the dreamer. The fantasy of escape is the
> same, whether one explains the guilt in Christian,
> Freudian, or any other terms.

It is no accident, then, that these early poems of Auden's
should be describable in the terms of Poe's fiction, for they
share the same landscape of fantasy, are all, in a sense, detective stories of the unconscious. The 'Who' which opens so many
of these poems is the guilty culprit of the 'Whodunnit', seeking
to become the innocent and knowing detective. The detective
for Auden, we might note, is the 'total stranger who cannot
possibly be involved in the crime'.

Uncertainty about our subject-position as readers is linked
to a larger anxiety of transit in which all sureties are unsettled.
The interrogative 'Who' which opens the poem later called
'No Change of Place' plunges into a journey across a shifting
landscape of antitheses, only to return in the end to the
recognition foregrounded by that title. The 'Who' which
endures these shifting dangers is itself not a unitary being,
but an instant of transit, reconstituted from moment to
moment. Yet for all the dislocations through which we pass

in reading, in the end we have got nowhere, find ourselves turned back by the patriarchal imago of 'gaitered gamekeeper with dog and gun'. The change of pronoun has trapped us into a deeper loss. For the opening 'Who' which 'will endure' has now become a merely negative pronoun: 'No one will ever know/For what conversion brilliant capital is waiting.' We too are denied our 'conversion', denied our 'change of place'.

The linking of 'conversion' in the self with the 'conversions' of capital is not fortuitous. The self is exchanged like money, an abstract commodity circulated through a range of subject-positions, yet nothing in itself. Reviewing a study of mental duality in April l930 (*EA*, pp. 301–2), Auden argued that dual conceptions, of a higher and lower self, reason and instinct, are apt to lead to 'the inhibition rather than the development of desires, to their underground survival in immature forms, the cause of disease, crime and permanent fatigue'. They are thus likely to produce that psychosomatic illness in which the repressed and unspoken makes itself felt in the semiotics of the symptom. 'The only duality is that between the whole self at different stages of development – e.g. a man before and after a religious conversion. The old must die in giving birth to the new.'

'Consider this and in our time', written a month before this, is clearly echoed in it. The poem is a crucial negotiation of the moment of conversion, enacting in its dual movement of 'concealment' and 'manifestation' that 'peripeteia' spoken of in 'The Guilty Vicarage': 'not a reversal of fortune but a double reversal from apparent guilt to innocence and from apparent innocence to guilt' (*DH*, p. 147). The reader is initially summoned into a point of view which offers identification with the superior gaze of the outsider, hawk or airman. But we are then plunged back to earth, from the detached synoptic view to the close-up scrutiny of the detective looking for clues:

> look there
> At cigarette-end smouldering on a border
> At the first garden party of the year.

At once, however, we are invited to 'Pass on, admire the view', and to join in a series of acts which increasingly implicate us in the privileged scene of the Sports Hotel. We are not allowed to sit content here, however, but are then 'Relayed elsewhere' along with the music.

Not only are we swept along through a variety of scenes. In the next paragraph we seem to have changed our identity as addressee, and become a mysterious 'supreme Antagonist'; and before we have assimilated the analogy that links us with Leviathan we have to make sense of the accusation that long ago and somewhere else our unanswered comments on 'the high-born mining captains/ . . . made them wish to die'. By this point we should be getting seriously worried. What, precisely, is it that the speaker wants us to do? Just who does he think we are?

But the catalogue of our crimes grows. We are vain, and talk to our admirers every day. What's more, we seem to be responsible in some way for the silted harbours, derelict works, and strangled orchards where we meet them. Confusion is compounded by the next lines, a series of injunctions which, despite the full stop which precedes them, may just carry over the indicative of the earlier sentence ('You talk'). But if they are orders, who is it that is addressing us now, ordering us to —

> Order the ill that they attack at once:
> Visit the ports and, interrupting
> The leisurely conversation in the bar
>
> . . .
>
> Beckon your chosen out. Summon
> Those handsome and diseased youngsters, those women
> Your solitary agents in the country parishes. . .

Are we in turn agents of his authority, or is his address that of an accomplice or, with irony, that of an enemy (we have been named the Antagonist)? The instructions which follow are not nice and suggest either that our addresser is not nice either or that he has no love for us, if he thinks us capable of such things. Not only are we bad-mannered, interrupting all those people, but we spread disgusting rumours and diseases.

Look, just who do you think you are? *I* only came for the view of the massif, and now I am transformed again for, in the final paragraph of the poem, I am addressed as 'Financier, leaving your little room/Where the money is made but not spent'. And before I can protest my innocence I am told that 'The game is up for you and for the others', and plunged once again into a web of complicity with people who, on second inspection, don't seem too bad at all – dons and bishops and nurses and people like that.

Now at least I seem to have found the right set: 'Seekers after happiness, all who follow/The convolutions of your simple wish'. But here comes the menace again: 'It is later than you think.' Good lord, is that the time? I must fly. Well perhaps you should have the last word, since you seem to have it all sewn up. Speak up:

> You cannot be away then, no,
> Not though you pack to leave within an hour
>
>   . . .
>
> The date was yours; the prey to fugues
>
>   . . .
>
> After some haunted migratory years
> To disintegrate on an instant in the explosion of mania
> Or lapse forever into a classic fatigue.

Oh, I say, is this your helmet on the seat?

The poem, that is, takes us through a series of powerful transformations in which, like money, we are always passing on, and yet always fixed in the same position, projected passively at the receiving end of a series of commands that attribute to us the power and authority that the speaker himself seems to possess. Auden subverts both speaker and addressee here, in a 'double reversal', recruiting us first into complicity against the contemned world, and then casting us back into it as the prime cause of its dereliction. Yet, as the cause of this catastrophe, we then become its victims, disintegrating, lapsing, exploding in the final instant into exhaustion, mania, the collapse of meanings. But the speaker too, casting us as his adversary, is caught up in that which he condemns, the very authority of his voice compromising him; his fixity against our fungibility calling his commanding position into question. As speaker and addressee at once, the subject here partakes of the duplicity of the text, simultaneously culprit and judge.

It is this crisis which lies behind the parable of conversion in the four poems that make up the sequence later called '1929'. Though he points out the allusion in the second poem of the sequence to 'final war/Of proletariat against police', Edward Mendelson is emphatic that 'The poem makes no move to embrace this socially apocalyptic future', seeing 'a global warning in the autumn air' as 'a psychological apocalypse ...only slightly updated from the Book of Revelation'.[2] Mendelson points out the contradictoriness of the sequence, which moves from metaphors of weaning in the first two poems to ones of drowning in the second two, the third poem being the point of transition between manuscript and published versions. That this shift of metaphor is not simply an unresolved contradiction of the text, but a key moment in its disruption of perspectives, becomes clearer if one gives a little thought to Auden's title.

For 1929 is not, of course, just any old year. It is a turningpoint in modern history, standing at the beginning of that 'low dishonest decade' whose obituary Auden was to write in September 1939. As J. K. Galbraith recorded in *The Great Crash 1929*:

> Some years, like some poets and politicians and some lovely women, are singled out for fame beyond the common lot, and 1929 was clearly such a year. Like 1066, 1776, and 1914, it was a year that everyone remembers. One went to college before 1929, was married after 1929, or wasn't even born in 1929, which bespeaks total innocence. A reference to 1929 has become shorthand for the events of that autumn.[3]

A shorthand everyone remembers, it seems, except the critics. Yet the clue is provided in a footnote Auden slipped into his essay on 'Psychology and Art To-day' in 1935 (*EA*, p. 334). Auden had been quoting Freud on the role of art in translating repressed 'phantasy' into an aesthetic gratification, whose 'origin in prohibited sources is not easily detected'. 'We only think', he says, 'when we are prevented from feeling or acting as we should like. Perfect satisfaction would be complete unconsciousness. Most people, however, fit into society too neatly for the stimulus to arise except in a crisis such as falling in love or losing their money.' And then, half-repressed into a footnote in a way which prefigures Mendelson's treatment of the same theme, he adds: 'E.g., the sale of popular textbooks on economics since 1929'. Auden does not need to spell out the reasons for his date. It is not an arbitrary choice any more than the different moments of the four-part sequence are arbitrary, corresponding as they do to the key moments in that financial crisis which ran in tandem with Auden's own crisis of identity. Even at the very end of his life, in 'Thanksgiving', he was to recall this as a year in which he did something unusual, when his personal experience of German culture offered him 'a new language', Brecht's, to explain an otherwise inexplicable 'external', 'social' disaster.

'1929' has a double subject. One is that person whose 'psychological crisis' of weaning is completed in the October of death and drowning of the last poem. But the other subject is the year itself, living itself out through all the individual lives it touched and transformed, whose own crisis also came in October, in the form of economic collapse. At the moment that the soul seemed 'weaned at last to independent delight' that collapse put an end to 'the summer talk', called instead for 'the destruction of error'.

Auden, seeking abroad in the first poem 'An altering speech for altering things,/An emphasis on new names, on the arm/A fresh hand with fresh power', is rebuked by a less inspiriting figure:

But thinking so I came at once
Where solitary man sat weeping on a bench,

Hanging his head down, with his mouth distorted
Helpless and ugly as an embryo chicken.

His response is to turn away from such sights. If the fertility associations of Easter pervade the first poem, transforming all grief into hope of renewal, it is May Day which presides over the second. The very ambiguity of this day – a pagan celebration of the present turned into a workers' celebration of the future – is reinforced by the events of May Week in the poet's neighbourhood: 'All this time was anxiety at night,/ Shooting and barricade in street', though it is experienced only vicariously, in the excited words of a socialist friend reporting events. The political storm passes him by; he is much more absorbed in contemplating his own thought-processes. As yet, the thinking, feeling subject makes no connection between the 'anxiety at night', riot and insurrection, and the 'solitary man . . . weeping' of the earlier moment.

The speaker begins, however, to put himself in perspective, a 'homesick foreigner', realizing himself a 'Tiny observer of enormous world' from his hill-top vantage point, and as if for the first time recognizing all those other lives and voices around him. In self-absorption, he turns to reflect on a Freudian account of the formation of the self, passing from mother to otherness, learning separation and loss in that entry into knowledge which is also self-division, 'knowledge in him now of other,/Cries in cold air, himself no friend'. Fear of the other person turns back into fear of oneself as other, distrust of the body itself as that which betrays – the origins, the poem suggests, of the death-wish and of its offshoots in 'hired' and 'ancestral' property:

Body reminds in him to loving,
Reminds but takes no further part,
Perfunctorily affectionate in hired room
But takes no part and is unloving
But loving death. May see in dead,
In face of dead that loving wish,
As one returns from Africa to wife,
And his ancestral property in Wales.

Writing in *Illusion and Reality* in 1937 of the processes by which consciousness is transformed, within limits set by 'necessity', Christopher Caudwell offered an account which might explain what is going on through the course of this sequence. Auden's preoccupation here with the relation between seeing, saying, thinking and feeling, and between forgetting and reminding, corresponds to that process which Caudwell describes by referring to the four functions of the psyche demarcated by Jung – intellect, feeling, intuition and sensation (a quartet Auden employed later in *The Age of Anxiety*). A transformation of personality takes place, Caudwell suggests, when the ratio between these different functions in a personality undergoes a shift. This change can be effected by a shift of external and internal forces, such as to bring about a conflict in consciousness. What happens for Auden is what Caudwell, drawing on Jung, calls an 'enantiodromia', in which an external crisis suddenly transforms that which is seen, and frees the repressed alternative function of the psyche which the conscious self had sought to forget. Speaking of Jung's 'functions', he says:

> All four functions exist in all psyches, and therefore individuation – the development of one function at the expense of the other – means that the functions not used sink into the unconscious. Thus in a thinker feeling sinks into the unconscious and becomes correspondingly barbaric and crude. Here it exerts a compensatory influence, and may eventually gain in power until, at first sporadically and then completely, it becomes the main function, and there is an *enantiodromia*, a kind of conversion or complete reversal of personality, as when the cold, Christian-hating Saul becomes the ardent apostle Paul, or when the dry mathematical person becomes a raving maniac.[4]

It is this last rupture with the past which occurs in the final section of '1929', when 'the loud madman/Sinks now into a more terrible calm', and 'the abrupt self-confident farewell' stands revealed as imposture, 'The self-confidence of the falling root'. In section 3, sporadic outbreaks of doubt and disturbance spread through August, the month of completion when the harvest is gathered. Signs of a deepening repression are apparent in the opening lines, with their emphasis on order, correctness control, even while the contrary 'slackening of wire' is taking place, only to meet 'sharp reprimand'. The English country cottage to which he has returned is a place of regression for 'the frightened soul'. It is 'No longer his'; but he 'falters . . . vexed' in his movement, like a child newly weaned, glad to return home, 'a place/Where no tax is levied for being there'. The fiscal metaphor hints at a larger world which exacts tribute. He is torn by insecurity, not knowing whether his present is the seed of some fructifying future, or the 'degenerate remnant' of an immense past, now 'Surviving only as the infectiousness of disease'. So far, some dreadful end has been 'glossed over by the careless but known long/To the finer perception of the mad and ill'. Insight, that is, has its costs – madness, illness – but so does ignorance. He is perched on the frontier between false and true seeing, resisting the break, trying to hold on to what he loves, losing and mourning it, but in that 'difficult work of mourning' coming to a new perception.

The 'homesick foreigner' of an earlier section must now find his home in the exile of language, out of its falterings and mistakes. In a strange country foreign settlers 'By mispronunciation of native words' create a new speech. What is taking place in the subject at this moment is the conflict of discourses out of which an 'independent delight' may emerge; but the section ends with a self 'Startled' out of its security, prepossessed by 'forethought of death', which it is hoped will avert being 'helplessly strange to the new conditions'.

Noticeable in the last section is the passivity of the agents. 'Orders are given to the enemy', but they have no specific source; rather they form a whole landscape of rumour, whisper, casual question, enforcing a collective destiny which abolishes individual wills, enforcing 'Conformity with the orthodox bone, / With organised fear, the articulated skeleton'. The last adjective indicates how the material has taken over from the mental, how the economic infrastructure now articulates events, not 'The intricate play of the mind'. 1929 has come into its own. The young man who thought to inherit has his legacy. Choice is now no longer what it merely *seemed* to be in the first section: 'a necessary error'. Error has now been destroyed, and with it, choice. This is not our day at all: 'This is the dragon's day, the devourer's.'

The 'free play of the mind' is over. This is 'the history of knowing' of which the 1930 version speaks. The crumbling of the economy reveals the fatuousness of all that personal preoccupation with the 'restlessness of intercepted growth'. The 'tiny observer' is dethroned from his eminence, marginalized by events, and can enter into that knowledge which obsesses the poem only by accepting supersession, recognizing that love needs, now, its opposite: 'Needs death, death of the grain, our death,/Death of the old gang'. This gang, the old ruling class, can no longer be described in terms of its personal charm and distinctive culture, but only in the cliché images of arbitrary power derived from Perrault and the Brothers Grimm. Parental imagos are transformed into the ogres of the nursery, just as the thaumaturge of the new age merges the fairy prince and the awaited messiah:

The hard bitch and the riding-master,
Stiff underground; deep in clear lake
The lolling bridegroom, beautiful, there.

In this early poetry, Auden exposes a world where subjects have no power, where they are overwhelmed by and secondary to objects, to external forces that can arrange and rearrange their loves. The death of this kind of subject is necessary before an active, engaged consciousness, sensuously involved in action, can be possible. This 'lolling bridegroom' is what awaits on the other side of catastrophe. *The Orators* is about the price that has to be paid.

There is no point of view outside the compromised and compromising perspectives of history, but in the early poems Auden tries by a deliberate deranging of the surface coherence of language to make them give up a few clues that might show us where we are and what we have done. His essay of 1946 in the *The Kafka Problem* (1975) argued that drama and novel present a 'feigned history', a spectacle to which one remains a spectator, 'firmly fixed in my own time and place'. But a parable requires that 'I have to surrender my objectivity and identify myself with what I read', and its meaning is 'different for every reader'. The hero of such a tale is not one of the elect, but under a curse, and his desire to reach a goal is proof of this. Unlike traditional quest heroes he does not ask 'Can I do it?' but 'What ought I to do?' What he does now matters enormously, and if he guesses wrong he will suffer and be as responsible as if he had chosen wrongly. If the advice he receives seems absurd or contradictory, this may be proof of his own folly, not that of his advisers. Kafka's K is interpellated into identity by the fact of his complicity in history. In the traditional quest, becoming a hero means acquiring the right to say *I*. 'But K is an *I* from the start, and in this fact alone, that he exists, irrespective of any gifts or deeds, lies his guilt':

> If the K of *The Trial* were innocent, he would cease to be K and become nameless. . . In *The Castle*, K, the letter, wants to become a word, *land-surveyor*, that is to say, to

acquire a self like everybody else but this is precisely what he is not allowed to acquire.

This could almost be a description of the opaque and baffling world depicted by *The Orators* in 1932.

Surveying and the desire to have a self like everybody else are intimately linked throughout *The Orators*. The link is foregrounded in the opening quatrains of the book, with their picture of a child entering into identity by learning to inscribe himself in the language which maps out his social landscape:

> By landscape reminded once of his mother's figure
> The mountain heights he remembers get bigger and
>   bigger:
> With the finest of mapping pens he fondly traces
> All the family names on the familiar places.

Accepting these names and places, he enters into an ideology which also puts him in his place, makes him the proud possessor of the self and phallus that endorse this act. Throughout the book, such surveying is associated with that Enemy who lies in wait in all our acts, seeking the moment to betray, suborn, appropriate us. He is there in the stout clergyman 'estimating on the back of the envelope the height of the waterfall for the hydraulic engineer'; in those helpful parental figures who bring 'a map of the country' to help the hero on his mission, who warn against the 'flying trickster' in the wood, and advise him to get a 'settled job' and 'keep their hours and live by the clock'. It is by refusing their maps and advice that he 'Finds consummation in the wood/And sees for the first time the country'. 'THE ENEMY', one aphorism tells us in urgent capitals, 'IS A LEARNED NOT A NAIVE OBSERVER', and it is in this learning to observe that consciousness is suborned, drawn into misrecognition of what it sees. The 'maps' are linguistic mappings of the 'real'. Only by rebelling against them can the subject find its own country and 'the hour of love'. The Enemy, that is, is that ideology and self-interest which contaminates consciousness, and the first lesson we have to learn is set out at the beginning of the

Airman's Journal: 'A system organises itself, if interaction is undisturbed. Organisation owes nothing to the surveyor. It is in no sense pre-arranged. The surveyor provides just news.' 'The Enemy as an Observer', however, has the 'half-true' awareness of invalids and precocious children: 'accuracy of description of symptoms' while he prescribes more of the same, like the vet who prescribes arsenic for the dog paralysed by arsenical poisoning. (Auden's thirties readers would have caught an allusion to current cant ideas in economics - that the cure for the Depression and unemployment was more of the same.)

In the thirties Auden's version of that question 'What ought I to do?' had been Lenin's more objective formulation: 'What is to be done?' Discussing the new Leavisian ideas of education in 1933, for example, and the need to assist 'children to defeat propaganda of all kinds by making them aware of which buttons are being pressed', he answered the question by addressing the cause, not the symptoms – the nature of consciousness itself. The crucial step is to realize that consciousness is not 'uncontaminated by its object', that it is not 'insulated' from the 'process of decay' it observes (*EA*, pp. 317–18). Reviewing Liddell Hart's biography of T. E. Lawrence in 1934, Auden detected in Lawrence's life 'an allegory of the transformation of the Truly Weak Man into the Truly Strong Man, an answer to the question "How shall the self-conscious man be saved?"' The way forward, he says, lies not in seeking to 'enlist in the great Fascist retreat', surrendering to despair, but in a unity of 'action and reason', for 'it is only in action that reason can realise itself, and only through reason that action can become free.' Citing D. H. Lawrence's dismissal of 'the Western-romantic conception of personal love' as 'a neurotic symptom only inflaming our loneliness, a bad answer to our real wish to be united to and rooted in life', he links both Lawrences to Lenin's revolutionary asceticism: 'The self must first learn to be indifferent; as Lenin said, "To go hungry, work illegally and be anonymous".' T. E. Lawrence and Lenin, he says, exemplify 'our nearest approach to a synthesis of feeling and reason, act and thought, the most potent agents of freedom and to us, egotistical underlings, the most relevant accusation and hope' (*EA*, pp. 320–1). T. E. Lawrence's enlistment as Aircraftsman Shaw, relinquishing heroic elevation for anonymous service, is the 'absolutely modern act'. The Airman likewise, in his Journal, is one trying to come to terms with the 'signs of mixed character' in his own identity. As he notes: 'Most people mixed characters – the two-faced, the obscure and amazed, the touchline admirers.'

The mixed character of Auden's own text has often been remarked on. Richard Johnson writes that it 'was evidently very significant during the thirties; everyone seems to have known what it was about. But, as G. S. Fraser has remarked, one is apt to find, coming back to it years later and in a different context, a meaning quite different from what everyone assumed it to have when it was published.'[1] Not only repentant ex-communists could clutch at Auden's own recantation, in the Preface to the third edition in 1967: 'My name on the title-page seems a pseudonym for someone else, someone talented but near the border of sanity, who might well, in a year or two, become a Nazi.' Auden's own perplexity is part of the meaning. His anxiety about the book's obscurity and 'swank' expresses that pattern of censorship which throughout his life led him to placate the paternal imagos of Censor and Scissor Man by suppressing some of his best poems. He wrote in reply to a reader's letter that the book 'is far too obscure and equivocal. It is meant to be a critique of the fascist outlook, but from its reception among some of my contemporaries, and on rereading it myself, I see that it can, most of it, be interpreted as a favourable exposition. The whole Journal ought to be completely rewritten' (*EA*, p. xv). In 1967 he wrote in his Preface that 'My guess today is that my unconscious motive. . .was therapeutic, to exorcise certain tendencies in myself by allowing them to run riot in phantasy . . . It is precisely the schoolboy atmosphere and diction which act as a moral criticism of the rather ugly emotions and ideas they are employed to express. By making the latter juvenile, they make it impossible to take them seriously.'

The most striking thing about *The Orators* is that we still don't know how to classify it. Auden is a poet who is keen on giving clues to the genre in which he is working: charade, oratorio, commentary or baroque eclogue, tragedy or melodrama, are all classifications which appear on his title pages. But the subtitle of *The Orators* – *An English Study* – gives no indication of what to expect and, therefore, of how to read the book. We're not even told whether this is prose or verse, and we have difficulties, therefore, in assessing the particular valency of individual passages, many of which were subsequently published separately. Coupled with this bewilderment is a larger one, which constantly presents itself in reading: does this text have a narrative that can be deduced from its clues and riddles, its nods and winks of meaning? It seems after all, to have a hero, though he shifts his ground before we can pin him down, merging at times with the authorial voice, and at other times offering his own internal texts, as in 'Letter to a Wound' and 'Journal of an Airman'. We too are enrolled in the ranks of the detectives invoked in 'Argument' as patron saints and protectors.

The Orators, that is, presents itself as a hermeneutic problem from the start. It offers as its *primary* concern the problematic nature of interpretation, implicating us as readers in the crisis of meanings it explores. It signals that it is doing this by importunately reminding us of the diversity of reading acts in which we can be involved, making us ask that question of the wayward text which is asked in the 'Epilogue': '"O where are you going?" said reader to rider.' These varieties of discourse include prize-day oration, argument, prayer and litany, statement, letter, diary, journal, an I.Q. 'test' with geometrical figures, sestina, 'Airman's Alphabet', lists, riddles, elegies, gnomic Welsh triads, interview, pamphlet and lecture, lampoon, dream narration and dream analysis, military despatches, scientific textbooks, bills, pindaric odes, newspaper reports, metrical psalms. The text confronts the reader with its own problematic textuality. As Auden wrote in 1932: 'The difference between different kinds of writing lies not so much in the writing itself, but in the way we look at it. . . . Literary forms do not exist outside our own mind' ('Writing', *EA*, p. 308).

The title must be taken seriously in its stress on the relation between discourse and power. It proposes that every speech-act is aimed to produce an effect, is never disinterested, even if that effect is only the reincorporation of our elusive impulses into a system of language and authority where we know our place. The repeated echoing of the word 'read' throughout, combined with an emphasis on the act of writing, turns round on the reader. If the text itself is evasive, riddling, cryptically hinting at and refusing a narrative progression or genre category, if its subject (both hero and theme) keeps slipping from our grasp, it is because the text wishes to make us see in a new and unfamiliar way all the forms of discourse we have taken for granted as our inheritance.

The guerrilla warfare spoken of in one of his final Odes, subsequently entitled for separate publication 'Which Side Am I Supposed To Be On?', becomes a figure of the larger move-ment of the text. Unlike positional warfare, in which each side has a clearly demarcated battle-line, and knows where it and its enemy are, guerrilla warfare has no fronts. Or rather, the front is everywhere and nowhere, surfacing for a moment in a little local struggle, then dissolving away, leaving hardly any trace. Infiltration, fifth column activities, spying, are the keys to such warfare. We have to acquire skills in reading the signs of the Enemy's presence, become permanently suspicious, live on our nerves. When the division runs right through the self, the most apparently loyal of impulses can suddenly turn round and reveal its treachery. Eternal vigilance is hardly enough, for the vigilance of the surveyor may itself reveal the hand of the Enemy. For the Airman, his own hands are traitors. 'Conquest', he notes, 'can only proceed by absorption of, i.e. infection by, the conquered', and this is 'The true significance of my hands. "Do not imagine that you, no more than any other conqueror, escape the mark of grossness." They stole to force a hearing.' Not only does this reveal the rebellious hands engaged in another form of discourse – forcing a hearing through the psychosomatic symptoms of kleptomania – it also shows the rebellious Airman imagining himself the figure of power he has set himself against. Struggle against the Enemy only increases his power: his 'power is a function of our resistance' and that power can only be destroyed by ceasing to resist, by 'self-destruction'.

The text itself becomes self-destructive, bisecting and dissecting the normal continuities, prising open the cracks, flaws and weaknesses in the terrain of bourgeois ideology. Codes and riddles hint at a world of meaning withheld, the real explanation of all these false connections and lost threads. The ostensibly seamless web of discourse affirmed by the orators is revealed in all its nakedness as a jangling mess of jargons, held together only by the voice of power that commands them into imaginary unity. The 'English Study' of the subtitle reflects on us. For it is a study of the English language, and the forms of power it articulates, and it is a study of the English. But it is also a study *in* English, the language we share with the text, and in the process we too presume upon systems of meaning which take over our thinking, subsume us within certain expectations. This text written and set in an English public school, has for author a schoolmaster who was only recently a rebellious schoolboy. The school, like the language, becomes a locus where we are simultaneously masters and equally surely victims of power. We too can never know, not which side we are on, but which side we are *supposed* to be on – which raises the whole question of who is doing the supposing, who is expecting us to take sides, and who is deciding what the correct side is.

The 'English study' finally is that cosy room where even our Marxist studies in a dying culture are written. But in the process of fixing ourselves in a secure position, wrapped up in a book, we are also rapt away, 'in a study', taken up and taken over by language. The final reply that the rider gives to the reader in the 'Epilogue', is that he is going '"Out of this house"'. The 'reader' has warned the 'rider' against venturing into a wilderness of disorder and madness beyond. In the second stanza the 'fearer' warns the 'farer' that he is foolish to believe his 'diligent looking' will 'discover the lacking' which his every footstep registers. The reply in the last stanza is that '"Yours never will"' – your looking will never find what is lacking because you refuse to go beyond the confines of your fear. The last stanza also turns the table on the harmless reading subject who warns the rider and farer not to venture beyond the confines of a shared culture. In the third stanza, the reader experiences 'horror', but this is still an emotional response to something external, against which he warns the hearer. In the last stanza he *is* the horror, as the departing rider tells him: '"They're looking for you". . ./As he left them there, as he left them there.' The Epilogue enacts that transit beyond the bounds of its own discourses, the various forms of language which seek to fix us in our subject-positions. We as readers are drawn to choose sides, between reading and riding, fearing and faring forth.

As readers, we are invited to challenge that which we have taken for granted: our selves, and the language which sustains those selves. This is the crisis the Airman goes through in his final days of mobilization, torn between two interpretations of his acts:

> I know that I am I, living in a small way in a temperate zone, blaming father, jealous of son, confined to a few acts often repeated, easily attracted to a limited class of physique, yet envying the simple life of the gut, desiring the certainty of the breast or prison, happiest sawing wood, only knowledge of the real, disturbances in the general law of the dream; the quick blood fretting against the slowness of the hope; a unit of life, needing water and salt, that looks for a sign.

> What have I written? Thoughts suitable to a sanatorium. Three days to break a lifetime's pride.

The two paragraphs catch the doubleness of an identity double-crossed by the very language in which it tries to explain itself. It knows its own artificial quality, knows how much of its identity is shaped by the Oedipal struggle of father and son, and knows too how the comfort of the breast is also that of the prison. 'Certainty' here is self-delusion, and it can only be fractured in a way that leads to truth, momentarily, when 'disturbances in the general law of the dream' – that ideological discourse in which we live all the time – give a glimpse of the 'real'. Writing desire out, externalizing it as signs, only confirms the madness of revolt. But refusing to follow the logic of that madness only incarcerates the self more absolutely in the prison-house of language.

Writing in *The Orators* offers scope for a fracturing of the dream discourse which may, at times, reveal 'the real'. In 'Letter to a Wound', the wound is not any specific illness or symptom, but rather the core of identity. The subject is constituted out of the experience of rupture, formed, at its deepest levels, by that moment which splits it off from the mother, the happy valley landscapes of the 'Prologue', and installs it as a separate being in the shadow of the father, subject to his law and language, enforced by the threat of castration. This breach in being does not merely leave it permanently scarred and incomplete. It thrusts identity into the very site of the wound, that rawness that opens up in all our discourses, as for example, 'when I was in the middle of writing a newsy letter to M., or doing tricks in the garden to startle R. and C., you showed your resentment by a sudden bout of pain.'

The scandal of the subject's formation is that it was not present at its own birth. All it knows is what it has gained – a discourse in which to figure itself – and what it has lost; for everywhere, in desire and melancholy, in anxiety and distress, it sees signs of that loss. This is the pain that makes itself felt in the middle of writing a letter, it is the thieving which the Airman's hands do against his will, it is the psychosomatic symptom, the tic, gesture, twitch that give away what goes on below the composed surface. It is, in fact, the site of the Enemy's presence. In *The Orators*, it happens to be homosexuality.

Later, in *The Enchafèd Flood*, writing about the romantic hero with his suffering, his scars and his symbolic and real castrations, represented by Ahab in *Moby Dick*, Auden was to offer an analysis of the sources of the hero which explains some of what is going on in *The Orators*. Hamlet, he observes, as the Romantic Avenger Hero, cherishes his situation, because if he lost it he would be ordinary again. He suffers from a 'dread of not having a vocation': '"My injury", he says, "is not an injury to me; it *is* me. If I cancel it out by succeeding in my vengeance, I shall not know who I am and will have to die. I cannot live without it". So not only does he cherish the memory of the catastrophic injury, but also he is not lured forward by the hope of happiness at some future date' (pp. 110–11).

This is the dilemma of the Airman, at once finding his identity in his injury, yet knowing he must go beyond the romantic personality, which has failed. This sense of failure is his first reaction to the discovery of the wound – 'I've lost everything, I've failed. I wish I was dead.' Then it becomes a consolation to him: 'knowing you has made me understand', able to penetrate all those other wounded and hidden subjects around him; and he feels now an almost cosy sense of self-satisfaction: 'And now here we are, together, intimate, mature.' But the smugness of this position identifies him with the Prize-Day speaker. He is fixated in his injury, gloating smarmily over it, narcissistically writing it letters. At the same time, the Airman knows he has to move beyond such traps. Recognition of the wound thus also involves a dislocation: 'I can't recognise myself. The discontinuity seems absolute.' It is in this gap that Ahab's fixation originates. Like the Airman, he becomes obsessed with the revenge which alone will free him.

Ahab is a figure of 'the exceptional hero' who suffers a tragic fall and is 'reduced to being lower than the average' (p. 136). But instead of accepting this, and assuming the position of the Truly Strong Man – i.e., '"To will to become nobody in particular in an aesthetic sense"' – Ahab takes the route of defiance, engaging in a parody of God's punishment, an 'extra wounding of himself' which is 'a goading of himself to remember his vow', a wilful remaking of that role he has been cast in by the power of the father to donate an identity he must embrace. This is how the paradox of resisting by showing no resistance works in *The Orators*.

It is in *writing* that the 'discontinuity' in the subject makes itself felt. For writing allows for rupture in its very textuality. This point is slyly made half-way through the 'Letter', when the writer breaks for dinner, to return with a simple indication that the times of writing and of reading are not the same – a new paragraph that begins *'Later'*. Similarly, after the 'Good-night and God bless you, my dear' that ends the letter, the last scribbled observation which he writes to himself is in sudden fear of the castrating reader: 'Better burn this'.

The essay 'Writing' in 1932 (*EA*, pp. 303–12) suggests that writing can be distinguished from speech in terms of its assumed community. In the oral tradition, 'the *feelings* meaning is transmitted with extraordinary accuracy, as the gestures and the tone of voice that go with the words are remembered also.' But 'With a statement in writing it is often impossible, after a time, to decide exactly what the author meant. Think how easy it is to misunderstand a letter.' At the same time, in speech, 'the *sense* meaning is apt to get strangely distorted. It is easy not to catch or to forget the exact words told to one, and to guess them wrongly; again we may be asked to explain something and add our own explanation, which is passed on with the story.' These distinctions give a hint as to what is going on in *The Orators*. Foremost among the Airman's subversive activities, after all, is the undermining of language, particularly in those oral public forms that posit an audience of participating equals. The Enemy's sense of humour may be based on 'Private associations', but 'he is serious, the associations are constant. He means what *he* says.' The only way to subvert such single-mindedness, the 'reason' of the 'usurper' who believes that 'man's only glory is to think', is through a double discourse that does *not* mean what it says: 'Practical jokes consist in upsetting these associations. They are in every sense contradictory and public, e.g. my bogus lecture to the London Truss Club.' The Airman's own example in turn upsets the seriousness of the discourse in which he too was almost trapped into the Enemy's single-mindedness.

What we see in the whole text of *The Orators* is a perpetual self-subversion in which meaning is refused. The reader, particularly the reader as critic, has to beware here, for we in turn may be trapped into the closure of the Enemy, seeking an assured and confident reading from the text. If *The Orators* is in one sense a prolonged practical joke, it is so in a highly serious way, for its technique of unsettlement hits us precisely where we are most vulnerable, in our desire for a unitary text that gives us a meaning and meaningful person with whom to associate.

The dilemma in which various critics have found themselves in reading this text becomes then the real site of that guerrilla war of interpretations which the book foregrounds. The poet, 'Watching in three planes from a room overlooking the court-yard', in the first of the Six Odes, seems to be a surveyor in a position of command over that which he sees. But he then has a dream which unsettles him, a voice urging him and his fellow writers to '"Read of your losses."' Each of the subsequent stanzas similarly interrupts the delusory happiness and certainty of the self with a pithy interjection, a cliché which takes on the ominousness of an aphorism, until all stand revealed as 'self-regarders' – the deserters, mechanics, conjurors, delicate martyrs alike. The next stanza brings the figure of oedipal anxiety, the castrating 'father,/Cold with a razor'. But nowhere are we shown 'One with power'. At this point the disembodied voice commands '"Save me!"' There is a peculiar doubling in this dream vision, for the self is at once a 'spectator' of what happens now, and yet seems to have fallen in sleep-walking from his eminence to be wakened by a voice asking '"How did you fall, sir?"' Before, however, we can come to terms with this, the whole earth is addressed, in the closing lines of this poem, by a beggar who speaks of our deepest terror, that a conqueror is coming even now, may already be 'seeking brilliant/Athens and us'.

The overthrow of the brilliant capital of intellect is what the text perpetually effects for the critical reader. If 'Letter to a Wound' has excited much contrary interpretation, the opening 'Address for a Prize-Day' (speech rather than writing) has created the same confusions. Justin Replogle in *Auden's Poetry* puts his finger on the raw nerve, speaking of it as 'another case of shifting persona, probably unparalleled for creating an almost incredible tangle of irreconcilables'. If the reader, he says, wishes to make the Address coherent, he has to decide whether Auden endorses its sentiments, or mocks them, or manages to do both simultaneously. Replogle's conclusion is that the passage, though 'in a perverse way it succeeds in spite of itself', is a text in which voices reverse and cancel each other: 'Auden could not make up his mind. . .he could not decide what he believed. . .Neither part is subdued, controlled, or subordinated to the other. . .and as a result we see Auden's own temperamental inconsistency pulling the speech to pieces'.[2]

It is certainly true that in his attack on 'England, this country of ours where nobody is well' and in his account of the various faulty loves that rule it, the speaker seems to echo Auden's own ideas on the collective neurosis of his age, its psychosomatic symptoms, and the cure required. At the same time, the speaker's address not only begins with pompously authoritative commonplaces, evoking the grandeur of the dead, but finally degenerates into a fantasy of revenge which seems less like a revolution than a spiteful pogrom. The clue to what is going on may lie in that language of power with which Replogle describes the authorial duty. The author should know his mind and stamp it on the text. Auden should Audain his meanings, issue textual Audenances to his Audience. But the nexus of authority and authorship is just what this Address denies. The speaker of the Address does not present a unitary speech because the culture which utters him is itself not unitary, but a web of contradictory discourses. Authority and rebellion may be tarred with the same brush, as the voice of power speaking from the dais reveals, at the core of his own unconscious, a text not of order and decency but of violence and revenge. As the Airman said of the Enemy, there is a contrast between his 'accuracy of description of symptoms compared with his prescription'. It is perhaps not accidental that these two words inflect 'script', writing, into mutually antagonistic modes. It is this double, self-cancelling discourse the book attempts to explode.

The Address, with its smooth elisions and oily self-congratulating articulacy, conceals all the snares, false analogies and arguments it cunningly slides over in recruiting the 'Initiates' to the role it wishes them to have in society. In a clear echo of Blake's Urizen and his hypocritic angels, the eminent old-boy links the call – interpellation – to the young boys with the apparently rational, modern desire to map the kingdom, bring it under a semblance of rule by census and surveying. He envisages a 'Divine Commission' of angels sent to compile a 'complete report' on England – something, he says, which would no doubt evoke anxiety in the boys. The implication is that, weighed in the balance, they know they would be found wanting. And it is on this anxiety that he now builds in order to recruit them to his project.

Power is here revealed as those Lords of Limit spoken of in 'The Watchers', seeking to delineate, delimit, define. But the superficial lucidity of the address is belied, as it develops through knee-jerk formulae, literary allusions, sly half-truths, by an increasingly surreal series of associative leaps in which the confidence and authority of the speaker is gradually undermined by his own Freudian slips and omissions. These analogies come dangerously close to giving the game away, as, for example, in his account of the 'defective lovers' aimed as a reproach to the boys, which alludes to systems running to a standstill, 'like those ship-cranes along Clydebank, which have done nothing all this year'. This degenerating sequence, which mimics the social collapse it describes, is arrested only by the abrupt call to direct violence. A saving exercise of brute force, exploiting the boys' repressed desire for revenge, but turning it against scapegoats in order to protect the real power that represses, is the strategy. The real return of the repressed, in this address, lies in the old-boy's nostalgia, not for the heroic ideals of the noble dead who have passed through this fine school, but for personal memories of bullying and fagging, the petty persecutions and guilt on which such an institution is founded, glorified in memory to daring deeds. At the base of all the talk of heroism and purity of heart are the shabby, furtive and Fascistic impulses of power. The hysterical conclusion, in retrospect, throws light on all the fine persuasive phrases that had gone before.

The passage recalls the jaundiced words which open *The Ascent of F6*, where Michael Ransom quotes Ulysses' famous appeal, in Dante, to sail into the sunset, pursuing Virtue and Knowledge. Ransom is contemptuous of the rhetoric, picturing Ulysses as 'a crook speaking to crooks', a bunch of 'seedy adventurers, of whose expensive education nothing remained but a few grammatical tags and certain gestures of the head'. He is adamant that this talk of Virtue and Knowledge is mere ideological camouflage for plunder and piracy; and that, for the exiled Dante, writing the *Inferno* involved not the worship of a disinterested God, but 'absolute revenge' on all those who had wronged him:

> who was Dante, to speak of Virtue and Knowledge? It was not Virtue those lips, which involuntary privation had made so bitter, could pray for; it was not Knowledge; it was Power . . .

Ransom is scathing in his cynicism about the ideological function of this rhetoric, a cynicism which justifies his own abstention from such a world in terms which recall the opening of *The Orators*:

> Virtue. Knowledge. We have heard these words before; and we shall hear them again – during the nursery luncheon, on the prize-giving afternoon, in the quack advertisement, at the conference of generals or industrial captains: justifying every baseness and excusing every failure, comforting the stilted schoolboy lives.

The play demonstrates that Ransom's abstemious withdrawal is no more disinterested. He learns that his own apparently 'clean' act, climbing F6, in its deepest motives belongs to the fallen world of Power. It is not simply that his desire for knowledge and his exercise of physical prowess have been *recruited* by that world. He is prepared to accept that the Imperial power and the popular media will use his deeds as justifications of Empire. The real shock is learning that his disinterested acts are *from the beginning* inscribed within the discourse of Power. At the mountain top, his companions dead, in delirium he has a vision of his Mother, welcoming him like an Ice Queen to a death which has always been his wish, but which is now seen to be fulfilment of the Oedipal dream. Behind all the noble justifications, we learn at his ritual Trial, 'There is always another story, there is more than meets the eye.' The 'wicked secret', the private reason' here is the incest motive itself, intimately linked, the play suggests, with the ego-structures of an imperial order.

The key to the whole procedure of *The Orators* lies in a section heading near the middle: *'Continuity and Discontinuity'*, which, the Airman notes, are 'Both true'. The work is structured on this proposition, and Auden's retrospective attempts to impose a unitary meaning on it express a desire for ideological closure in which we all share as reading subjects. To seek a definitive reading is to subscribe to the ego's impulse to map, delineate, survey. But the very process of imposing a 'line' upon the text generates an excess of meaning elsewhere that cannot be reconciled. 'The enemy's two waves of attack', the Airman continues, are 'Flux-mongers (shock troops for destruction)' and 'Order-doctrinaires (establishment of martial law). The latter of course do not admit collusion into the former, claim rather to come as redeemers.' Nevertheless, 'One must draw the line somewhere. . . . Not to confuse the real line with that drawn for personal convenience, to remember the margin of safety. By denying the existence of the real line, the enemy offers relief, at a price, from their own imaginary one.'

It's significant that this continuity/discontinuity antithesis points back to the break of the 'Prologue', in which the child comes into existence in learning to trace lines on the familiar map of a landscape, but enters at the same time into falsity. Learning, it seems, 'worshipping not lying' from the maternal landscape around, he learns the value of endearment and bravery, to carry 'the good news gladly to a world in danger', ready to argue with any stranger, to propagate the self and the world that goes with it in all his encounters. And yet, in the last quatrain, homing, he is welcomed by the country he defended only with reviling and insult, unmasked in the words of others not as a 'Dear boy' but as 'Coward' and 'Deceiver', denied by the very discourse he served.

In the same way, the continuity/discontinuity is reproduced in the exchanges between reader and rider in the epilogue, with its fretful riddling catechism and its contrast between staying here in an illusory safety and crossing a frontier into admitted danger. What immediately precedes this, balancing the Prize-Day Address that succeeds the 'Prologue', is the distorted language of the metrical psalm parody. What we see here is a brutal forcing of speech into grotesque, violated forms, in which power inscribes itself in the forced syntax, the unnatural inversions and torsions which celebrate an omnipotent patriarch. The psalm is a plaintive anthem of abjection and surrender, redeemed only by the satisfaction that, in pleading for absolute defeat, accepting castration and weakness, the subject ceases to resist the Enemy, and so offers him a taste of defeat in victory, hastening that second coming in which power and its subjections will be overthrown, 'self-destruction, the sacrifice of all resistance, reducing him to the state of a man trying to walk on a frictionless surface'.

In one of his early poems Auden warns that 'To ask the hard question is simple'; but it is 'The simple act of the confused will.' What *The Orators* undertakes is an exploration of that 'confused will', dissolving its surface simplicities back into the complex processes that generated them, dissolving, too, the unitary voice of the speaking subject back into the many discourses that go to make up its illusory unity: powers we pretend to understand. The answer is 'hard and hard to remember', for consciousness is everywhere engaged in the repression of its genesis, of that moment before language when it was born out of separation and loss. Thus it is 'the strangely exciting lie' that moves us, impels us to act and think in certain ways. Formed by 'losing memory' of these primal scenes, the subject seems no more than a collection of ghosts, suppressed voices and texts, forced in a compulsive repetition endlessly to re-enact its formative traumas: 'And ghosts must do again/ What gives them pain.' In the process, it lays itself open to the commanding voice – of the state, the Leader – which seeks only obedience and surrender, masochistic self-punishment for the crimes committed *against* the subject. Thus 'Cowardice cries/For windy skies,/. . .Obedience for a master.' But these ghosts can be laid. The way involves memory restoring that which was lost, 'The face and the meeting place'; means going beyond those systems of power where the subject is constructed in subjection. This can itself be no more than a question now –

> Can love remember
> The question and the answer,
> For love recover
> What has been dark and rich and warm all over?

– a question of recovering some sense of being at ease with the carnal, of reconciling the cold, sharp air of the ego with the warm folds of the body, the valley, the material maternal landscape. The subject, to put together question and answer in a mutually satisfying catechism, has to join, too, what should never have been sundered, conscious and unconscious moieties of the double man. But the utopian hope, already distanced by being mererly a question, carries a sub-text. For 'What has been dark and rich and warm all over' recalls another riddle of identity: 'What's black and white and read all over?' The answer, as every schoolboy knows, is *a text*. The dream of recovering the sensual darks of the body must always encounter this sub-text. The body carries in its deepest recesses the signature of another. This is its wound.

4   The Look of the Stranger

Auden didn't like the title *Look, Stranger!* foisted on him by Faber and Faber. He wrote in 1936 to his American publisher: 'Faber invented a bloody title while I was away without telling me. It sounds like the work of a vegetarian lady novelist. Will you please call the American edition *On this Island*.'[1] It may be that Auden came to think better of the English title. Whatever the case, the book has stubbornly retained it, even in American critical discussions.

Faber's title, bringing the gaze of the stranger to bear on Auden's text, saw things its author didn't – saw, for example, that the politics of the volume is focused in the look of the stranger; saw the recurrence of that word 'look' (and of the perceptual leitmotiv) throughout the book; and saw too that the hortatory tone, half bullying and half pleading, is the key to the book's urgency and impulse. Much later, in a 1948 essay 'The Greeks and Us', Auden wrote that the Greeks had taught us 'to think about our thinking', to examine why we and other people think the way we do, and to follow the logic of *supposition* in order to understand why things are as they are. 'To be able to perform either of these mental operations', he continued,

> a human being must first be capable of a tremendous feat of moral courage and discipline for he must have learned how to resist the immediate demands of feeling and bodily needs, and to disregard his natural anxiety about his future so that he can look at his self and his world as if they were not his but a stranger's. (*FA*, p. 32)

In *Look, Stranger!* he attempted this feat, rejecting the culture whose intimate he remained in order to discover the startling conditions behind even the most ordinary scenes of middle-class life. One of those conditions he had noted in a journal entry in 1929: 'The middle class: an orphan class, with no fixed residence, capable of snobbery in both directions. From class insecurity it has developed the family unit as a defence. Like the private bands in the tribal migrations. It is afraid of its fortunate position' (*EA*, pp. 299–300). In order fully to explore the ambivalence of this 'orphan class', Auden had in turn to make himself an orphan. In *Look, Stranger!* the moment had arrived to take politics head on, to reveal that what we take to be 'nature' – the way the universe is made – is actually a product of history, the outcome of past conflicts and evasions, that 'the immediate demands of feeling and bodily needs', 'natural anxiety' and the struggle to resist all these, are themselves a secretion of 'class insecurity'. Or as one un-collected poem of the period says (*EA*, pp. 123–4), addressing a supposedly representative petty-bourgeois,

> You certainly have a good reason
> For feeling as you do
> No wonder you are anxious
> Because it's perfectly true
> You own a world that has had its day.

Reviewing Herbert Read's 1936 study of Shelley, with its attempt to trace 'the origins of the work of art in the psychology of the individual and in the economic structure of society', Auden concurred that Shelley, 'like every neurotic, had a just grievance, that his neurosis was the source of his insight'. Auden himself wished to push the argument further. Not only does he insist that 'Every psychology...every economic analysis contains therapeutic intentions, i.e. they presuppose an idea of what the individual or society could and should become.' He also requires the poet to offer the same: 'a lack of interest in objects in the outside world', a refusal of partisan '"passions – party passions, national passions, religious passions" is equally destructive'. In fact, 'the more "autosexual" a poet,' he concludes, 'the more necessary it is for him to be engaged in material action.' (*EA*, pp. 356–8).

In an article for the Workers' Educational Association a few months later he is even more explicit:

> When we are confronted with an emotional difficulty or danger, there are three things we can do. We can pretend that *we* are not there, i.e. we can become feeble-minded or ill; we can pretend that *it* isn't there, i.e. we can daydream; or we can look at it carefully and try to understand it, understand the mechanism of the trap. Art is a combination of these last two; there is an element of escape in it, and an element of science, which only differs from what we generally call by that name, in that its subject is a different order of data. (*EA*, pp. 358–60)

'The artist is the person who stands outside and looks, stands even outside himself and looks at his daydreams.' He is not a social reformer, but 'the truths he tells' can be of use to one, and, in the end, 'The secret of good art is the same as the secret of a good life; to find out what you are interested in, however strange, or trivial, or ambitious, or shocking, or uplifting, and deal with that, for that is all you can deal with well.' Auden's gloss on this is his variation on a famous nostrum from the *Communist Manifesto*: '"To each according to his means; from each according to his powers", in fact.'

The purpose of *Look, Stranger!* is to stand outside the self and look at its daydreams, to 'understand the mechanism of the trap' as an alternative to running away or succumbing. It is a strategy for dealing with psychological and economic deadlock which winkles out the secrets of a society, and naughtily broadcasts them, not from malevolence but as therapy, a kind of collective psychoanalysis. But to do this, to investigate 'the beatings of man's heart', the spy has also to be an insider. He is not only *interested in* this society as an observer; he also, in the root sense of the word, has his being *in-among* it (*inter-esse*). It is this double sense of the word 'interest' that makes for the complexity, and the richness, of Auden's insight in *Look Stranger!*, opening up, in the words of the 'Prologue', that 'ring where name and image meet'.

There is a remarkable contrast between the 'stranger' of the title poem and the one addressed in an earlier poem, 'Who stands, the crux left of the watershed'. The earlier stranger, initially only an empty part of speech ('whoever should stand there would see...') becomes by the end a situated subject, with a past and a future:

> Go home, now, stranger, proud of your young stock,
> Stranger, turn back again, frustrate and vexed:
> This land, cut off, will not communicate.

In that refusal of communication there is a whisper, too, of a castrating isolation, a refusal of patrimony and a denial of impulse. The stranger is excluded from a reified landscape it seems he should inherit, to which he has made his claim by accepting his place as the subject of the sentence 'Who stands...', filling out its empty signifier with his actual body. He is, then, estranged from the landscape in the same way as the empty speaker who addresses him, who seems to be standing nowhere in particular, merely establishing a hypothesis from which all perceptions follow. Between the two, though there is a kind of address, a silence falls. The subject who speaks and the subject of whom he speaks may be the same, but they are both empty beings, turned back from meaning and position, 'orphans', frustrated by the very terms of the discourse which constitutes them. How does this negative vision square with the exuberant 'delight' of the later poem?

This 'delight', first of all, is merely putative. The 'leaping light for your delight discovers' the richness of the island; but the onlooker may not respond in kind. In the gap between 'light' and 'delight', objective and subjective, both denial and desire may flourish. This antithesis echoes that opened up by the first two words of the poem. For it is in the gulf between the subject who commands and the subject addressed that a primary estrangement occurs – an estrangement reproduced throughout by those pairings that enforce division in what the poem insists is a unitary experience: leaping and standing stable, speech and silence, the channels of the ear and of a river, the sound of the sea and the sea itself. At every turn a unitary world of experience breaks down into proliferating dualities. The common feature this poem shares with 'The Watershed' is that of an interface. The earlier poem had placed this between rural and industrial, past and present; here it is between land and sea, between a world which discovers itself in all its multiplicity to the ready eye, and a world which is all homogeneous surface, withholding its secrets.

In the earlier poem, the speaker saw through a class darkly: his class position imposed upon him the vision of a dying culture which held no promise for the proud young stock of a new looker. But now a new marriage is possible between seer and seen, just as the light 'discovers' and thus simultaneously enables the stranger to discover. The stranger has a stability and sureness of foot denied the speaker. He is silent, not because the speaker commands him, but because words are superfluous. Language lives in division and distinction, whereas for the stranger reality is not estranged, but enters through all the portals of the sense, mingling subject and object in the way tidal estuaries not only pour waters into the sea but also receive waters from it. He is a stranger to the speaker, not to the landscape. Rather he is its inheritor, and Auden's language here recalls that ecstatic moment in the *Canticles* which celebrates the marriage between bride and bridegroom as one prefiguring that between the expected messiah and his people (*Canticles*, II–III and VIII).

The sub-text of 'Look, stranger', like *Canticles*, is about stewardship. The difference between fertility and drought depends upon the look that is brought to bear on the inheritance. The flood that cannot drown love may instead fructify, like the 'crumpling flood' of 'A Summer Night', or, much later, that ambiguous element which, in *The Enchafèd Flood* and *The Sea and the Mirror*, is a place both of desolation and regeneration. There is a delighted whirling of perspectives which belies fixity, inserting motion right into the heart of stasis, but also bringing a peculiar calm to exuberant action. This paradoxical unity of motion and stasis is enshrined in the final metaphor. Fixity and flux are reconciled in the mirror's frame, which holds the turbulence of the sea within its own calm two-dimensional surface. Here too, the analogy is between mind and world. The ships diverge on 'urgent voluntary errands': the two adjectives offer a utopian unity of freedom and necessity, and the noun reconciles a self-delighting wandering with a sense of imposed mission.

Consciousness is not a void craving objects, but a self-delighting plenitude, into which 'the full view / Indeed may enter/And move in memory as now these clouds do', simultaneously entering and entered, mirror and harbour for the floating impressions of a world where all is movement. Divergence is thus balanced by that act of entry. 'Memory' may imply a sundering of viewer and viewed, but the poem in the end appropriates all these external motions to the movements of the heart. These images will 'move in memory' in a double sense, moving pictures which move the subject to emotions recollected in tranquillity. Recollection, in its strong sense, the gathering in of the subject's inheritance, is the utopian core of this poem. In the end, the addresser and the addressee are reconciled too, in a movement of desire that seems to close the gulf between them. Lack, however, persists in the echoing muted urgency of the appeal. Such momentary utopian epiphanies still carry within them the shadow of loss against which they protest.

Look, Stranger! is a major locus of the struggle between the authentically 'objective' gaze and that parody of it summed up in Christopher Isherwood's famous phrase from 'A Berlin Diary': 'I am a camera.' In a reprise of 1930s attitudes, Auden was to claim in 'Memorial for the City' that 'The steady eyes of the crow and the camera's candid eye/See as honestly as they know how, but they lie.' In 'Consider this and in our time' we have seen how the poem itself overthrows any claims to an objective viewpoint outside the compromising positions of history. *The Orators* had rehearsed the extent to which all seeing is ideologically charged. In 'Look, stranger' that Nietzschean word ' delight' indicates that clarity leads not to passive reflection but to involvement. In 'May with its light behaving' the ambiguity of the adjective alerts us to this same process. The light behaviour of a playful spring contains a hint that all this stirring of 'vessel, eye, and limb' is no more than the light behaving itself, behaving as it should. Even 'The singular and sad/Are willing to recover' in this careless picnicking, leaving the dead 'remote and hooded/In their enclosures'. We, however, have broken from the 'vague woods' of childhood, into clarity and definition. The light may be too strong to face without a 'shaded eye', the apple we have taken may be 'dangerous', but in that danger of recognized complicity lies a prospect, too, of 'The real world [that] lies before us'. This may be a paradise lost; that 'lies' may resonate with all Auden's regular duplicities; but it is the doubleness of the inheritance which counts. The world that has been gained in the real is both 'Animal motions of the young' and 'The common wish for death', a world of both 'The pleasured and the haunted'. It is not, however, a question of simple confrontation between those who are pleasured and those who are haunted, for it is the very condition of the Fall that we are *all* both pleasured and haunted. If 'The unjust walk the earth' we ourselves are among them, fallen creatures, torn between the death-wish and that urging to pleasure and love which makes us 'impatient' along with the tortoise and the roe (in another echo of *Canticles*). Love 'lays/The blond beside the dark' in a pun which indifferently combines the love-bed with the serried ranks of graves. But to respond to that urging, we have to move beyond passivity, the empty speculative gaze of the uninterested.

Love, the poem ends, 'Urges upon our blood,/Before the evil and the good/How insufficient is/The endearment and the look'. It is clear here that Auden is speaking of a joyous knowing, in Nietzsche's terms, that takes us 'beyond good and evil', beyond the casual endearment and the 'objective' look, into a deeper encounter of self and world – an encounter based not on passive reflection of a passive and passing reality, but on an active grasping and delighting, capable of affirming and denying, commanding and destroying, 'Love or Hatred'.

'Love and hatred' is one of the antitheses in 'The Creatures', not collected until *Another Time* but written a few months after 'Look, stranger'. The creatures, recognizably the creatures of the night of the Freud elegy, are both our past and our future, 'the poles between which our desire is unceasingly discharged'; yet it is in this place of discharge – of empty transit or eddying joy – that the utopian suspension of time in 'Look, stranger' is revealed as an actual deadlock. The silence of desire at the heart of that poem cannot be broken without confessing all the contradictory feelings hinted at in its language of opposition, antithesis and paradox. Here such a discharge of desire can be effected only by some catastrophic interruption of an inertia in which 'love and hatred so perfectly oppose themselves that we cannot voluntarily move; but await the compulsion of the deluge and the earthquake.'

The deluge is a recurrent and perhaps inevitable motif of leftist writing in the thirties. In C. Day Lewis's play of 1936, *Noah and the Waters*, it is a revolutionary flood which presents Noah – type of the middle class intellectual – with a 'choice that must be made . . . between clinging to his old life and trusting himself to the Flood'. In Stephen Spender's widely influential critical study of 1935, *The Destructive Element*, it is both social revolution and the collective unconscious. Taking its cue from Conrad's advice for the modern individual in *Lord Jim* – 'In the destructive element immerse. That is the way' – Spender combines diagnosis and therapy along the lines Auden had required above. For Spender the modern world is driven by the death-wish, and the anxiety of a dying culture is revealed in a recurrent motif of castration, real or symbolic. The only way forward from this, Spender suggests, is by embracing that flood which is coming anyway. One can survive by immersing in the destructive creativity of the proletariat, which is linked obscurely with the anarchic regenerative powers of the unconscious. Spender quotes the ending of '1929' in support of his argument that Auden's poems are 'the literature of "the destructive element"', defining 'a void between two worlds' (p. 20).

In 'The Creatures', the creatures of the unconscious can be friends or enemies, depending on how we respond to them. In their 'affections and indifferences' alike they belong to an order beyond good and evil. Now, amid all our 'dreams of machinery' they offer a utopian vision of a world beyond repression, 'nude and fabulous epochs'. But we can only recover such a world by charity and generosity. In the poem 'Now the leaves are falling fast' Auden traces the origins of repression. Nurses and neighbours alike, pretending to care, actually 'Pluck us from the real delight', deny and drive us into deathly separation with 'Arms raised stiffly to reprove/In false attitudes of love'.

A decade later, Auden was to supply in *The Enchafèd Flood* a reflection on various motifs of European literature which also provides a gloss to the image clusters here. The sea, he says, 'is that state of barbaric vagueness and disorder out of which civilisation has emerged and into which, unless saved by the efforts of gods and men, it is always liable to relapse' (p. 6). It is 'that which separates or estranges' (p. 7). But it is too, as for example in the later Shakespeare, 'the place of purgatorial suffering: through separation and apparent loss, the characters disordered by passion are brought to their senses and the world of music and marriage is made possible' (p. 11). The sea, that is, is both a place of desolation, like the desert, and a realm of possible vitality and freedom. The desert, however, may require the flood to restore it to that potential vitality, for –

> the desert may not be barren by nature but as the conse-
> quence of a historical catastrophe. The once-fertile city
> has become, through the malevolence of others or its own
> sin, the waste land. In this case it is the opportunity for
> the stranger hero who comes from elsewhere to discover
> the cause of the disaster, destroy or heal it and become
> the rebuilder of the city and, in most cases, its new ruler.
> (p. 15)

Later Auden goes on to discuss the Oedipus story and the castration of the hero (pp. 133–41), and it is clear that the figure of Oedipus lurks behind this familiar narrative too, complicating its image of the 'stranger hero' with the half-recognition that this stranger who 'comes from elsewhere' is also the rightful heir of the realm he saves; but, as a corollary to this, that he also shares in the curse he seeks to end – may, indeed, be its source. It is this combination of complicity and detachment which makes the figure of the stranger so difficult to pin down in Auden's early verse.

For the stranger is, on the one hand, the complete outsider who looks in on the world of the bourgeoisie, weighs it in the balance and finds it wanting, of that famously suppressed poem, 'A Communist to Others'. But as that poem also reveals, he is also a compromised accomplice of the society he denounces, himself a victim of those repressions which thwart and frustrate the self. He may be, like the watcher of *Paid on Both Sides*, a 'watcher in the dark' who holds us accountable for all our derelictions and, significantly, like the sea will roll in to claim his own:

> you wake
> Our dream of waking, we feel
> Your finger on the flesh that has been skinned,
> By your bright day
> See clear what we were doing, that we were vile.
> Your sudden hand
> Shall humble great
> Pride, break it, wear down the stumps of old systems
>   which await
> The last transgression of the sea.

But on the other hand, in the words of 'A Communist to Others', he must admit: 'We cannot put on airs with you/The fears that hurt you hurt us too.' The only difference is that 'we say/That like all nightmares these are fake', ideological inversions of the real.

The contradictoriness of this posture explains the peculiar mélange of mystical euphoria and historical anxiety of the poem subsequently called 'A Summer Night', which ends with a vision of the liberating flood. Encouraged by Auden's later alterations to the poem, and by his retrospective anecdote about the experience in which it originated in 'The Protestant Mystics' (*FA*, pp. 49–78), critics have stressed the extent to which it prefigures his later Christian commitment. Yet even this 1964 account of what Auden calls a 'Vision of Agape', or spiritual love, has remarkable political resonances. Auden distinguishes such a vision from that of 'Dame Kind', or nature, and that of Eros, or personal love. It is in terms of the look brought to bear by the subject that this distinction is made. In the Vision of Dame Kind 'there is one human person, the subject, and a multiplicity of creatures whose way of existence is different from his.' The relation between the subject and his objects is thus 'one-sided'; there is no reciprocation. The Vision of Eros is, by contrast, an unequal relation between two subjects. The Vision of Agape, however, 'is multiple but it is a multiplicity of persons', 'a mutual relation; but unlike any of the others, this relation is a relation between equals.' And, in an afterthought which takes us right back to the preoccupations of the thirties, Auden adds:

> Not the least puzzling thing about it is that most of the experiences which are closest to it in mode, involving plurality, equality and mutuality of human persons, are clear cases of diabolic possession, as when thousands cheer hysterically for the Man-God, or cry bloodthirstily for the crucifixion of the God-Man.

A common theme of the Left in the thirties was that the devil had all the best tunes, that Fascism knew how to mobilize the repressed forces of the unconscious in the service of its own repressive mission. In 'The Creatures', Auden had suggested that desire could be the guide of tyrant and reformer alike. In the elegy for Freud he was to argue that the 'delectable creatures' of the unconscious are 'exiles who long for the future that lies in our power', and that they too would 'rejoice/ if allowed to serve enlightenment like him'. How we respond to these excluded, 'the injured', who 'lead the ugly life of the rejected', whether we acknowledge them as our own or continue to deny them, will determine whether we can overcome evil or not. For seen in the right way, evil is not 'deeds that must be punished, but our lack of faith,/our dishonest mood of denial,/the concupiscence of the oppressor'.

The trajectory of 'A Summer Night' is the attempt to rescue delight from this 'concupiscence', by drawing in the ugly and rejected. The poem offers a complex seeing which constantly undermines the assurances it seeks. It opens with the poet lying out on the lawn at night, looking up at the moon and stars, enjoying the delights in his privileged, 'chosen' position. For the moment, the idyllic mood is free to evolve into a vision of Agape, as he sits 'Equal with colleagues in a ring' in an enchanted mutuality where 'Fear gave his watch no look' and 'eyes in which I learn/That I am glad to look, return/My glances every day'. Already, however, this charmed circle of looks, ostensibly cut off from the outside world of grief and fear, is being subverted. The moon becomes the figure of this larger estrangement.

Initially the moon seems part of this generalized benevolence, the figure of a gaze that collectivizes in imagination even those loved ones physically absent, for it 'looks on them all', bringing them within the enchantment. But this all-encompassing look also requires a general indifference. The moon climbs the European sky and looks down on churches and power stations with equal unconcern. She peers into art galleries, unmoved by 'the marvellous pictures'. She 'blankly as an orphan stares' on them all, attentive only to gravity. If she notices nothing, 'we/Whom hunger cannot move' suffer a similar blindness. 'From gardens where we feel secure', we return that look, in the process translating its coldness and the real brutalities of politics into a merely frivolous metaphor: 'Look up, and with a sigh endure/The tyrannies of love.'

It is eastward that Auden's gaze now turns, admitting that this delightful mood is founded on *wilful* ignorance. 'Gentle', he says, with an ironic play on the class privilege which underlies such an attribute, we 'do not care to know,/Where Poland draws her Eastern bow,/What violence is done'. They, too, like the moon, are in reality indifferent, 'do not care'; but, unlike the moon, they *choose* not to know.

What the poem does not care to know is the whole historic hinterland of its timeless privileged moment. The poem was written in June 1933. On 28 May the Nazis had won the elections in Danzig, setting the seal on a half-year of triumph. In January Hitler had come to power; in February he suspended civil liberties and the freedom of the press; in March an election confirmed his majority, and an enabling law allowed him to assume dictatorial powers until 1937; in April the persecution of the Jews began, with a national boycott of all Jewish business; in May the trade unions were suppressed. 'Orphan' recalls Auden's characterization of the middle class. But it also points to a people disfranchised and a Europe soon to be overflowing with orphans. In post-war versions of the poem Auden changed 'orphan' to 'butcher', and while this is appropriately subversive of an arcadia where hunger and carnivores are alike allayed, its main effect is to turn the moon simply into a philistine shopkeeper, insensitive to the great art treasures which we more 'gentle' souls appreciate. But this muting is nothing compared with that achieved by the suppression of the next three stanzas of the original.

Not only the politics of a far-away country are ignored thus, but also the more immediate tyrannies of economics. The company are unmoved by hunger in a double sense: their own actions are not impelled by it, and they are insensitive to the hunger of others. In the gap between caring and knowing, however, loss and anxiety may take root:

> The creepered wall stands up to hide
> The gathering multitudes outside
>   Whose glances hunger worsens;
> Concealing from their wretchedness
> Our metaphysical distress,
>   Our kindness to ten persons.

If the privileged company do not care to notice the physical distress of the wretched, they can hardly expect the wretched to show much consideration for their merely personal kindnesses and their profoundly sensitive souls. I cannot share with some readers of this poem the sense that it offers a true Edenic vision. This Eden is already flawed, and the rhyming of 'wretchedness' and 'distress' indicates a contempt like that in an omitted stanza of 'A Communist to Others', which speaks of the poet fleeing the 'horror' of the real world to private islands 'Where thoughts like castaways find ease/In endless petting'. Only a threat will move the privileged from their complacency, the new stanza indicates, speaking of every path on which they move showing already 'traces of/Intentions not our own'. Such alien intentions are 'able to achieve/What our excitement could conceive,/But our hands left alone'. Kindness to middle-class 'persons' of one's own kind is not really the basis on which to build a visionary metaphysics. Such a metaphysics, says 'A Communist to Others', tells the poor 'That wealth and poverty are merely/Mental pictures, so that clearly/Every tramp's a landlord really/In mind-events'. What's more, they reassure the unhappy rich that the world 'has no flaws/There is no need to change the laws.'

In 'A Summer Night', the fine tradition in which these privileged individuals were nurtured 'has no wish to live'. At the beginning of the poem the opening light had drawn enchanted flowers out of hiding. Then the creepered wall had hidden the gathering multitudes, concealed their own metaphysical distress. Now it is the 'river-dreams' themselves, their Edenic fantasies of fulfilment and of time suspended, which hide a vigour that alone could turn the private dreams into public reality. But such a revelation, inviting to a different kind of pleasure and power, also discloses death. It is the death-wish, that '"reinstatement of the earlier condition"' to which Auden referred in his journals, 'Entropy [as] another name for despair' (*EA*, p. 299), which lies behind these 'river-dreams' of bliss:

> Soon the through the dykes of our content
> The crumpling flood will force a rent,
>   And, taller than a tree,
> Hold sudden death before our eyes
> Whose river-dreams long hid the size
>   And vigours of the sea.

Mendelson sees the whole structure of this poem 'directed single-mindedly towards its reconciling cadence'.[2] I am less convinced that the concluding moments involve anything more than a painfully insecure appeal. The Oedipal stress which desires to hear 'through a child's rash happy cries/The drowned voices of his parents rise/In unlamenting song' adds a peculiar distress to the tone, cancelling out the strength and the belonging, harking on loss and dread. Even 'unlamenting' concedes what it tries to deny. The 'dove-like pleading' of the opening stanzas turns almost into the bleating of the shorn lamb in the concluding one, with its strangely negative prayer:

> After discharges of alarm
> All unpredicted may it calm
>   The pulse of nervous nations;
> Forgive the murderer in his glass,
> Tough in its patience to surpass
>   The tigress her swift motions.

After all that unmoved emotion earlier, the shift into 'swift motions' in the last line, like that ambiguous 'discharges', is as 'unpredicted' and contrary as the calm it also envisages. The indeterminate 'it' and 'this' of the last two stanzas could be either the flood of the contentment in which the poem started. The difficulty of reconciling them, like the difficulty of putting a name to the pronouns, reinforces that final and most powerful of anomalies, the intrusion of 'murderer' and 'tigress' at this moment of supposed resolution and closure. The last impression is of an unresolved contradiction, and a deeper anxiety, like that more forcefully uttered in 'The Witnesses': 'Something is going to fall like rain/and it won't be flowers.' The hungry and possibly vengeful glances of the poor decentre the mutually returned glances of the 'lucky'.

Auden's poetry in this period is full of such interruptive procedures, in which the text tells us more than it knows. 'Let the florid music praise', for example, is one of those compact lyrics which packs enormous subversive force. Superficially, it is a poem exploring the Renaissance trope which draws an analogy between the campaigns of Love and War. But the poem itself transforms the analogy by linking it to another conflict, that between the rhetoric of consciousness and the silence of an unconscious that seems to be the ally of death. Death's natural allies in turn are those 'secretive children', excluded now from the arrogant discourse of Love and Beauty, whose hour will nevertheless come. It is a poem, again, about the supersession of bourgeois power, in which that whole language of 'conquest', 'citadels', 'imperial standards' is subverted by the unacknowledged power of the excluded, waging a guerrilla war of attrition on such arrogant mastery. For 'the unloved have had power/. . .Always.' They keep their council, but they also infiltrate the lines of the powerful – military lines which are also lines of florid self-praise – passing through his 'vigilance of breath/To unpardonable death'. Language in the end cannot help or pardon; supersession of breath leaves the master speechless: 'And my vows break/ Before his look.' The silent look of the stranger decentres the whole discourse of beauty, founded as it is on the discourse of power.

   The poem later known as 'A Bride in the 30's' opens as a gracious celebration of a love which moves easily through 'the night's delights and the day's impressions' without any concern for the darkening skies of Europe beyond. Love, luck and looking seem intertwined in a happy conjunction, so that the look of love becomes transformed into the good looks of the well-fed:

> Looking and loving our behaviours pass
> The stones, the steels and the polished glass;
> Lucky to Love the new pansy railway,
> The sterile farms where his looks are fed,
> And in the policed unlucky city
>   Lucky his bed.

Yet that separation of looking subject from behaving body (an illusion, one notes, since 'looks' have to be fed), the play on words that links 'polished' and 'policed', the sneer of 'pansy' and the edge on 'sterile', culminating in the antithesis of public and private lucks, point towards the vision of desolation in the next stanza. Love may transform the 'lands of terrifying mottoes' into 'worlds as innocent as Beatrix Potter's', may pursue his 'greens and lilies' through bankrupt countries; but the darkness spreads its stain through the celebration. Love is too 'easy', finding in the beloved's face 'The pool of silence and the tower of grace'. Echoes of the *Canticles* come too pat;

love's ways are conjuring, the simple excitements of a glance. And, in the human dispositions of love, it cannot be separated from hunger and all the dark images that 'Hunger and love in their variations' summon up:

> Hitler and Mussolini in their wooing poses
> Churchill acknowledging the voters' greeting
> Roosevelt at the microphone, Van der Lubbe
>   laughing
> And our first meeting.

For the lovers, such political scenes are a mere backdrop to their encounter; but the word 'wooing' suggests a deeper, more sinister link. The tyrants too speak the rhetoric of desire.

If love must work its public spirit 'through our private stuff' (with its carefully modulated innuendo), the dictators too can use the desires of the desperate. The poem proceeds through a chronicle of repressions, of desire refused, choices killed and promises fractured out of which the particular life was constructed. For as the plans, 'Schemes for a life and sketches for a hatred', in each life grow clearer, the repression deepens till the desiring subject is ready to have his 'ghosts' – all that has been repressed but remains unspoken – manipulated by these powers of hatred and 'fascinating rubbish'. The voice the speaker hears and would rather not hear is a compromising one, linking the apparently easy personal realm with the forces that impel the darker public world:

> The voice of love saying lightly, brightly –
> 'Be Lubbe, Be Hitler, but be my good
>   Daily, nightly.'

Desire is undiscriminating, amoral, seeking only its own discharge, ready to subscribe to any scheme that satisfies its craving. It is thus malleable material for those who wish to exploit it, and it is 'The looked instruction' which betrays it to 'join the lost in their sneering circles,/Forfeit the beautiful interest and fall/Where the engaging face is the face of the betrayer'. 'The power that corrupts, that power to excess' by which beauty exploits desire draws deep on the death-wish, taking advantage of 'all who long for their destruction,/The arrogant and self-insulted' alike. Desire cannot be divorced from power. As, earlier, the speaker would rather not hear the tempting voice of love, so, as the poem ends, it is the voice of the heart which repeats what we would rather not know: that the choice is ours, and cannot be avoided. 'The language of learning and the language of love' could work together to avoid such devious routes for love's satisfaction; but if it is the crooked paths of moneybug and cancer rather than the straight flight of the dove which prevail, it will be our responsibility. If we refuse to bring the clinical gaze of the surgeon spoken of in the 'Prologue' to bear on our backslidings, wait instead for the 'looked instruction' of the despot, we will have made our own doom. As Auden wrote at the end of 'The Malvern Hills':

> These moods give no permission to be idle,
> For men are changed by what they do;
> And through loss and anger the hands of the unlucky
>   Love one another.

'The chimneys are smoking' starts in a world beyond the personal, its speaking subject deferred to the end of an opening stanza which shifts its gaze from chimneys to crocus to mountains, offers as its first human agent the 'political orator' (in *New Country* a 'communist orator') landing at the pier like a sea god, and only comes to its uttering subject through loss and separation. The departure of the loved one is implicitly balanced by the arrival of the orator. Though now 'I stand on our world alone', the aloof spectatorial view is explicitly refused in the next stanza. The speaker is merely one figure in the configuration of a field, 'the distribution of forces':

> Over the town now, in for an hour from the desert
> A hawk looks down on us all; he is not in this;
> Our kindness is hid from the eye of the vivid creature;
> Sees only the configuration of field.

If the speaker does not identify with the hawk, however, its simultaneous arrival and exterior view identifies it with the orator, who is also here for a purpose, and who is not interested in our kindness to ten persons, but only in 'what is to be done'.

The collectivizing view of the stranger knows that the whole precedes and generates its parts, that the loving subject is secreted by the field and does not construct it, that the division of inherited power is what shapes the inheriting selves, and that they find themselves and each other only as they become carriers of this secret:

> For the game is in progress which tends to become like
>   a war,
> The contest of the Whites with the Reds for the
>   carried thing
> Divided in secret among us, a portion to each:
>> That power which gave us our lives
>> Gave us, we found when we met,
>> Out of the complex to be reassembled
>> Pieces that fit,
>> Whereat with love we trembled.

The temptation for the privileged, trembling subject is to assume that the landscape, in some pathetic fallacy, can be appropriated to their personal love, so that, embracing in the dunes, they can think of the dunes approving, pleased. The contrary view, induced by separation, is equally distorted, believing now that the landscape is actively 'hostile, apart/ From the beloved group', that the trees may be 'spies on the human heart', seeking to catch them out. This paranoia of the watched is in its way as self-important as the arrogance of a watcher who thinks himself the absolute voyeur. In reality, the landscape is indifferent: 'the white death, friendless, has his own idea of us', has his own 'private saga he tells himself at night' in which he is the central hero, has 'His eye on all these people about us, leading/Their quiet horrified lives'. In reality:

> We ride a turning globe, we stand on a star;
> It has thrust us up together; it is stronger than we.
> In it our separate sorrows are a single hope.

The 'sundering streams' can nevertheless be loved. The

personal and the political wish for solidarity are founded in the same desires. Those working on a bank facade, conferring at a health resort, like the harbour master and colliers and doctors earlier, like 'boatmen, virgins, camera-men and us' of the next stanza, and those around goal-post, wind-gauge, pylon or bobbing buoy, share that 'wish to be one' which is 'Like a burglar...stealthily moving' among them. The simile, like 'crooked', or 'camouflaged' later, implies no anti-social impulse to deceive, but rather the furtive obliquity praised in 'Our Hunting Fathers', with its Leninist dedication to 'hunger, work illegally,/And be anonymous'. It is the subterfuge of the spy for life who, to deceive death, shams dead, but is in fact 'quick' and 'real'. If earlier their kindness was 'hid from the eye' of the hawk, now 'our joy abounding is, though it hide underground'. In his later writings, Auden will repeatedly use Marxist and Freudian motifs to defamiliarize and enrich Christian themes. Here he uses Christian allusions, to the messiah who comes like a thief in the night, to that crooked relation between sin and grace abounding resolved only by a spiritual death and rebirth, to give a shock of familiarity to the unfamiliar themes of psychological and social revolution. Taking the crooked routes, hiding underground, are the means by which desire can not only survive but be fulfilled, linked by circumstance with all those other separate desires which together may 'More clearly act our thought', achieve a social revolution. It is such an 'interest' that 'August for the people' (the penultimate poem in *Look, Stranger!*) takes for its theme.

The poem opens in an order not of landscape but of human activity, the collective rhythms of the holiday season. Holiday, too, like the 'good-natured habit' of the everyday city, has its routines. But excess bursts through these simple patterns. A universe in ferment is evoked by a language which attributes gaiety and volition to the inanimate and impersonal. Steamers 'sidle' to meet 'The effusive welcome of the pier', the waiting coaches catch their passengers, who are passively 'laid bare' beside a sea which is both literally and anthropomorphically 'undiscriminating'. The personalized self-aggrandizement of all this is revealed by a mock-heroic tone which attributes to all the same illusion of unique importance: the yachts on the little lake seem theirs alone, the gulls ask for each of them, to them alone the band makes its tremendous statements. To each of them it seems that they alone 'control/The complicated apparatus of amusement'. In fact, that apparatus controls them.

The contrast between the feeling of being a unique beneficiary, and the actual reduction to the ciphers of an objective process, is continued in the movement to the personal speaking 'I' of the third stanza. Yet his interest in 'All types that can intrigue the writer's fancy,/Or sensuality approves' carries with it the dangerous hubris that the 'writer' is after all different, and to be distinguished from these types. 'I' emerges to distinction only by setting itself off against 'The defeated and disfigured marching by', as if only by denying them the chance to cut a literal or literary figure can he, in watching and dismissing them, sustain his own superior gaze.

Nine years ago he and Isherwood were, Auden sees now, mere empty carriers of a class discourse, 'behind us only/The stuccoed suburb and expensive school'. Now 'writer's fancy' and 'artist's wish' are seen to be part of an illusory world of subjective pleasure like that of the holiday-makers. Then their 'hopes were still set on the spies' career', but now they know 'all the secrets we discovered were/Extraordinary and false'. It seemed then that 'one fearless kiss would cure/The million fevers' of generic man. But this was an illusion. The 'insensitive refuse' is not so easily brushed away from 'the burning core'; 'the dragon who had closed the works/While the starved city fed it with the Jews' is not tamed by the 'trainer's look' of love. Another look is needed. 'Private joking' and 'solitary vitality' are insufficient, like 'the studied taste' and 'the whisper in the double bed'; one can seek only pardon for them 'and every flabby fancy'. It is the proud subject who is the 'insensitive' one, realizing only belatedly to what it is an accomplice –

> For now the moulding images of growth
> That made our interest and us, are gone.
> Louder to-day the wireless roars
> Its warnings and its lies, and it's impossible

Among the well-shaped cosily to flit,
Or longer to desire about our lives
The beautiful loneliness of the banks, or find
The stoves and resignation of the frozen plains.

Their interest in the world has been a vested one, an interest
from investments, the *double entendre* of 'banks' implies. But,
as in 'A Bride in the 30s', one must forfeit one 'beautiful
interest' in order not to be betrayed into loss of the other. The
impasse which afflicts so many of the poems in this volume
arises here, in this frozen attitude where 'The beautiful
loneliness of the banks' means that loss and betrayal attend
the isolated subject whatever choice he makes. For the two
interests depend on each other. That earlier deadlock is thus
summed up as the shrewd self-interested look of the mother's
boy, whose 'close-set eyes. . ./Saw nothing to be done', able
to refute Lenin himself. But times have changed: 'we look
again.'

The poem here moves into gracious eighteenth-century
personifications of a far from gracious world, turning the
devices of the tradition against itself. The personifications allow
for a new simplicity and clarity, like that sought in the
'Prologue' to the volume. It is the look of the stranger which
is able to abstract all these personal derelictions into a general
pattern, to extract from all the petty frauds and peculations
an apparatus of deceit, a system of exploitation where one
finds –

Greed showing shamelessly her naked money,
And all Love's wondering eloquence debased
To a collector's slang. . .

The list of generalizations ends with an ironically specific non-
event, a holiday, or holy day, which never comes: 'And Justice
exiled till Saint Geoffrey's Day'. This false specificity of the
future brings us back to our own time and place, 'this hour
of crisis and dismay', in which the writer of this letter submits
his own writing to the invigilation of another writing, the 'strict
and adult pen' of Isherwood which –

Can warn us from the colours and the consolations,
The showy arid works, reveal
The squalid shadow of academy and garden,
Make action urgent and its nature clear.

The subject of the final stanza, then, has moved on in the course of the poem to define a new 'interest', watching the night from what he now recognizes as a 'narrow window'. Seeing is no longer falsely disinterested, but recognizes both its situated limitation and the urgency of having 'nearer insight to resist/The expanding fear, the savaging disaster'. The landscape outside seems abandoned, the pianos are closed in the houses, but the clock strikes the same hour for all, and all alike are brought together in the final contradictory embrace of a history which combines fire and flood, personal responsibility and personal weakness, to which no Faustian ego can say 'Be still':

And all sway forward on the dangerous flood
Of history, that never sleeps or dies,
And, held one moment, burns the hand.

The 'Epilogue' of *Look, Stranger!*, not reprinted after 1950, sums up the many looks that are brought to bear during the course of the volume, more in sorrow than in anger indicating how the virtues of the fine tradition are inseparable from its viciousness, the modern suburbs dependent on 'the byres of poverty'. This is a city in which we are all duplicitously involved –

Built by the conscience-stricken, the weapon-making,
By us. The rumours woo and terrify the crowd,
    Woo us. The betrayers thunder at, blackmail
    Us . . .

If betrayal runs as a theme through *Look, Stranger!* it is because the heir of this island now has to exile himself from it, betray it, in order to save it, like the stranger hero who is the lost inheritor in that passage from *The Enchafèd Flood*. But in so far as he is an heir, he is also an accomplice to its crimes, and even his Oedipal revolt against that tyranny and desolation compounds it, a continuing of the curse.

The only way out of such a double-bind is to effect that complete rupture with the past, that interruption of normality which revolutionary commitment involves, seeking in one's own class death the death, too, of the old gang, that the 'lolling bridegroom' may come. Yet the resonances of Christian apocalypse and Arthurian myth are too strong in such imagery to root it effectively in the real world. It is no accident that Merlin figures in the 'Prologue' to the volume, or that he is strangely endowed with the epithet of the doomed hero Hector, 'tamer of horses'. It is no accident, too, that the voyage of exploration celebrated there as the beginning of a new world echoes the extended Homeric simile that closes Arnold's 'Scholar Gipsy'. 'The Malvern Hills' likewise combines the millennia of geological time with the millennial myths of a Grail legend whose immediate progenitor is Eliot's *Waste Land*. The Lawrences of that poem are suspected, in a suppressed stanza, to be false prophets, yet D. H. Lawrence returns in the 'Epilogue' as one of those writers who has shown us our condition, neither liar nor false comforter, but one who 'revealed the sensations hidden by shame', in the company of Kafka who recorded the sense of guilt, and Proust who exposed our 'self-regard'. In their estranging and thus truthful gaze they share the credits with those others 'Who without reproaches shewed us what our vanity has chosen', 'unlearnt our hatred, and towards the really better/World had turned their face' – Nansen, Schweitzer, a Lenin significantly not named but identified by his acts, Freud and Groddeck 'at their candid studies'.

It is an eclectic bunch, yet perhaps Auden was right in seeing that each, in his way, even the doubtful Lawrence, had set his face against 'the great retreat,/And the malice of death'. The retreat from reason of 'The feverish prejudiced lives' was certainly real enough in 1936; the 'wicked card' had been dealt, the plague was about to be loosed 'on the ignorant town'. Perhaps it was too late to break that ignorance, as, in a final withdrawal from the reassuring destructive intimacy of the usual moon and the necessary lovers, Auden cast one last estranging gaze on this troubled planet, 'through years of absolute cold...rush[ing] towards Lyra in the lion's charge.' Can, he asks in the last words of the volume,

> Can
> Hate so securely bind? Are they dead here? Yes.
> And the wish to wound has the power. And
> to-morrow
> Comes. It's a world. It's a way.

Poetry makes nothing happen. What it can do, however, is discover the conditions of that happening, reveal the startling picture that lies within even the most ordinary scenes of middle-class life.

Auden wrote in *Letters from Iceland* that 'an effect of travelling in distant places . . . is to make one reflect on one's past and one's culture from the outside.' More succinctly, 'Journey to Iceland' affirmed the necessary condition for this outsider's view: 'North means to all: "Reject!"' All Auden's discoveries of the artifice of cultural identity, the source of that anthropological interest that runs through his work, occur at moments of dislocation. It was the experience of Germany in 1928–9 which opened his eyes to the real meaning of economic collapse. *The Orators* derived its sharp edge of insight from his residence at Larchfield Academy, Helensburgh, where it was written, in 1930–1 – the experience of teaching in an *English* public school in Scotland gave him a sense of the edges of Englishness, its status as a cultural construct, not a natural thing.

Yet Auden's journeyings constantly reflect back on that which he is ostensibly leaving behind. In *Spain 1937* the alien landscape of the peninsula is a place where we find what has been gripping *our* unconscious, where 'Our thoughts have bodies, the menacing shapes of our fever/Are precise and alive.' The fears that made us prey to the advertiser's patter now stand revealed as 'invading battalions', and 'Our faces, the institute-face, the chain store, the ruin/Are projecting their greed as the firing squad and the bomb.' At the same time, those apparently isolated, privileged 'moments of tenderness' by which we have lived our private lives now 'blossom' into a collective solidarity,

'Our hours of friendship into a people's army'. One should not underestimate, even in the 'Red Thirties', how much against the grain of the English literary tradition is that sense of the inseparability of personal and political. In the words of *On the Frontier*, 'Truth is elsewhere': going abroad, Auden brought it home.

The traveller has to learn in 'Journey to Iceland' that –

> our time has no favourite suburb; no local
>   features
> Are those of the young for whom all wish to care;
>   The promise is only a promise, the fabulous
>   Country impartially far.

In *Journey to a War* the travellers are not heading to some peripheral conflict. Rather they are engaged upon a double journey, in which the war in China only brings them closer to the war about to erupt in Europe when their book was published in 1939. The war is a global war, and it is their future. As all the little local fronts converge, Austria, Spain, Nanking, Dachau, it becomes clear that they are not isolated struggles but part of a total conflict in which all are involved, though few in the privileged West as yet realize it. While Auden and MacNeice sojourn in Iceland the Franco rebellion breaks out in Spain. Isherwood and Auden arrive in Hankow, and it seems to them that 'History, grown·weary of Shanghai, bored with Barcelona, has fixed her capricious interest upon Hankow. But where is she staying? Everybody boasts that he has met her, but nobody can exactly say.' Four days later, they hear that the German army has marched into Austria. Suddenly, 'If we are killed on the Yellow River front our deaths will be as provincial and meaningless as a motor-bus accident in Burton-on-Trent' (*JW*, pp. 39–51).

This is why 'Journey to Iceland' not only begins but also ends *in medias res*, with the driver once more heading out into the snowstorm, the writer again running howling to his art. For if there is no privileged space in history, there is also no privileged time. History, for the individual, always begins and ends in the middle of things. All lands are equally and impartially distant from that 'fabulous country' which is 'only a promise'. 'Journey to Iceland' enacts that same decentring of consciousness effected at greater length in Isherwood's prose narrative, shows the peripatetic self trying repeatedly to organize the world as circumference around its centre, only to find its own desire to name, to place, to organize overthrown by a proliferation of antitheses: local/far, here/there, city/sea, continent/island, real/unreal, language/reality.

'Journey to Iceland' presents a radically decentred, de-humanised world, '"far from any/Physician"'. There is only here a plurality of elsewheres, for, if 'Europe is absent' this is also 'an island and therefore/Unreal'. Fixity is an illusion, 'the steadfast affections of its dead'. The subject is a 'mendicant shadow' presenting the world to itself, but 'the world is, and the present, and the lie', for inside mendicancy lurks mendacity. Traveller and native share the same concern: 'When/Shall justice be done?'

The introductory sonnet 'The Voyage' in *In Time of War* raises the same question. The traveller, setting out, seems to be leaving to the watcher on the quay, 'Standing under his evil star', an inheritance of injustice he is abandoning. But there is no 'Juster Life' elsewhere. The journey is false, 'really an illness/On the false island where the heart cannot act and will not suffer'. As the linked sonnet 'The Traveller' makes clear, he may seek 'the hostile unfamiliar place', but he will not find it so long as he carries with him that England where no one is well. 'Holding the distance up before his face' like a fan which shields him from the native gazes, he is reassured by the fact that these are far-away countries, 'lands where he will not be asked to stay'. Knowledge is withheld because all the time the travelling subject 'fights with all his powers to be the same,/The One who loves Another far away,/And has a home, and wears his father's name'.

Another introductory sonnet, 'The Ship', puts the point even more bluntly, speaking of the complacency of passengers who never ask why the beggars are in the bows and the rich in the state-rooms, for they carry with them everywhere the bland assumptions of their culture. Nevertheless, somewhere ahead they will be called on to justify themselves, and found wanting: 'Somewhere a strange and shrewd To-morrow goes to bed/ Planning the test for men from Europe; no one guesses/Who will be most ashamed, who richer, and who dead.' It is not only China which holds this judicious strangeness, but the future itself, which is going to unsettle all the smug illusions. The evil star under which some stand in 'The Voyage' has been transformed into the star on which all alike stand, without discrimination, by the end of the 'Commentary' which concludes the sequence, replacing that 'fate' passively suffered with a justice which has to be actively constructed. This is a goal like that envisaged at the beginning: a place 'Where hearts meet and are really true', and the fever is cured. But it is 'the distant murmur of guerrilla fighting', mingling with the 'voice of Man', that has brought this peripety. The listener now finds his 'frozen heart' compelled by circumstance to be 'awkward and alive,/To all it suffered once a weeping witness'. Renewal requires not only sweeping the madness and 'masses of impressive rubbish' out of his head. In terms which recall that guerrilla war he has to 'Rally the lost and trembling forces of the will', to 'gather them up and let them loose upon the earth,/Till they construct at last a human justice,/The contribution of our star...' The transformation enacts a major *political* shift.

In a poem of 1937 published in *Another Time*, 'Dover', the same marginalizing realization is explored. 'Nothing is made in this town': it exists simply as a point of transit, a place of 'Not here, not now' where time is killed. 'Above them.../The aeroplanes fly in the new European air,/On the edge of that air that makes England of minor importance.' But it is not only England that is marginalized. The tides warn bathers of 'a cooling star,/With half its history done'. The full moon over France 'returns the human stare' with a cold dangerous flattery. Human beings are simply 'recruits' to the night, 'pilgrims' whose 'Mecca is coldness of heart'. This coldness everywhere grips the star, the moon, the heart, in a world where language is a mere pocket of delusive safety:

Within these breakwaters English is spoken; without
   Is the immense improbable atlas.

Those who leave, however, carry this falsity with them in
the stories they tell of their future, trying to 'conjure their
special fates from the impersonal water', in self-deluding sorti-
lege imagining there all they wish for and have been denied
at home:

'I see an important decision made on a lake,
An illness, a beard, Arabia found in a bed,
   Nanny defeated, Money.'

Returning, the beaten and the successful alike 'thank the
historical cliffs', telling another story to themselves, which lies
as it announces an end to lying:

'The heart has at last ceased to lie, and the clock to
   accuse;
In the shadow under the yew, at the children's party
   Everything will be explained.'

Dover, in fact, 'has built its routine upon these unusual
moments', makes a profession of catering for 'The vows, the
tears, the slight emotional signals' which are here not unique
experiences but generic patterns of behaviour, 'eternal and
unremarkable gestures/Like ploughing or soldiers' songs'. Each
of these individual subjects imagines itself the centre of the
universe, marginalizing all the others; and each is in turn
marginalized in the endless shifting of perspectives: 'The
soldier guards the traveller who pays for the soldier;/Each one
prays in the dusk for himself, and neither/Controls the years.'

Such control comes only when the myths of a bankrupt
culture have been grasped and exposed. In *The Ascent of F6*
the ordinary citizen Mrs A wakes momentarily from her
media-trance to realize that 'I have dreamed of a threadbare
barnstorming actor, and he was a national symbol.' Ransom,
the heroic image constructed by that media packaging, similarly disenchanted with himself, seeks escape in suicide, not
humility and renewal. But in *Letters from Iceland* the writer runs

howling to his art to find another solution. Writing a letter home to an earlier enemy of British cant, Auden composes a poem which simultaneously exposits and exposes that supercilious upper-class manner in all its smug complacency, and enters the tradition as itself a masterpiece of irony and authorial voice. Byron is a brilliant choice as model and fictive addressee, for in his contradictions he embodies the crisis of Auden's generation: a privileged radical, a democratic aristocrat, an *homme de société* who was also a social outcast and self-made exile, dying finally for a marginal cause, in a Greece which the English tradition nevertheless looked to as the mainstream of its own political and moral values.

Auden was to write, of Byron's *Don Juan*: 'One should be wary, when comparing an author's various productions, of saying this piece is an expression of the real man and that piece is not – for nobody, not even the subject himself, can be certain who he is' (*DH*, p. 401). 'Letter to Lord Byron' begins with an almost bumptious self-confidence, the young poet brashly buttonholing his predecessor in a tone which is simultaneously deferential and overfamiliar. The repeated word-play on titles stresses both the respect and the presumption of assuming that the writer, like the reader, belongs to an elite culture which can agree in looking down on the impertinence of the 'common' public. The flip confidence recurs throughout the text in this presumption of a shared knowledge, a common knowingness, announced in that second line as a *class* endowment:

> Excuse, my lord, the liberty I take
>   In thus addressing you. I know that you
> Will pay the price of authorship and make
>   The allowances an author has to do.
>   A poet's fan-mail will be nothing new.
> And then a lord – Good Lord, you must be peppered,
> Like Gary Cooper, Coughlin, or Dick Sheppard,
>
> With notes from perfect strangers starting, 'Sir, . . .'

On the one hand, this repeated 'I know' can be presented as a member's card, guaranteeing *entrée* to the club; on the other hand, it reveals a deeper anxiety, a fear of being ejected from the true *cognoscenti*. The writer is disturbingly aware that there are other forms of knowing, and the unpronounceable Icelandic names can remind of this: 'In Seythisfjördur every schoolboy knows/That daylight in the summer never goes.' His (inadequate) pencil thus figures a larger unsettling:

> To get to sleep in latitudes called upper
>   Is difficult at first for Englishmen.
> It's like being sent to bed before your supper
>   For playing darts with father's fountain-pen.

This abuse of father's pen is Freudianly close to what Auden is attempting here, already acknowledged in that moment of Oedipal diffidence in which he defers to the 'master', falters before the prospect of taking him on in the full challenge of ottava rima:

> Ottava Rima would, I know, be proper,
>   The proper instrument on which to pay
> My compliments, but I should come a cropper;
>   Rhyme-royal's difficult enough to play.

Propriety and knowledge are here intimately linked, even in the recurrence of that other concept, 'play'. But there is yet another concept which reverberates through the poem, hinted at in that enjambement 'pay/My compliments', taking up the opening stanzas reference to 'pay[ing] the price of authorship' and to making 'allowances' (paternal, financial, moral).

The community of knowing on which Auden presumes, the shared assumptions of an unbroken lineage, are found to be inadequate throughout the text. 'Beauty of soul should be enough, I know', he says, in a statement which implicitly concedes its refutation. What we know we are and what we intend are not the final words on the matter. We are dispossessed of our very self-possession. Wordsworth the romantic rebel is now the darling of the pupil-teachers whom Milton so despised. But Milton the revolutionary has also been co-opted into the canon, 'learnt by heart in public schools,/ Along with Wordsworth and the list of rules', made into the ideological underpinning of an imperial tradition. 'William, to change the metaphor, struck oil.' The idea of the spontaneous overflow of powerful feeling, the self-expressive, self-constituting voice, has become the mainstay of a political order, a threadbare barnstorming actor fending off revolution: 'His well seems inexhaustible, a gusher/That saves old England from the fate of Russia.' The translation of emotional gush into a piece of ideological capital is an irony extended in Auden's confession that he thinks it time 'to take repressive measures' (which is a neat pun), 'When someone says, adopting the "I know" line,/The Good Life is confined above the snow-line'. The '"I know" line' stands revealed as a strategy of ruling-class power, laying claim to all acceptable knowledge as received opinion. What the *right* people *believe* is, by and large, what is *true*. But Auden's knowledge brings unsureness:

> I know I've not the least chance of survival
>   Beside the major travellers of the day.
> I am no Lawrence who, on his arrival,
>   Sat down and typed out all he had to say;
>   I am not even Ernest Hemingway.
>   I shall not run to a two-bob edition,
>   So just won't enter for the competition.

The authorial ego-jostling is intimately linked to the idea of economic competition, suggested by the 'two-bob edition'; linked, too, with the idea of a self totally defined by its utterances, able to type out all it has to say. Auden's whole text, however, works on a principal of deferring that unspeakable totality. It cannot all be said, and the author has repeatedly to break off arbitrarily at the end of each part, stopping to beg everybody's pardon, interrupting his screed to write home to mother, summoned by the clock to lunch, deferring his finish to another day, ending his 'conversational song' not because it's really finished, but simply because it's 'already far too long,/Just like the Prelude or the Great North Road'. In an act which links its deference to authority with the deferral of closure, Auden involves his imaginary addressee in a complicity which presumes upon that familiarity he is now, once again a stranger, in process of apologizing for:

> I hope you don't think mail from strangers wrong.
> As to its length, I tell myself you'll need it,
> You've all eternity in which to read it.

This closing remark raises the most problematic question of the whole poem. For one person who will *never* read this is Byron himself. Byron now is no more than a 'verbal contraption', a set of aesthetic effects produced by the reading of his texts. 'When one talks to another', Auden remarks in 'Hic et Ille', 'one is more conscious of him as a listener to the conversation than of oneself. But the moment one writes anything, be it only a note to pass down the table, one is more conscious of oneself as a reader than of the intended recipient' (*DH*, p. 105). The writer, that is, becomes his own reader. But he is not only writing a letter *to* Lord Byron. He is also assuming the magisterial mantle *of* Lord Byron. The whole poem is an act of plagiarism, in which Auden writes to himself by stealing the voice of his master, speaking ventriloquially as if he *were* the person he claims to be addressing. That this is an Oedipal escapade of the most outrageous kind hardly needs to be stressed. What is less clear is the status assigned to the *actual* reader of the two-faced text.

The subject as writer and reader of his own productions is, in his doubleness, the site of a conflict within the structures of authority and authorship themselves. It is as writing and reading subjects that we become citizens, and it is as such, too, that we enter into that unfreedom of employment where we may have to write what we do not believe, and believe what we read, even when such subscription and conscription is to our detriment. As long as 'Each poet knew for whom he had to write', the parasite of a particular class, there was no problem. But the artist doesn't like to be a 'scivvy'. He wants a patch 'he can call/His own', wants to 'style himself the master', 'to have a circle where one's known' and 'expert knowledge' is exchanged. Instead, the modern writer is flung into a world where he is neither his own man nor sure any longer whose 'man' he is. He is fractured into disparate discourses, depending on whom he is writing for at the moment, and who he reads himself to be:

> So barons of the press who know their readers
> Employ to write their more appalling leaders,
> Instead of Satan's horned and hideous minions,
> Clever young men of liberal opinions.

Signing the usual pledges to be a better man, Auden has now returned, as writer and reader, to the familiar lines of English life, 'To read the papers and to earn my bread'. But part of his newly acquired knowledge is not so easily forgotten, though it can be played down:

> I know – the fact is really not unnerving –
> That what is done is done, that no past dies,
> That what we see depends on who's observing,
> And what we think on our activities.

Who's observing also depends on what we see. It is the blind spots of a culture and its texts which tell us most about them.

In this New World of the ostensibly 'democratic vision', the very act of reading, of universal literacy, becomes the grounds for a deeper exploitation, the site of the modern subject's ideological recruitment:

> Again, our age is highly educated;
> There is no lie our children cannot read
>
>   . . .
>
> Advertisements can teach us all we need,
> And death is better, as the millions know,
> Than dandruff, night-starvation, or B.O.

Don Juan could move easily in the highest society because the English milord 'could introduce [his] hero to it/Without the slightest tremor of anxiety;/Because he was your hero and you knew it,/He'd know instinctively what's done, and do it.' Such 'instinctual' knowingness is really a 'second nature' acquired from an uncontested and unapologetic privilege. Now the mixing of the social drawers by Industry leaves us with a populace whose half-knowledge is worse than ignorance, exploited by the newspapers and the cinema:

> Now for the spirit of the people. Here
>   I know I'm treading on more dangerous ground:
> I know there're many changes in the air,
>   But know my data too slight to be sound.
>   I know, too, I'm inviting the renowned
> Retort of all who love the Status Quo:
> 'You can't change human nature, don't you know!'

In fact, human nature *has* changed. The phrase has never defined an ideologically untainted *de*scription of actualities. Rather it has referred to an ideologically charged *pre*scription. The 'average man' is 'another man in many ways:/Ask the cartoonist first, for he knows best.' John Bull, 'The swaggering bully' of the good old days, has gone, his 'acres of self-confidence' put up for sale since the Great War. The modern hero is found in the work of Disney, 'The little Mickey with the hidden grudge' who kicks the tyrant only in his dreams. That bluff 'don't you know' speaks here with the smugness of an ideological consensus closed off from true knowledge, and already out-of-date.

It is this public that provides Auden's actual, as opposed to his imaginary, reader. He had toyed with addressing Jane Austen, but had feared he would outrage her sense of propriety. She shocks Auden more, however, making him uncomfortable to see –

> An English spinster of the middle-class
> Describe the amorous effects of 'brass',
> Reveal so frankly and with such sobriety
> The economic basis of society.

It may even be that her economic *nous* accounts for her literary success: *she* knew what the public wanted. Auden, by comparison, does not, but at least is confident that his publishers know: 'I love my publishers and they love me,/At least they paid a very handsome fee/To send me here.' Nevertheless, he's afraid of 'Obtaining money under false pretences'.

Such a fastidious concern for property and propriety, however, contradicts that other impulse behind this poem, the Oedipal desire to outdo the tradition. The poet wants *entrée*, but is not sure he wants to join any club that would have him as a member. He thus turns the tables on the tradition's sense of superiority, starting out with the challenge of Yeatsian greatness but ending by outdoing a Byron who found perverse greatness in the heroisms of mediocrity, refusing the Oedipal challenge and triumphantly topping it at once, in the very admission of failure:

> 'The fascination of what's difficult',
>   The wish to do what one's not done before,
> Is, I hope...
>   The proper card to show at Heaven's door
>
>   . . .
>
> Et cetera, et cetera. O curse,
> That is the flattest line in English verse.

Outraged at its own lowly status as a commodity, bought and sold on the market, the text deliberately rebels against the heroic postures expected of a poet. This is the 'proper explanation' for writing to Byron, cocking a snook at the commercial reader by writing to a poet who also despised the bourgeoisie from a position of aristocratic superiority, while knowing how to screw every penny out of the public and his publisher. The clash of two proprieties reveals that commercial relation, that idea of 'property', which underlies the writer's contract with his reader, and is embodied in the very idea of a 'proper self' speaking with its 'own' voice. The whole poem works at this level of double-take, engaged in masterly turns of style and extravagant rhymes and syntax at the moment that it dishonestly apologizes for its honest incompetence. The poetry dons the mantle of Byron's *picaro* in a double sense, rambling picaresquely over a changing verbal terrain as it deliberately picks the pockets of as many authors and readers as it can lay hands on, finally revealing itself as a confidence trickster who has all along assumed another man's guise, the more artfully to deceive us. The final joke is on us, and the publishers. This carefully improvised self-delivery is already published and purchased as a 'masterpiece'. For us to read it at all, the anxieties of its composition and transmission have to be resolved, as the lines which close the first section admit, begging Fabers' pardon lest the book's a flop, and that of the critics lest they're 'hard on/The author when he leads them up the garden'; begging of the readers 'Permission now and then to pull their leg'. In the process, a whole tradition has been turned on its head, and its economic base revealed. The writer, like every other citizen, is himself a party to that 'crack between employees and employers' – feels the crack, perhaps, running down the middle of his *rentier* position. What the 'Letter' finally records, setting out on its postal journey, is the uneasy relation between the resonant voice of great art, 'That marvellous cry with its ascending phrases', and the vulgar material world with which it rhymes and consorts, 'Capitalism in its later phases'.

At the moment that Auden writes himself into acceptance of his textuality ('My name', he says, 'occurs in several of the sagas') he sits down to tell himself all over again, in a brief *c.v.* which accepts that he is being rewritten by an estranging history:

A child may ask when our strange epoch passes,
    During a history lesson, 'Please, sir, what's
An intellectual of the middle classes?'

His *c.v.* becomes thus no more than 'A plain, perhaps a cautionary tale' for a future reader, significant only in its exemplary typicality. Writing to a dead man who lives only as a collection of reading-effects, Auden accepts that he too has become an oft-told tale, a literary commodity. Both as text and historic individual, the poet prepares diplomatically to disappear up his own sense of an ending. He is only a book – said so in the opening section. What is more, he is not a unitary one:

Every exciting letter has enclosures,
  And so shall this – a bunch of photographs,
Some out of focus, some with wrong exposures,
  Press cuttings, gossip, maps, statistics, graphs;
  I don't intend to do the thing by halves.
I'm going to be very up to date indeed.
It is a collage that you're going to read.

And he reminds us of this at the end: 'This book has samples of MacNeice's art'.

From undergraduate experiments in the Surrealist technique of group writing, through Isherwood's memories in *Lions and Shadows* of a poetry made from 'a little anthology of my favourite lines, strung together without even an attempt to make connected sense', down to his delighted acceptance of a printer's error as a happy improvement in 'Journey to Iceland', Auden's deference to the objectivity of the text is frequently revealed in attempts at a writing that transcends individual authorship. It is this perhaps, as much as any desire for privacy, that led him to deny that biography revealed anything about a writer. It is this, too, which led him into collaborative work, with Isherwood on the drama and *Journey to a War*, with MacNeice in *Letters from Iceland* and later, with Chester Kallman on the libretti, with Benjamin Britten, Stravinsky and Brecht.

A collaborative work is not simply the joint production of two authors, even when their specific contribution can be identified. In his *Paris Review* interview Auden said that 'When a collaboration works, the two people concerned become a third person...different from either of them in isolation.' The conflict between the two authorial voices can open up a gap in discourse where the collective unconscious of language may raise its head. Isherwood records (*New Verse* 1937) that he always had, in the plays, to struggle with Auden's Anglican ritualism – 'I have to keep a sharp eye on him – or down flop the characters on their knees.' Auden's own choruses at times acquire a satiric and satyric venom from their proximity to Isherwood's barbed burlesque. It is significant that those works which most conspicuously insist on their status as texts, not representations of the real, but aware of their own artifice, are precisely those works which Auden produced in collaboration with others. They are also the works which most directly confront the artifice of a capitalist society in crisis.

The plays foreground their own artifice to show the way in which all subjects of discourse are subjected to an authority that transcends them, uses them as its agents and carriers – as, precisely, 'actors'. The more exaggerated and unreal the action, the more ludicrous the assumptions the audience is required to accept, the more critical the posture it should take towards the 'facts' of the 'Status Quo', particularly that most arty fact of all, that 'common knowledge' summed up in 'Letter to Lord Byron': '"You can't change human nature, don't you know!"'

It is this lesson, the abdication of the imperious ego and the English ideal it sustained, which Auden takes further in his final collaborative work of the thirties, *Journey to a War*. The sonnet sequence is traditionally a vehicle for the expression of 'sexual infatuation', Auden remarked in his introduction to Shakespeare's Sonnets (*FA*, pp. 88–108). After the Romantic upsurge, when 'confession becomes a literary genre', this tendency deepens. But 'Sonnets from China' turn the genre inside-out, evacuating the personal, using it instead as a vehicle for an objective history of the species. The original title of the sequence was 'In Time of War'. This war has always existed: it is that war with nature, objective necessity, material circumstances, of which Auden wrote in his 1939 contribution to the volume *I Believe*, a war which there he sees turning into the history of class struggle. This history, diachronic, mythic, impersonal, complements the personal, synchronic, auto-biographical prose account of two young men's journey towards realizing and accepting that history. The tension between the relaxed informality of the picaresque prose, and the formal, structured narrative episodes of the poetry, carrying an accumulated message of history forward from sonnet to sonnet, bares the device of story-telling itself, and sets the self-centred subject on a collision course with the realities of an evolution which decentres that subject, where 'History opposes its grief to our buoyant song.'

'In Time of War' downgrades the West's barnstorming threadbare individual, convinced of his own centrality, from protagonist to chorus. Macao and Hong Kong prefigure this decentring. The former is a displaced 'weed from Catholic Europe'; far from home, it preserves only the childishness of its origins: 'nothing serious can happen here.' In Hong Kong, 'The leading characters are wise and witty', men of substance, breeding, education. They are nevertheless marginalized, out-of-date, clinging to the edge of an alien continent, 'Ten thousand miles from home and What's-her-name', on a 'Late Victorian hill'. The theatricality of their self-importance is farcical, while 'off-stage, a war/Thuds'. The plot actually belongs to those they regard as minor parts – the servants who 'enter unexpected', whose silence 'has a fresh dramatic use'. In its parody of Englishness, the colony the bankers have erected is 'A worthy Temple to the Comic Muse'. There is no excuse: 'For what we are, we have ourselves to blame.' History will not say alas or pardon.

By taking the personalized, self-regarding lover of the sonnet sequence, and dispersing him into the multitude of collective subjects who make a history, Auden deconstructs the political and literary traditions of bourgeois individualism. Moving from the mythical Fall to the present, the sequence traces a repeated rhythm in which successive social formations emerge, rise to hegemony and collapse under their own contradictions, to be superseded in turn by a new order. This reproduces (in the terms of *I Believe*) at the level of 'the instruments of production' those processes in which, 'in the transition from parent to child, the whole pack of inherited genetic characters is shuffled . . . The entire pattern of talents and abilities is altered at every generation.' Each social formation has its own epistemological system and crisis. The 'Commentary' speaks of our era as 'the epoch of the Third Great Disappointment', the First being the collapse of the slave-owning empire 'Whose yawning magistrate asked, "What is truth?"', the Second that of the Universal Churches brought to an end by the Renaissance and Reformation, which dispelled their 'certain knowledge' in a new, anthropocentric relativity – that of Galileo's *sed movet* and Descartes' '"I am because I think."'.

Each of these crises of disappointment is a social and an epistemological one, and 'In Time of War' links the two by situating each sonnet as a moment of knowledge in a particular knowing subject – a moment which carries with it, too, a complementary ignorance, that finally puts an end to that moment. Each sonnet has a new subject, though in the opening sequence nearly everyone begins with the same 'he' (occasionally 'they') without any indication that the subject has changed from one sonnet to the next. We never inhabit a fully civilized community, Auden says in *I Believe*, and 'All advances in knowledge, from Galileo down to Freud and Marx, are, in the first impact, humiliating; they begin by showing us that we are not as free or as grand or as good as we thought; and it is only when we realise this that we can begin to study how to overcome our own weakness.' Thus each historial moment spotted in the sonnets is a moment of humiliation and learning, as well as of progress, and the motif of learning/teaching runs though the whole sequence, from the opening sonnet on the Fall onwards:

> So from the years the gifts were showered; each
> Ran off with his at once into his life:
> Bee took the politics that make a hive,
> Fish swam as fish, peach settled into peach.
>
> And were succesful at the first endeavour;
> The hour of birth their only time at college,
> They were content with their precocious knowledge,
> And knew their station and were good for ever.

'Man' alone never settles into a fixed positionality in which knowledge and circumstances are totally coincident. History originates in this fall into knowledge, which is also the discovery of a new kind of ignorance – the knowledge that we don't know enough. Man 'looked for truth and was continually mistaken'. The forbidden fruit 'taught . . . nothing new'.

Initially, leaving Eden, 'They knew exactly what to do outside'; but as soon as they left 'the memory faded/Of all they'd learnt'. History is a finishing school in which they are never finished, as the 'Commentary' tells us, seeing the present as 'but the local variant of a struggle in which all,/ . . . In all their living are profoundly implicated'. We live now 'in a world that has no localised events'. But if we are always at risk, always in college, the present becomes our own kind of gift, in a motif that takes up the pun of the opening sonnet and runs through the sequence. Sonnet XX speaks of that present moment, in China, where the people huddle after a bombing raid, 'Like children sent to school'. Space has rules 'they cannot hope to learn', Time 'a language they will never master'. But the peripatetic Englishmen have learnt a little. In sonnet XIV the appearance of the bombers had startled them out of complacency, 'Who never quite believed they could exist,/Not where we were'. Taken by surprise, they have learnt that they too 'dwell upon the earth', and are as vulnerable to the impartial bomb as any native. Sonnet XX repeats this lesson, using a 'We' which is no longer exclusive, but implicates the two travellers with all those others whose local war they had previously thought it to be. Now, they realize, they have completed their journey to a war, grasped that it is theirs too:

> We live here. We lie in the Present's unopened
> Sorrow; its limits are what we are.
> The prisoner ought never to pardon his cell.

Enjambement allows for the unwrapping of the Present as the unfolding of a lie, a dangerous gift: it may only be sorrow, the poem suggests, but it is *our* sorrow, and for that we should be grateful. It teaches, in the words of the 'Commentary', that we are only 'apparently immune', and will be 'compelled to realise that our refuge is a sham'. For if, in Galileo's words, *sed movet*, this objective movement which dethrones our confident knowledges is also the guarantee that we will not be allowed to persist in our error. 'Nothing is given; we must find our law', sonnet XXV advises. 'Nothing is certain but the body'; but it is in having a body that we are subject to the general laws that move the universe – laws quite different from our own interpretative theories or legislative codes. (The difference is that between a human law which says 'Thou shalt not jump off a roof', and a material law which says 'Falling bodies are subject to gravity'.) Nowhere is Galileo's phrase more consoling than when we contemplate the dictators who feel that their *logos* commands history, who tell us, in the 'Commentary', to '"*Leave Truth to the police and us; we know the Good;/We build the Perfect City time shall never alter;/Our Law shall guard you always . . ./Your Ignorance keep off evil like a dangerous sea . . .*"'. They bring their train of willing or reluctant philosophers in their wake. But time moves on, 'Night falls on China; the great arc of travelling shadow/Move over land and ocean, altering life', and in its movement dethrones them, revealing philosophers and leaders alike as 'humbugs full of vain dexterity'.

Grasping this, in the words of sonnet XXV, we discover 'We have no destiny assigned to us' and thus 'We learn to pity and rebel.' All human institutions, from the humblest tools to the most complex civilizations, have taken their cue, appeared, and moved on. The humbling of political and intellectual pride has recurred repeatedly as one moment of this processive history. The earliest scholar-priests systematized their studies of the heavens into a framework made up of scientific prediction and lucky guesses, for which they were rewarded well by those with power. The mage 'fell in love with Truth before he knew her,/And rode into imaginary lands', feeling himself increasingly superior to 'those who served her with their hands'. But, summoned by Truth, he found reflected in her eyes 'every human weakness,/And saw himself as one of many men'. It is this humbling recognition that comes to the arrogant Western intellectuals abroad in China. In sonnet XXVI this process begins outside the personal – 'Always far from the centre of our names,/The little workshop of love'. But it sweeps in from the margins to engulf that personal, and suddenly we realize that it has been there all the time, the unconscious, unnoticed ground bass of all our acts.

In China, the decentring is a double one, as sonnet XIII indicates. It begins in that personal realm of the speaking, singing voice: 'Certainly praise: let the song mount again and again' in a celebration of beauty, patience, grace, happiness, greatness. But there is another world which puts this enclosed and privileged one in perspective:

> But hear the morning's injured weeping, and know why:
> Cities and men have fallen; the will of the Unjust
> Has never lost its power; still, all princes must
> Employ the Fairly-Noble unifying lie.
>
> . . .
>
> The Good Place has not been; our star has warmed to birth
> A race of promise that has never proved its worth...

Such a realization reveals that 'The quick new West is false', decentred by the Eighteen Provinces of this ancient China whose people for so long 'have constructed the earth'. But it reveals that China too, decentred by the West, is 'prodigious, but wrong'. No construction of the earth is equivalent to the vastness of the earth itself. (The ambiguity of 'construction' makes it both a physical and an intellectual act). The honest intellectual and political method is one which lives in a perpetual 'As If', starting not with 'rigid Certainty' but with the speculative 'The Chances Are'. This is what Auden now espouses as an authentic socialism, to set against the dogmas and murderous confidence of Stalin and Hitler alike. In a world where man is 'abject/And to his own creation... subject' (III) and is easily 'imprisoned in possession' (IV), Auden's way lies in a deeper identification with that 'College of the Humble' he invokes in the 'Commentary'.

We too have had our famous, Auden says, of the progressive camp. But they would not care about fame, for in their disinterested researches they shared the strangeness of those estranged from power, those also with nothing to lose:

> Some looked at falsehood with the candid eyes of children,
> Some had a woman's ear to catch injustice,

> Some took Necessity, and knew her, and she brought
>   forth Freedom.

Such forms of knowledge are collective, not private property, for 'goodness needs the evidence of all our lives,/And even to exist, it must be shared as truth,/As freedom or as happiness.' They remind us of those who really make history, the anonymous multitudes who built the Sphinx of the opening sonnets, who wait upon the Europeans in Hong Kong, who fight the wars the Generals arrange on maps in sonnet XVI, whose unacknowledged labours inform all our acts of intellection, including writing and criticizing poetry. This 'Invisible College' is not just a collectivity, but a place of learning and teaching as much as that privileged Oxford left behind, whose stones even, the poem 'Oxford' tells us, are 'utterly/Satisfied still with their weight', in 'quadrangles where Wisdom honours herself'. Outside that complacent sanctuary, 'Eros Paidagogos/Weeps on his virginal bed'; and it is the widows and the fatherless ignored by that cosy enclave who now 'find a hearing' in the 'Commentary' –

> Who through the ages have accomplished everything
>   essential,
>
> And stretch around our struggle as the normal
>   landscape,
> And mingle, fluent with our living, like the winds and
>   waters,
> The dust of all the dead that reddens every sunset;
>
> Giving us courage to confront our enemies,
> Not only on the Grand Canal, or in Madrid,
> Across the campus of a university city,
>
> But aid us everywhere, that in the lovers' bedroom,
> The white laboratory, the school, the public meeting,
> The enemies of life may be more passionately attacked.

What the voice of the Humble says, in reproach, is a challenge to Knowledge and Virtue alike. Speaking not in the privileged accents of *F6*'s Ransom, but in those of history's human dust, they reveal the Power that lies at the base of all quests for freedom, truth and justice, if these three are separated out instead of apprehended in their unity:

> '*You talked of Liberty, but were not just; and now*
> *Your enemies have called your bluff; for in your city,*
> *Only the man behind the rifle had free-will.*'

One such mote of 'human dust' (the phrase is Trotsky's) gave his portion back to history in sonnet XVIII. But this is not the act of 'voluntary personal commitment' Edward Callan envisages.[1] This soldier was 'used', 'far from the heart of culture' – our culture, mine, yours and Callan's. 'Abandoned by his general and his lice', when he died he simply 'vanished'. 'He will not be introduced/When this campaign is tidied into books.' Even in Auden's sonnet he is not one but many, all of a type, lacking 'vital knowledge', and even here 'His name is lost for ever like his looks.' Yet he enters into the record, for:

> He neither knew nor chose the Good, but taught us,
> And added meaning like a comma, when
> He turned to dust in China that our daughters
>
> Be fit to love the earth, and not again
> Disgraced before the dogs; that, where are waters,
> Mountains and houses, may be also men.

He teaches what the equally unnamed Rilke teaches in sonnet XXIII, to 'remember all who seemed deserted'. Rilke too 'through ten years of silence worked and waited,/Until in Muzot all his powers spoke,/and everything was given once for all'. The gift is the reward of waiting patient like a peasant for the fulfilment of that truth: *sed movet*. Empires fall. The dead are not to be remembered as names, but redeemed by our *actions* in the present, where their hopes may like seeds grow again. The same point had been made in IX: 'We bring them back with promises to free them,/But as ourselves continually betray them:/They hear their deaths lamented in our voice,/but in our knowledge know we could restore them.' It is this restoration that the poet is about here.

Rilke does not belong to the self-centred West satirized in the preceding sonnet (XXII), with France putting her case before the world, proclaiming joy above everything, America asking '"Do you love me as I love you."' Instead, like Auden, he belongs to that Western tradition prepared to give witness, to remember, as Auden caustically indicates with his request to –

> Think in this year what pleased the dancers best:
> When Austria died and China was forsaken,
> Shanghai in flames and Teruel re-taken.

The dance of the capitalist powers is still the dance of death, the dance marathon with increasingly desperate stakes. Maps are abstract, and generals can move their troops about them without caring for the 'living men in terror of their lives' who, 'unlike an idea, can die too soon'. The poet, too, in his concern for the personal and immediate, can easily fall into that abstraction in which *his* feelings, *his* experience alone are real, while those soldiers out there, those struggles in Spain and Austria and China are reduced to abstractions on a map. The heart must have its maps too, and refuse the facile antithesis of abstract and sensuously immediate, as it must refuse the separation of the collective life from the excitements of the personal. Maps can *really* point too, and they point to *real* places:

> But ideas can be true although men die,
> And we can watch a thousand faces
> Made active by one lie:
>
> And maps can really point to places
> Where life is evil now:
> Nanking; Dachau.

Sometimes a single name on the map can tell us more of human evil and of good than all the poets can.

It is a travesty of this sequence, which ends up with the ortho-dox 'Marxist' proposition, 'We live in freedom of necessity,/

A mountain people living amoung mountains', to cast it as a rejection of socialism, as, for example, Callan does.[2] It is illicit to import Auden's subsequent biography into the poem to justify this reading, like Mendelson.[3] Auden's departure to America, seen by many of his old comrades as a defection from the struggle, brought an impassioned response from him in a letter to Stephen Spender in 1941:

> If I thought I should be a competent soldier or air-raid warden I should come back tomorrow...As a writer and a pedagogue the problem is different, for the intellectual warfare goes on always and everywhere, and no one has a right to say that this place or that time is where all intellectuals ought to be.[4]

It might seem that, for the mature Auden, running away was a continuation of the struggle by other means. But this is only if we insist on speaking of him as 'the English Auden', as the misleading title of Mendelson's collection suggests, rather than 'the socialist Auden'. The England Auden turned his back on had looked away 'When Austria died and China was forsaken'. Its policy of so-called 'Non-Intervention' had betrayed the legitimate Spanish Republic to Fascism. Teruel was re-taken on 15 February 1938. Five days later Anthony Eden resigned as British Foreign Secretary in protest against the Prime Minister Neville Chamberlain's Spanish policy. On 11 March Nazi troops marched into Austria. In April Britain recognized Italian sovereignty over Ethiopia and in September Chamberlain personally signed away Czech independence at Munich. For any decent radical in the thirties, England was not a *patria* to be proud of but a burden of betrayal, shame and perfidy presided over by that 'Beethameer, Beethameer, bully of Britain' lampooned in *The Orators*, a composite newspaper proprietor made up of the Lords Beaverbrook and Rothermere and by a venal and hypocritical elite based in the Home Counties. 'England our cow/Once was a lady – is she now?' Auden asked rhetorically in *The Orators*. By 1938 he had his answer. There was nothing, really, to abandon.

Auden's trips to Spain, Iceland and China had shown him

clearly enough that 'our time has no favourite suburb'. The struggle for democracy and socialism is one that goes on everywhere, all the time, a guerrilla war like that he saw in China, which has no fronts, because everywhere is the front. In this struggle, ideas are not vague abstractions floating above a landscape, but the very stuff of reality, everywhere shaping the very terms and conditions in which that struggle is waged. His affectionate portrait of Voltaire, in *Another Time*, caught the discrepancy between the great man's *amour propre* – a humble little human failing – and his real contribution to the cause of enlightenment and justice, in terms which recalled the peasants of that far-away country. He would write:

> 'Nothing is better than life.' But was it? Yes, the fight
> Against the false and the unfair
> Was always worth it. So was gardening. Civilise.
>
> Cajoling, scolding, scheming, cleverest of them all,
> He'd led the other children in a holy war
> Against the infamous grown-ups; and, like a child, been sly
> And humble when there was occasion for
> The two-faced answer or the plain protective lie,
> But patient like a peasant waited for their fall.

Ideas are material things, as real as the books in which they are printed, the brains in which they form, the 'printing presses turning forests into lies'. In *I Believe*, he had urged us to 'remember that while an idea can be absolutely bad, a person can never be'. But to 'defend what we believe to be right' may require 'the cost of our lives and those of others'. In two quatrains he dropped from the typescript of sonnet XIV of 'In Time of War', he put it in terms less absolute and abstract than Michael Ransom's triad of Knowledge, Virtue, Power:

> There is a power that has the will to kill us.
> Resist then; be destructive and as strong:
> All killing hurts, but it will always matter
> Whose dust the twelve winds lift and scatter;
> All people are not equal; some are wrong.

6 Conscripts to Our Age: *New Year Letter*

Many of the poems Auden later suppressed, including most famously *Spain*, find their focus, and the cause perhaps for their suppression, in fretting over 'The conscious acceptance of guilt in the necessary murder'. It has been conventional to see these agonizings as the moral peripeteia of a born-again Christian distressed by the attitudinizings of a misspent youth. This would be fair enough if Christianity were unequivocally a religion of pacifism, with no doctrine of the 'Just War' up its voluminous sleeves. But the most striking evidence against this cosy myth is the fact that it was the Christian socialist Reinhold Niebuhr who dissuaded Auden in 1940 from veering towards pacifism.[1]

What Auden found in Niebuhr's *An Interpretation of Christian Ethics* (1936) was confirmation of his own (impeccably left-wing) thesis that liberalism was the godfather of a Fascism whose direct progenitor was a capitalism in crisis. For Niebuhr, Christianity alone, restored to its disinterested and stateless original form, could provide 'a transcendant perspective upon the issues at stake'. In Niebuhr, as in the existentialism of Kierkegaard, whom he began to read at about the same time, Auden found a mode of historical interpretation which did not supersede his earlier mentors, Marx and Freud, but which like them justified the positive value of scepticism about all confident subject-positions, all absolutist claims to knowledge, all doctrines which identified truth with the state and the status quo. In *Modern Canterbury Pilgrims* in 1956, Auden identified this latter position as that of the 'conventional Christian... who does not distinguish between his faith and his culture', who 'believes in the Nicene Creed as unquestionably and in the same way as he believes that no gentleman wears a celluloid collar' (p. 34), for whom faith is merely conformity. In his Christian apologia in the *Partisan Review* symposium in 1950, 'Religion and the Intellectuals', he wrote of the 'abandonment of hope for a general social improvement' as leading 'not to Christianity but to one of those religions which hold that time is an illusion or an endless cycle' and insisted instead on Christianity's *materialism*, enshrined in the concept of the incarnation and resurrection of the body.

In fact, he argued, 'Man is both a historical creature creating novelty and a natural creature suffering cyclical recurrence and no religion is viable which does not do justice to both aspects.' The definition recalls that interplay of cyclical return and historical progression we have traced in 'Sonnets from China'; it points too toward the theme of *New Year Letter*, announced in the 'Prologue', later dropped, which balances the 'season of repetition and return' of nature, reassembling our bodies 'to hold/the knowledge they cannot get out of', with those dark uni-directional walks into 'the unknown unconditional dark' of history. It is this balancing of nature and history which is, indeed, the condition of the 'Double Man' spoken of in its last stanza.

Auden found in a passage from Paul Tillich's *The Interpretation of History* which he included in the notes to *New Year Letter* a confirmation of his own historical interpretation, linking the changing subjects of 'In Time of War' with the ostensibly fixed, secure authorial stance of the later poem:

The absolute position of the *knowing subject* became doubtful when the break which the Middle Ages sought between nature and super-nature was found in nature itself, and when super-nature was done away with, as happened in Protestantism... The fundamental Protestant attitude is to stand in nature, taking upon oneself the inevitable reality; not to flee from it, either into the world of ideal forms or into the related world of super-nature, but to make decisions in concrete reality. Here the subject has no possibility of an absolute position. It cannot go out of the sphere of decision. Every part of its nature is affected by these contradictions. Fate and freedom reach into the act of knowledge and make it a historical deed: the Kairos determines the Logos.

The 'knowing subject', knowing the historical relativity of its knowledge, cannot get out of having to make decisions in the pressing moment. There is no outside to history, and success or failure depends upon the correct conjunction of cir-cumstance and decision: in 'Balaam and His Ass' Auden defines the Greek notion of *kairos* as 'the propitious moment for doing something' (*DH*, p. 140). But (as 'In Time of War' revealed) 'man' is perpetually out of sync with himself, ahead of his time or lagging behind it in consciousness, and it is this lack of synchronization which has made history a record of half-achievements, unfinished revolutions, a movement of uni-directional forces which nevertheless repeatedly lapses back into the cyclical returns of nature, without ever fully succumb-ing. The present, that package always about to be unwrap-ped, is never the most propitious time to carry out the historical tasks the past has donated to us; but there is no other time in which to act.

Auden's original choice of title for *New Year Letter*, preserved in the American edition, was *The Double Man*. It focuses many dualities. Arising from the contradiction between natural and historical being – this body in space, born to this moment in time – is another one, indicated in the epigraph from Montaigne: 'We are, I know not how, double in ourselves, so that what we believe we disbelieve, and cannot rid ourselves of what we con-demn.' This is the tension between 'Kairos and Logos' of the poem of that name, aware of 'The shadow cast by language upon truth', yet knowing that there is no other way than through language that reality can be apprehended and defined.

Such a dualism opens into that wider one discussed a decade later in *The Enchafèd Flood*, which explains the endlessly processive nature of the subject and its history, 'a process in a process', in the poem:

> Man's being is a copulative relation between a subject ego and a predicate self. The ego is aware of the self as given, already there in the world, finite, derived, along with, related and comparable to other beings. It is further aware of the self not only as existing but also as potential, as not fully actual but as a self which becomes itself. (p. 117)

Auden's antitheses repeatedly spawn new ones which drown any crude schema in plurality. So, here, this self which 'cannot initiate anything' but only respond to the ego's urge to 'self-realisation' itself breaks down into a duality, able to 'welcome or resist the decision when it is taken'. 'The desire of the ego is a double one' also, freely owning a self and desiring a self of which it can approve, but also desiring to be approved for the self it has (p. 118). In its isolation, this ego 'cannot compare its egoship with the other egos, as it can compare the self it is related to with other selves' (p. 117). And this leads to a further duality, between self and others, who can be known as bodies but not as experiencing subjects, except at second hand. Charles Williams's *The Descent of the Dove,* which provided the epigraph and much of the incidental language and imagery of *New Year Letter*, also supplies patristic authority for this dualism, in a quotation which recalls Auden's own socialist ponderings on the nature of solidarity in 'In Time of War':

> 'It is right for a man to take up the burden for them who are near to him . . . to put his own soul in the place of that of his neighbour, and to become, if it were possible, a double man, and he must suffer, and weep, and mourn with him, and finally the matter must be accounted by him as if he himself had put on the actual body of his neighbour, and as if he had acquired his countenance and soul, and he must suffer for him as he would for himself'. (p. 56)

This brings us back to the most significant duality of the whole work, indicated by its double title.

Depending on which title we give priority, Auden's poem changes its significance for the reader. One emphasizes its textuality, as a piece of writing. The other stresses that pseudo-person into whose voice and soul we seem to enter, whose suffering becomes, for a while, our own, when we read the poem. A book, Auden had said in the thirties, 'is not only the meaning of the words inside it; it is the person who means them'. *New Year Letter* is a double text, in that it is both writing and the imaginary presence of a man. But if that man is double, so is the writing, for on the one hand it is 'this private minute for a friend' spoken of at the end of Part I but, on the other, is 'under Flying Seal to all/Who wish to read it anywhere,/And, if they open it, *En Clair*'. The image of a dispatch addressed to Whitehall reinforces this paradox. For although Whitehall deals with public business, it also conducts that business with the utmost secrecy. Auden's epistle is both a private missive, to its dedicatee Elizabeth Mayer, and a public document. In the same way, by making the closing line of the first Part refer to the act of opening the letter, Auden alerts us to that larger paradox, which engulfs text, subject and history alike, and which runs as a leitmotiv through the poem, from the opening lines, which open on a moment of closure – New Year's Eve, the end of an inglorious decade in retrenchment and sacrifice – to the closing, which end on an expansive movement (and a metrically extended line) out into renewed travelling, refusing closure.

One of Auden's prose notes to the poem spells this out. Artists, as citizens, he says, are 'the *only* people for whom a capitalist democracy is a completely open society', and the successful artist is 'always an anarchist at heart'. But in his own work the artist is 'the only person who is really a dictator', for 'Works of art really are closed societies...made...by the artist alone.' This is of course too simple an antithesis, and the whole poem struggles with its implications only to find them wanting. Nevertheless, it points to the continual paralleling of order in art and in society which the paradoxes of closure and openness repeatedly subvert. Early on the poem tells us:

To set in order – that's the task
Both Eros and Apollo ask;
For art and life agree in this,
That each intends a synthesis.

But that 'intends' is a weasel word. The discrepancy of intention and effect is where Auden's supposedly 'closed society' perpetually deposes its overweening 'dictator'. For dictators need publics as letters require readers, and once the text enters the hermeneutic circle it ceases to be a world closed on the outside. Existing in language, it has to derive its significances from the meanings of words, and those meanings depend upon the interpretative acts of its readers.

Art may present 'Already lived experience', 'Autonomous completed states', but those 'Unique events that once took place' in the artist's life now occupy a 'new field' in the text. As 'An abstract model of events' a poem returns to fleshy multiplicity in the readings of its multiple readers, saying different things to each. Experience, 'Trapped in a medium's artifice', is paradoxically released 'To charity, delight, increase', the 'changeless presences' of art sent forth to multiply in the public world. Ironically, by contrast, the multitudes outside the poet's window are reduced to uniformity, moving 'in loose formations of good cheer,/ . . . Towards the habits of next year', and he joins them in the realization that all their 'reflections turn about/A common meditative norm'. The actual relations between 'art and life' are various, involving not only analogy, but antithesis. What in their asymmetry they share, however, is a constant deferring of finality, synthesis. For if, unlike history, stories come to an end, they do so only in deferral and deference, deferring to those readers who make them start all over again, just as history has to, each New Year's Eve.

The doubleness of the subject is matched then by the doubleness of a text which is constantly turned against itself, which cannot be pinned down to its authorial intention. And this arises out of a larger slipperiness of language, which is always at odds with the reality *it* intends to pin down. In his commonplace book *A Certain World* Auden reiterates a point from Werner Heisenberg also made in the notes to *New Year Letter*: 'When we speak of the picture of nature in the exact science of our age, we do not mean a picture of nature so much as a picture of our relationship with nature . . . [B]y its intervention science alters and refashions the object of its investigation . . . method and object can no longer be separated' (p. 333). A note to section III tells us an idea has two purposes: as 'reflection of our material life' it 'cannot re-enter history as an effective agent because it does not want to'. But at the same time it shares our doubleness, for, whether it is true or not it can 'suggest a way to relieve our wants', change our behaviour and thus become 'an agent of historical change'. Whether an idea 'reflects' reality, then, can be less important than whether someone believes it, and by believing it, commits an act which has effects in that reality.

Each language carves up the world in certain ways, assuming that the ideal objects it thus creates correspond to some actually unknowable essential reality. That these ideal objects are creations of thought, working on that reality, only becomes apparent at moments of social and economic disruption, when the language by which we normally map out the real begins to falter. Thus, emergent capitalism created a 'new *Anthropos*, an/Empiric Economic Man', quite different from any previous concepts of the human. This 'Man' –

> did what he was born to do,
> Proved some assumptions were untrue.
> He had his half-success; he broke
> The silly and unnatural yoke
> Of famine and disease that made
> A false necessity obeyed . . .

until he too succumbed to the depravity he had set out to expose, that of taking 'useful concepts' as 'universals'. To avoid fetichizing this 'useful concept', Auden makes it clear that this is not a real *man*, but an ideologically constructed idea, an item in a complex anthropology. He does this by ripping out of its context that key word from an older discourse, *Anthropos*, thrusting it gratuitously into this new verbal arena to reveal the provisionality and shiftingness of all concepts. Under that older discourse 'necessity', the *Anangke* of famine and disease that lies behind Greek tragedy, was felt to be coterminous with 'nature'. This new 'Man', however, revealed such assumptions to be 'unnatural' and even 'silly', brought about not by nature but by the uneven development of the forces of production, which confused the historical with the cosmic. But 'Empiric Economic Man' in turn created his own false necessity, against which new discourses rose in rebellion and dissent, as the Enlightenment turned on itself in Romantic reaction.

Even at the height of its ascendancy, such a discourse did not hold unchallenged sway, 'could not silence all the cliques'. What Auden demonstrates throughout the poem is the extent to which reality is not a single, homogeneous continuum, in which an unproblematic world is reflected in a seamless, totally transparent language, but a babble of discordant jargons, contending for dominance, or slinking away in defeat from contestation. The language of his own text reproduces this effect. Critics have repeatedly spoken of its 'neo-Augustan' qualities, its coherence and lucidity and its sense of an urbane, worldly and experienced subject confidently articulating an argument through careful periphrasis, discursive illustration, moral exempla and shrewdly representative personifications. This is all true, in part. But there is another side to it. Auden may well employ the couplet form, but it is not, significantly, the stately heroic couplet of Pope and Dryden, which is a spacious enough measure to allow for sense to be repeatedly contained within its formal antitheses. He uses instead the rather more hectic octosyllabic measure of Marvell and Butler, a form which is constantly in its compactness overflowing its couplets, spawning a syntax that can find its resolution only after a proliferation of sub-clauses and amplifications, which seems to move in a permanent future tenseness. Such a style is flexible enough, but its pace is considerably more urgent and impulsive that the pentameter.

Similarly, the remarkable enfilade of loan-words from most of the major European languages scattered throughout the poem testifies, perhaps, to the cosmopolitan accomplishment and intellectual sprezzatura of this much-travelled Seigneur. Nothing provincial here. There is about all this, though, not only the suspect showiness of a Byron, but also the larger anxiety of the émigré, desperately affirming his common European culture to the refugee German Jewess he addresses, while the continent they have both abandoned, one by choice, the other by necessity, goes up in flames behind them. At times, Auden's style approaches the macaronic, the decadent mode of a late-imperial culture. The larger purpose this polyglot style serves, spanning not only a range of languages but also a multitude of intellectual disciplines and their various jargons, is to break open the closed verbal universe of the poem, revealing that, if the United States is a cultural melting-pot, so is the English language. The difference, for example between *civitas* and *polis*, both words used in the text, defines a whole grammar of other differences between Roman and Greek society; but also, since both words have been taken up into different intellectual traditions, between Christian and secular definitions of the Just City spoken of in the closing pages of the poem as our goal and hope.

Each of us knows, Auden says in Part III, that 'Whatever nonsense we believe,/Whomever we can still deceive,/Whatever language angers us', our day is drawing to its close, and all the tasks begun by the Renaissance are done. The objects defined by our language are now unclear, its beliefs woozy, and that line 'Whatever language angers us' indicates why. In one sense, Auden is saying that as Anglo-Saxons, for example, we could be moved to anger by German, and Germans by English. But Elizabeth Mayer is German, and the language she speaks is one in which Auden himself experienced those political and sexual illuminations, in 1928–9, which made him the man he is. Indeed, when he comes to speak of the primal sources of identity, in Part III, in those adits and entrances of the limestone landscape where he first became aware of Self and Not-Self, and of that 'deep *Urmutterfurcht* that drives/Us into knowledge all our lives', he lapses as if naturally into the German which is the mother tongue of psychoanalysis and Romantic drama alike. 'Whatever language angers us' then has another sense – not of an external language, to be turned into the Outlawed and the Other, rejected from the community of tongues; but of that language which constitutes our being, which drives us to anger or to love, without which we would be subjectless selves. When this language falters, all is lost.

The poem's effortless transitions from the phraseology of diplomacy to that of theology, and from this to philosophy or military or political science, psychology, music or geometry, affirm that the 'true' language does not belong to one particular nation. Diplomacy may largely derive its vocabulary from French, music largely from Italian. But the very opening paragraph, that speaks of the babble of voices in the street outside, and prefigures the larger polyphony of the whole poem, hints at how all the discourses in which we engage cut at a tangent across the 'pure' national languages, just as the spectrum of human reactions cannot be contained by any one mental discipline. The voices are 'Singing or sighing as they go:/*Exalté, piano*, or in doubt'. Part I ends likewise on the doubleness of language, which may be 'useless', since 'No words men write can stop the war' or measure up to 'its immeasurable grief'. But often when the Oracle is dumb, truth may speak 'through the Janus of a joke', two-facedly. As if in jest, Auden speaks of this with a pompous classical allusiveness as 'The candid psychopompos' – the epithet being that of Hermes, 'leader of souls' to the underworld, who is also the carrier of messages. The circumlocution that is, refers to a letter he is about to commit to the postman, but it also reveals just how different language is from the pure representation of a given world. Periphrasis, in this poem, becomes not only a way of presenting a message, but a message itself, warning us of language's traps for the unwary.

The equivocation built into all language stalks abroad, too, in all the puns and paronomasias of the poem, in its puzzles and *double entendres*, riddles and teasing innuendos. Just how arbitrary language is is indicated by two words, one French, the other Greek, it conscripts from totally different conceptual discourses, which are distinguished only by a shift of accents – the mountaineering term *'arête'*, and the Aristotelian concept of *'areté'*. This shiftiness of language requires what the concluding lines of Part II refer to as 'the gift of double focus'.

The devil controls, we're told, the moral absolutists, the 'either-ors, the mongrel halves/Who find truth in a mirror'. They seek in the external world a mirror reflection of their own ideological constructions. For them, language has to correspond to a fixed reality and its sole purpose is to ensure that fixity. They are, according to a note to the text, the 'impatient romantics', and Auden defines Romanticism as 'Unawareness of the Dialectic', locked in ideological closure. But 'The Devil indeed, is the father of Poetry, for poetry might be defined as the clear expression of mixed feelings. The Poetic mood is never indicative.'

It is the very provisionality of poetic language which allows it to move in this dialectic, refusing to confuse signifier and signified either with each other or with that referent that lies outside the play of language altogether. The devil 'may never tell us lies,/Just half truths we can synthesize'. His half-truths depend upon collapsing the difference between the word and the concept, and the concept and the thing. For a word neither corresponds to a concept, nor does that concept necessarily name a real thing out there in the world. Auden demonstrates this at once by turning his favourite trick on the word 'lies', changing its grammatical function from noun to verb as its semantic function too is converted from language to physical position: 'So, hidden in his hocus-pocus,/There lies the gift of double focus', which is compared to Aladdin's magic lamp, dull but, used correctly, 'a sesame to light'. We are invited in this prestidigitation to see the process enacted. 'Open sesame' are words of power, gaining entrance to and exit from the caves of the real, ironically coming as the section itself rounds into closure, but promising us a new beginning in the next section, which indeed opens with Manhattan 'ablaze with light'. Hidden within the hocus-pocus of language lies that truth which can be opened unto us.

Auden speaks here not simply of the dialectic of history Marx derived from Hegel. He reaches back to that dialectical method

employed by Socrates to pursue a truth which, though somewhere fixed in its ideal forms, always seems to elude its
pursuers down the phenomenal forms of history and dialogue.
Its most immediate source is Kierkegaard, whom Auden
described in a review in *New Republic* in 1944 as 'a secular
dialectician. . .one of the greatest exponents of an approach
equally hostile to Cartesian mechanism and Hegelian idealism,
to which the Germans have given the name Existential', an
approach which 'is typical of what is most valuable in Marx
and Freud'. As an interpretative method, this dialectic does
not supersede the Marxist one, but supplements it, rescuing
the truth from its half-truths.

At the beginning of this section Auden had spoken of the
human reluctance to accept provisionality and process, 'The
mere suggestion that we die/Each moment and that each great
I/IS but a process in a process/Within a field that never closes'.
We imagine ourselves fixed in identity, and –

> As proper people find it strange
> That we are changed by what we change,
> That no event can happen twice
> And that no two existences
> Can ever be alike; we'd rather
> Be perfect copies of our father,
> Prefer our *idées fixes* to be
> True of a fixed Reality.

In a 'swelling universe' we have in fact to 'stretch imagination/
To live according to our station'. Ideal forms are not the end
(goal) of knowledge; rather, as fixed ideas that get in the way
of the cognitive act, they *put* an end to it. We have repeatedly
and with difficulty to 'Learn who and where and how we are'
in a process that constantly lags behind all the displacements
that undermine any knowledge we already have. Shifting
between an imaginary 'Reality' and discourse, the lines
redefine these fixed 'ideas' as foolishly arrested signifiers,
detached from the play of signification, perpetually transfixed
as arbitrary, 'artificial' foreign words, interrupting the 'natural'
flow of English meaning, wrenched into a displaced fixity out

of their own, 'natural' context. The strangeness in the end is our own, as we too sense our endless displacement down the chain of signifiers, pursuing an elusive fixity and comfort.

That is, indeed, the 'trap of Hell' described in Part III, initially a paradisal place where the moment has come to a stop, and language is the pure play of transparency over an unambiguous reality:

> The field of Being where he may,
> Unconscious of Becoming, play
> With the Eternal Innocence
> In unimpeded utterance.

Held for more than an instant, such a blessing turns into a curse, paradise into that 'being of the lie' where we too 'lie' 'locked/Each in a stale uniqueness'. This illusion of a fullness of self-presence blinds us to our being in time, which in Kierkegaardian terms lies in an openness to the future, that which is-not-yet.

It is not a Hell confined to abstract conditions. Part III had begun with a celebration of a recent dinner-party at Elizabeth Mayer's which had vouchsafed a vision of harmony, an 'unexpected power/That drove our ragged egos in/From the dead ends of greed and sin/To sit down at the wedding feast'. An excess of delight floods the actual so that all are reconciled, but only at the expense of those larger exclusions. This party may celebrate plenitude, but it contains its own contradictions, where that surplus of feeling in excess of the situation can be contained only by an inflationary spiral in which he feels out of place in finding himself happily in place:

> Each felt the *placement* to be such
> That he was honoured overmuch.

The deliberate Frenchification of a word that would be perfectly acceptable as English (only the italics change its pronunciation and provenance) creates a leak in this closed circle, alerting us to the real displacements under the excessive mutual congratulation of this 'privileged community'. This dialectical movement, which turns the tables on the happy symposium, is implicit too in the party's imaginary guests, for 'SCHUBERT sang and MOZART played/And GLUCK and food and friendship' made them feel their 'privileged community' was the real republic not only of the politicians but, by implication, of Plato himself. Schubert, Mozart, Gluck are no more present as bodies and subjects than Auden and Elizabeth Mayer are present to each other now in this dispatch of texts, or than Auden and we as readers. Within the imagined fullness an absence already lurks, whether it is that of the uninvited or of those present only in their effects – not merely the providers of music but of food too. Auden acknowledges this by a shift of pace which undercuts the uniqueness, reducing it to the commonplace: 'O but it happens every day/To someone', and the disembodied vagueness of this last empty pronoun leads us on to that vision in which the field of Being turns into the place of the lie where we coddle our 'stale uniqueness' for all eternity.

Plato and Socrates, absent guests at this feast as throughout the text, provide an effective image of the double focus Auden is applying here. For if Plato is associated with the concept of the unchanging ideal forms in which the truth abides, Socrates' use of the perpetually deferred closures of dialogue as the model of intellectual enquiry totally belies the fixity he seeks. That this duality rules over the text is confirmed by Auden's comments in 'The Greeks and Us' in 1948 (*FA*, pp. 3–32), speaking of the drawback of the Greek 'Contemplative Hero'.

By identifying the Good with Reason instead of Will, he says, the Greeks 'doomed themselves to finding the ideal form of society which, like the truths of reason, would be valid everywhere and for everyone, irrespective of their individual character or their historical circumstances'. This leads either to 'political despair' or to 'a defense of tyranny', the abjection of failure or the arrogance of apparent success which then feels obliged to force its 'truth' on everyone. (The terms here are little different from the essay on Voltaire in 1939.) The 'Socratic dialectic', however, educates the intellect in the same way that free-association in psychoanalysis educates the emotions. It does not impose its truths authoritatively, but leaves the pupil to find them 'from the process of enquiry which each individual must live through for himself at first-hand'. As a method, then, the dialectic lives in history, but aspires to a truth which transcends it:

> A concept is either true or false. A mind which entertains a false concept may be brought through steps of argument to entertain the true one, but this does not mean that a false concept has grown into the true; there is always a point in the dialectic, like the moment of recognition in tragedy, when the revolutionary change happens and the false concept is abandoned with the realization that it was always false. The dialectic process may take time, but the truth it discovers has no history.

Nevertheless, such discoveries themselves have a history, for only a propitious time can discover *their* truth. Auden invokes the historian as well as the philosopher here, in a way which throws light on 'September 1 1939' as well:

> The *Republic*, the *Laws*, even the *Politics* should be read in conjunction with Thucydides; only a political situation as desperate as that which the historian describes could have produced in the philosophers who were looking for cure at once a radicalism which would break completely with the past to build up society again *ab initio* and a pathological horror of disunity and change. Living as we do in an age of similar stasis on a world-wide scale, we have witnessed a recurrence on both the Right and the Left, at both the economic and the psychiatric epicenters, of similar symptoms.

Having 'seen with our own eyes the theory of creative politics put into practice, and the spectacle is anything but Utopian', the Platonic system has to be reconsidered. What Auden finds in its place is that focused on the 'Comic Hero', particularly that of Don Quixote, and 'The nearest approach to such a figure among the Greeks is, of course, Socrates':

> In his person he exhibits the contradiction, so disliked by Nietzsche, between his subjective *arete* of soul, and

his manifest lack of objective *arete*; he, the best man, is the ugliest man. Further, he suffers death at the hands of society and does not regard his fate as a tragic one. To the Greeks, however, he is either, as he is to Aristophanes, a comic butt who is justly punished, or as he is to Plato, a tragic martyr who suffers because the wrong party was in power, the individual who represents the Right Society.

Socrates, that is, is the archetype of the double man, and we need the gift of double focus to see him clearly. This can be provided by his own and Kierkegaard's processive dialectic, which deconstructs all absolutes, knows that all syntheses break down into incoherence if pushed, and that language, while it is a vehicle to truth, is also a prison van carrying us to gaol. It is in the light of these observations, which on first sight seem rooted in the ethos of the Cold War, that we can return to the most significantly misunderstood relationship in *New Year Letter*, that between the author and the Karl Marx who is considered at length in Part II of the poem.

For John Fuller, Marx is clearly one of the Devil's Party, along with the early Christians and the millennialist Wordsworth, associating the truth with a lie and thus persuading us to throw out the baby with the bath-water.[2] This reading leads Fuller to surprise when some of Auden's concluding moralizings 'strangely echo the famous dictum of Marx' – 'strangely' indicates the strain of such a reading.[3] For the baby that the Devil tempts us to throw out with the bath-water is Marx's materialist methodology itself. Auden speaks of his Marxist disillusionings towards the end of Part II. We all waited, he says, for the day 'The State would wither clean away,/Expecting the Millennium/That theory had promised us would come:/It didn't.' That abrupt reversal on the enjambement enacts the dialectical process, setting up an antithesis of theory and event. Specialists may explain why it didn't; the layman may learn that it is the *hubris* of the all-too-self-assured elite which has led to this fall; but this does not detract from the greatness of the ideas, merely confirms 'that they grow small who imitate/The mannerisms of the great,/Afraid to be themselves, or ask/What acts are proper to their task'. The desire to turn that interpretative method into a fetish, a support for one's ego, is what is attacked, and Auden's image for this intellectual awakening is that of coming round with a hangover. Fuller is ready to jump in here: 'Disappointed political idealism gives the worst hangovers'.[4]

What Auden says is different. When the disenchanted wake up, he says, the lying devil is waiting for his opportunity, 'Who knows nothing suits his book/So well as the hang-over look,/That few drunks feel more awful than/The Simon-pure Utopian'. This blunt but sympathetic devil calls to ask after 'our Socialist', professes not to say 'Let this be a warning' and offers a convenient rationalization: students will always sow their wild oats, all the best Conservatives have done the same, 'I'll fix you something for your liver.' That 'fix' is the giveaway, and Auden seizes on it:

> And thus he sells us down the river.
> Repenting of our last infraction
> We seek atonement in reaction
>
> . . .
>
> Perceiving that by sailing near
> The Hegelian whirlpool of Idea
> Some foolish aliens have gone down,
> Lest our democracy should drown
> We'd wreck her on the solid rock
> Of genteel anarchists like LOCKE,
> Wave at the mechanized barbarian
> The vorpal sword of an Agrarian.

As Socrates is to be disentangled from his absolutist disciple Plato, so Marx is to be distinguished from his absolutist mentor Hegel. If 'some foolish aliens' – a clear allusion to Stalinism – have been tempted by the authoritarian elements in Marxism – which is not after all a unitary discourse but itself an ensemble – this is no reason for us to adopt the class-based rationalizations of the English tradition, or the organicist

fantasies of the American Southern school. It is not the booze
Auden denounces here, but renunciations of the booze made in
the shadow of a hangover, too much affected by the heat of the
moment to have any substance. This is why Wordsworth is a
potent warning. For his error is not that he espoused the French
Revolution, but that he saw in it 'The Parousia of liberty',

> And weaving a platonic dream
> Round a provisional régime
> That sloganized the Rights of Man,
> A liberal fellow-traveller ran
> With Sans-culotte and Jacobin,
> Nor guessed what circles he was in,
> But ended as the Devil knew
> An earnest Englishman would do,
> Left by Napoleon in the lurch,
> Supporting the Established Church,
> The Congress of Vienna and
> The Squire's paternalistic hand.

The early Christians made the same mistake. Disappointed
in the Second Coming, their 'heavenly worldliness' led them
to do a deal with the State, turning *agape* into 'a late lunch
with Constantine'. Critics who read this as Auden's renunciation of Marxism should perhaps ask why it does not also
indicate renunciation of the Christian logos. It is the discrepancy between Word and World which brings down all
these high-fliers into 'heavenly worldliness', as is indicated in
the foregrounding of the earlier poet's name. A word has no
fixed worth, but is a provisional regime imposed upon the
real, sloganizing it, driving its bearers round in circles they
think are revolutions, but which are really the circles of Hell
or the circulations of an empty abstract signifier, till they lapse
into Wordsworthlessness.

Auden, on the contrary, rescues from Wordsworth's folly
and his own a remarkable bonus – a doubleness indicated by
the way 'luck' combines both accident and privilege, and 'rare'
both infrequency and value:

> Like his, our lives have been coeval
> With a political upheaval,
> Like him, we had the luck to see
> A rare discontinuity,
> Old Russia suddenly mutate
> Into a proletarian state,
> The odd phenomenon, the strange
> Event of qualitative change.

That some saw this as the realization of 'the potential Man'
does not detract from the oddity and strangeness of this discontinuity, from which, considered properly, we can learn
much. Others (Auden implies himself among them) –

> settled down to read
> The theory that forecast the deed
> And found their humanistic view
> In question from the German who,
> Obscure in gaslit London, brought
> To human consciousness a thought
> It thought unthinkable, and made
> Another consciousness afraid.

Marx is not dismissed here. Rather the dialectic is applied
to his own dialectic. If, as he demonstrated, all discourse is
ideologically charged, then his own discourse can in turn be
deconstructed. His premises become the very ground upon
which his premises can be dismantled, thereby paradoxically
asserting their truth-effect. Bringing to consciousness a
previously unthinkable thought opens a Pandora's box of other
thoughts, calls into question the objectivity of knowledge itself.
Such a disclosure would not have been possible without the
distorting emotions that fuelled its intellectual drive. Yet, in
a sharp twist of argument, these emotions too, while they
deflect thought from its goal, have a rationality to them which
confirms their thesis:

> What if his hate distorted? Much
> Was hateful that he had to touch.
> What if he erred? He flashed a light

On facts where no one had been right.
The father-shadow that he hated
Weighed like an Alp; his love, frustrated,
Negating as it was negated,
Burst out in boils; his animus
Outlawed him from himself; but thus,
And only thus, perhaps, could he
Have come to his discovery.

Marx, that is, is a double man, outlawed from himself, and in that exile able to look at his experience from the outside. If his methodology involves negating the negation, in a dialectic whose synthesis is always deferred (for 'the Revolution' has not yet taken place), his self-division as a bourgeois intellectual becomes itself the site of a contradiction, as the paternal imago strikes back in illness and psychosomatic eruptions. The Oedipal rebel punishes himself for his illicit knowledge. The heroism of such achievements should not be underestimated. Marx too, like Kierkegaard, has sailed out alone over seventy thousand fathoms, and his lack of charity in raging against the fathers and the masters has to be matched with the larger and 'rare' charity of his service to human self-understanding:

Heroic charity is rare;
Without it, what except despair
Can shape the hero who will dare
The desperate catabasis
Into the snarl of the abyss
That always lies just underneath
Our jolly picnics on the heath
Of the agreeable, where we bask,
Agreed on what we will not ask,
Bland, sunny and adjusted by
The light of the accepted lie?

The doubleness is revealed in that unitalicized 'catabasis', which is both Xenophon's word for a military retreat and the medical term for a decline in fever; just as Marx's descent into the abyss is both a defeat for one kind of human self-delusion and at the same time its cure. In Part III, Auden is to use the language of Freud to speak of a similar confrontation with the Outlawed, the Others of the personal unconscious. Here Marx explores the economic unconscious of bourgeois society, revealing its dirty secrets. The war in whose ambit this poem is written then becomes on a larger scale a symptom of disorder like Marx's boils, the return of a repressed in which we have, finally, to pay for all those adjustments that reconciled us to 'The light of the accepted lie'.

The imaginary relations into which we enter as bourgeois subjects are dissolved by a method which discloses the doubleness of a class-divided society, revealing that 'The other other side to Him-who-steals/Is He-who-makes-what-is-of-use,/ Since to consume, man must produce.' The love of money likewise reveals that, deep down, love is not determined by tribal, ethnic, social or religious ties, but by 'universal, mutual need'. Capitalism, in reducing all relations to those of the cash-nexus, also creates the possibility of a human being no longer confined by these limiting contexts, able to enter into equal relations with all others on the basis of co-operation. If Auden's text now moves into a kind of closure, it is not to bid farewell to a sinking Marx, but to link him in a brother-clan with those others who 'brought an epoch to a close': Galileo who ended 'The slaveowners' mechanics' of the Ptolemaic system, Newton who 'Drew up a Roman code for Force', and Darwin who 'brought/Man's pride to heel at last and showed/His kinship with the worm and toad'.

These do not, *pace* Fuller, represent the end of an era,[5] for none of them in fact belongs to the era he closes. Rather they impose its closure, seal off its limits, reveal that what was previously thought of as knowledge was an ideologically deformed half-truth-at best, translating interest into ostensibly disinterested ideas. Darwin's pituitary headaches reveal that he too was a double man, struggling against the fathers and the flesh in himself to attain that outlawed knowledge in which an illusory pride is humbled. For, as Part III is to confirm, 'we wage/The war we are' in a subject which is the site of a class struggle, between the lines written for us and the truth we desire. Galileo, Newton, Darwin, Marx thus *initiate* an era by creating new forms of knowledge, setting the seal on those now obsolete forms their enquiries have deposed. These 'Great sedentary Caesars' have 'pacified some dread tabu', withdrawn 'The *numen* from some local law/And with a single concept brought/Some ancient rubbish heap of thought/To rational diversity'. But they will be betrayed unless we see that 'No *codex gentium* we make/Is difficult for Truth to break;/The *Lex Abscondita* evades/The vigilantes in the glades.' We may progress from *tabu* to *numen* and then to *codex gentium* (in an increasing secularization which also widens the general scope of its application), but Truth itself is always one step ahead, an absconding law like that absconding self we also try to fix in formulae and phrases.

Loyalty to the struggle of such intellectual patriarchs means precisely not allowing ourselves to sink into an ideological closure which preserves the letter but not the spirit of their law. It is not Marx but Stalinism which is rejected in *New Year Letter*, as the figure of all ideologies which distort the methodologies on which they are founded. For this reason, Voltaire and Kierkegaard can coexist in the text, as purveyors of Socratic doubt, representing that scepticism which, in Marx and Freud too, questions all motives, including its own. This is 'The Hidden Law' celebrated in the poem which is a note to these lines, the negative moment that lurks within all our positive acts and utterances, the other side of our escaping and forgetting, which resides within and deconstructs the positive laws of any system. In the final paragraphs of the poem it is addressed, *in absentia*, as the 'Unicorn among the cedars,/To whom no magic charm can lead us'.

It is not surprising then that, self-summoned to appear before a tribunal of poetic father-figures also of his own summoning in Part I, Auden should find himself faltering as he reads, stammering, and sitting down with hung head. It may be that in the summary tribunal, they 'Accept our rules of evidence/And pass no sentence but our own' – but this last *double entendre* indicates just how chilling this can be. We judge our own (poetic) sentences, but the only law against which we can measure them are the sentences we choose to admire from those poets we choose as our progenitors. The faltering and stammering, like Marx's boils and Darwin's headaches, are the site of an Oedipal conflict, where love of the father wars with the son's need to rebel, and it is in the failure of the voice that the struggle discloses itself. This ambiguous relation to the father is a feature of all Auden's work. But here it takes on a wider dimension, in a somewhat unexpected move from a literary trial to the historical and political one. Regretting his own derelictions, that 'slubbering through' his work with 'slip and slapdash', adopting what he would disown, 'The preacher's loose immodest tone', Auden moves on to consider 'The situation of our time' which 'Surrounds us like a baffling crime'.

The corpse on the carpet is one we all had cause to detest, the father-figure of late capitalism. But the only one so far sent to investigate the crime is 'one inspector dressed in brown' who 'makes the murderer whom he pleases/And all investigation ceases': Hitler. It's not clear whether we are supposed to feel guilty about this crime or not, and this ambivalence reinforces the Oedipal confusion. For if Hitler finds a scapegoat culprit for the collapse of capitalism in the Jews, is this to suggest that capitalism should not have been killed – that there is a *real* culprit who should be punished? But isn't capitalism itself the culprit? Isn't the corpse the real murderer? This, perhaps, is why we extend the area of the crime 'Until the guilt is everywhere'. But the misery and howling too now rise from Asia, Spain, Abyssinia, Austria, Poland, the Jews, the unemployed.

These are the real victims, and the corpse on the carpet their oppressor. Perhaps this is why the crime is baffling, and perhaps it explains too why even the best are tempted to succumb to the apocalyptic dream of vengeance on the oppressors, the 'evil Aryan lives' and the 'bleeding tyrant'. For of course, if one takes Auden's logic far enough, if we are all guilty, then no individual in particular can be singled out for blame. The Nazi is as much a victim of history as the Jew. At this point Auden abandons the Oracle, like Oedipus at

Delphi, for 'the Janus of a joke'. But Oedipus too was a double man, who had to unravel the riddle of his identity, discover that he was other than he seemed. It is in this awareness of duplicity that Auden returns, after the speculative detours of Part II, to the 'situation of our time' in Part III.

The relation between Fascism and socialism, Auden implies in a note to Part II, is something to do with these Oedipal accommodations: 'Fascism is Socialism that has lost faith in the future. Its slogan is Now or Never. In demanding a dictator it is demanding the advent of the Good Life on earth through a supernatural miracle.' That imaginary resolution of real conflicts by the father's magic is what the third section exposes as a Faustian delusion. That is why Hitler returns here, not as a monster, but as a theologian, dressed up so well that he convinces Edward Callan this passage refers to Kierkegaard.[6] The future now is not like that facing the last days of Rome, for it is not primitive barbarians but 'the refined/Creations of machine and mind' that lie behind the present lust to destroy:

> As out of Europe comes a Voice,
> Compelling all to make their choice,
> A theologian who denies
> What more than twenty centuries
> Of Europe have assumed to be
> The basis of civility,
> Our evil *Daimon* to express
> In all its ugly nakedness
> What none before dared say aloud,
> The metaphysics of the Crowd,
> The Immanent Imperative
> By which the lost and injured live
> In mechanized societies
> Where natural intuition dies,
> The international result
> Of Industry's *Quicunque vult*,
> The hitherto unconscious creed
> Of little men who half succeed.

Hitler speaks to the injured and incomplete creatures we all are, offering a magical release in vengeance. Unlike Marx, he does not uncover a previously unthinkable truth, but merely expresses a nasty commonplace previously repressed out of fear of disapproval. In an analogy from quantum theory, Auden suggests that the modern mechanized societies have turned us all into discrete particles, yearning to be part of a wave. The raving demagogue sets himself up as 'A quantum speaking for the waves' but such a unity as he offers is not possible and, 'A particle, I must not yield/To particles who claim the field.' Within Niels Bohr's theory, to which Auden refers in his notes and again in *A Certain World*, energy can be defined in two ways – either as a mass of particles, or as a wave motion. The two descriptions are mutually exclusive, but each, in discontinuity from the other, works. Hitler's hocus-pocus is to propose a merging of the two accounts. The 'double man' is permanently divided because he stands at the intersection of two incompatible yet equally valid discourses, two 'maps and languages and names', 'two atlases'. One atlas defines 'The public space where acts are done' which is 'In theory common to us all'. As the account goes on, that 'in theory' turns into a major reservation:

> The *agora* of work and news
> Where each one has the right to choose
> His trade, his corner and his way,
> And can, again in theory, say
> For whose protection he will pay,
> And loyalty is help we give
> The place where we prefer to live.

In this marketplace the odds are actually stacked against the competing individual, feeding that resentment which issues in Fascism. Elizabeth Mayer paid her taxes but could not choose to be protected by the Nazi state, which refused her citizenship of any place except the concentration camp. But Auden too, in a lesser plight, abandoned an England where he could have no effect on the larger polity. The rights of the citizen to effect the totality are largely abstract, except when individual will is merged in the 'metaphysics of the Crowd'.

But that other map is no more satisfactory, describing 'the inner space/Of private ownership, the place/That each of us is forced to own.../Where he is sovereign indeed'. This subjected sovereignty is no freer than the other, as 'forced' suggests, casting self-possession as in effect something imposed on the self by the same market-forces that render it powerless in the *agora*. These atlases are not *places* but *descriptions*: 'Two worlds describing their rewards,/That one in tangents, this in chords'. England itself exists only in discourse ('England to me is my own tongue'), but language never rests in identity. It is simply a play of differences, as he had indicated in Part II:

> If in this letter that I send
> I write 'Elizabeth's my friend,'
> I cannot but express my faith
> That I is not-Elizabeth.

What language demarcates is 'certain patterns in our lives,/Effects that take the cause's name'. Language is the ground of exile on which these 'two aliens in New York' meet. The epistolary form underwrites this solidarity in exile, which is the condition of real community too, for 'all real unity commences/In consciousness of differences.'

In a draft of an earlier section, Auden had spelt out this warring of worlds as a conflict in discourse, where each state claims to be 'The patrios of civility/For which no man will question why/It's sweet and decorous to die', substituting its own empty signifier as a magical object of loyalty: '"England", "La France", "Das Reich", their words/Are like the names of extinct birds/...And the plain proletarian lie/Is held up in position by/Noble police and the ornate/*Grandezza* of the Russian State.'

Auden's binaries dissolve into pluralities when he comes to think of England, in a series of metonymic emblems which become the very site of desire. His sentence overflows with instances, yet none of them offers a *nunc stans* to the subject, for in their proliferation they indicate that continual deferral of fullness in which desire is born. England cannot be grasped as a totality, even in memory, but remains stubbornly evasive, its rapidly resumed locales merely the traces of a desire which exists only in loss, where we too are perpetually held back from self-identity.

The limestone landscapes of Northumbria then become 'my symbol of us all', that place where 'Man faulted into consciousness', punning on moral and geological processes for that entry into difference which gives each of us an 'original address'. The coincidence of subject and place has to be constantly reiterated, if we are not to fall prey to that slippage in which signifieds slide under and abandon their signifiers. This, perhaps, is why Auden foregrounds names so much in this poem, giving them an eighteenth-century solidity by capitalizing them. Yet the one name which remains under erasure, not even mentioned let alone capitalized, is that of the author of *Capital* himself. This suppression of Marx's name has to be set against his omnipresence in the text, as a system of thought which organizes consciousness.

The central idea of Marx's *Economic and Philosophical Manuscripts*, first published between 1927 and 1932 and much discussed then in left-wing circles – 'alienation' – is not, as it is usually represented, a mental phenomenon like Kierkegaard's 'dread', though it gives rise to such. Rather it is an objective process in which relations between human beings, in the words of *The German Ideology* (1932), are transformed into relations between things: the commodification of reality. It is in these terms that Auden describes the fall from an imaginary primal unity into the differentiations of the symbolic:

> Now in that other world I stand
> Of fully alienated land,
> An earth made common by the means
> Of hunger, money, and machines,
> Where each determined nature must
> Regard that nature as a trust
> That, being chosen, he must choose,
> Determined to become of use;

For we are conscripts to our age
Simply by being born; we wage
The war we are...

The play on the two meanings of 'determined', the ambivalence of that 'use' (recalling Marx's distinction between
exchange value and *use value*), the paradox that the world is made
common in the very fullness of its alienation, the concept of
the subject as the site of a war; all these are commonplaces
of the Marxist tradition. 'Empiric Economic Man' is, then,
quite literally a self-made 'Man' erroneously perceived as a
fact of nature, driving about creation 'In the closed cab of
Occupation'. Auden echoes here the critique of Adam Smith
in *Capital*. His exposition of alienation as an *objective* condition
is equally to the point:

Man captured by his liberty,
The measurable taking charge
Of him who measures, set at large
By his own actions, useful facts
Become the user of his acts.

Lest this should be too abstract, Auden offers more concrete
images of the economy as a process without a subject, by
inverting the normal language of causality. This defamiliarizing invites us to look with a stranger's eyes at the world, to
ask whether it is not a more accurate picture of what really
happens than the conventional one of us as self-directing agents
in a society subordinated to human ends:

Boys trained by factories for leading
Unusual lives as nurses, feeding
Helpless machines, girls married off
To typewriters, old men in love
With prices they can never get,
Homes blackmailed by a radio set,
Children inherited by slums
And idiots by enormous sums.

In a powerful metonymic account of an increasingly
irrational capitalism, Auden depicts a world enmeshed in

struggles to break down or ensure the reproduction of the means of production, the rich discussing the best technique for enforcing labour discipline and protecting their privileges, while the Disregarded are 'poisoned by reasonable hate'. Yet both sides of the struggle are 'symptoms of one common fate', effects, not causes, of what is really a 'self-governed beast'. What each fails to recognize in the mirror each morning, reassembling an identity for work, is that they all 'face/A member of a governed race'. Sovereignty is the ideological mystification of an actual subjection. What really looks back at them from the mirror is 'The neuter outline that's the plan /And icon of industrial man', that castrate subject drawn by Thurber and Edward Lear.

Each private citizen, however, still finds it easier to congratulate himself on his uniqueness, making politicians and hired officials scapegoats for his unfreedom. And it is here that Fascism gains its purchase. In the witholding of love and sensitivity lie the causes of 'the soldier's violent touch'. The 'possible societies' that swarm around our actual one are denied realization because they lack formulation, 'craving a language and a myth/And hands to shape their purpose with'. But, repressed, the community all desire returns in the perverted forms of blood, soil and race, and 'The average of the average man/Becomes the dread Leviathan'. Fascism is the imaginary resolution of real conflicts, the alienated object of real desires. It is not then a specifically German or Italian or Spanish phenomenon, but a function of the general crisis of capitalism, in which we all have a hand, both as free and unfree agents – as, that is, double agents, determined by circumstance but also capable of determining to be and do something:

> Upon each English conscience lie
> Two decades of hypocrisy,
> And not a German can be proud
> Of what his apathy allowed.

Neither the left-wing English intellectual not the German Jewish refugee are exonerated.

New York, 'the great Rome/To all who lost or hated home',

becomes in these closing pages the Eternal City of Mammon and 'the Dynamo', the place where the wanderings of Capital, which lives only in movement, cause and are caused by a restlessness in ideas and economy alike. In a compact résumé Auden scans the wanderings of the Word through American history. At the level of the economic 'flesh' the same *Völkerwanderung* occurs: America is one great turmoil of displacements. For all the migrants truth is always elsewhere, and their apparently free choices – in their very genericness – reveal 'The choice of patterns. . .the machine imposes'.

In what is an orthodoxly Marxist move, Auden does not simply decry industrialism. Rather he sees that it opens certain possibilities, breaks down 'local customs', 'bonds of blood and nation', even the various languages evoked throughout the poem, to clear away all those heaps of cultural garbage which stand in the way of a 'personal confederation' of free individuals – the withering away of the state, in fact. No longer, he says, can we learn our little local 'good' from the chances of neighbourhood, class or party. A greater good can be imagined, once the secret has been let out of the bag by the machine. This secret is that 'Aloneness is man's real condition', that all social bonds and ideologies are ways of conscripting the subject to a discourse which evades this, which claims that true identity resides in this or that particular loyalty. The individual is alone not in any Lockean sense, freely entering as a constituted subject into the Social Contract and the laissez-faire economy. Rather this 'aloneness' is a condition of pure possibility in which, like money, the self has no real existence until it is cashed in some particular purchase and discourse. But this fungibility means also that all possibilities are open to a self alerted to its freedom.

That '"Nowhere without–No" that is/The justice of societies' remains as remote as Kafka's 'near-distant' Castle, 'The Truth where they will be denied/Permission ever to reside'. Auden closes off this overflowing city, with its multitudes of subjects and dreams, by a characteristic move outwards, back to that 'weary Asia out of sight' he had visited a couple of years before, where already a restless race stir in their sleep, clocks shooing the feudal childhood from their face, as 'accurate machines begin/To concentrate its adults in/A narrow day to exercise/ Their gifts in some cramped enterprise'. In Japan, the first oriental nation to adopt the techniques of capitalism, life has already begun to be transformed by the rhythms of the machine. All is malleable, in the transformations of the global economy. They, like us in our cramped enterprises, know what the good society is like, 'The seamless live continuum/Of supple and coherent stuff/Whose form is truth, whose content love'.

But this imaginary unity is belied by the very language in which we formulate it, which insists on the fracturing of our 'pluralist interstices' and wrenches assunder even the concepts, such as the republic, which we have come to assume a unity – for this utopia is a place where 'The largest *publicum's* a *res*,/And the least *res* a *publicum*'. Just as public and things are sundered here, so is the dream and the reality in the next paragraph, for 'wishes are not horses, this/*Annus* is not *mirabilis*'. Even day *breaks*, upon a world at war, which is the only world we know, where 'civilians come to grief/In brother-hoods without belief'. Democracy is now no more than 'a ready-made/ . . . tradesman's slogan', the poor are betrayed, and truth whipped out of youth, in a world controlled by 'A butch and criminal *élite*' and 'Rheumatic old patricians'. We are as 'Lost as our theories', which 'Veer round completely every day'.

There is no surprise at all, then, in Auden's deployment of Marx, overlaid with Christianity, in the closing paragraphs of the poem. He does not now, it is true, envisage a saving revolution. He has no need to. Those inter-imperialist rivalries he had written about in his plays have already started a war between the major capitalist powers which ensures that 'A day is drawing to a close', and there are 'millions brave enough to die/For a new day'. This, he had told us earlier, is common knowledge now. Nor does Auden refrain from 'preaching' to us, though the more covert way in which his socialism is presented, for an American audience, means that he has received fewer rebukes for it in this poem than in *Journey to a War*.

Nevertheless, preach he does. True democracy, he says, 'begins/With free confession of our sins'. This democracy is to be founded on a shared weakness, not a hierarchy of strength. None of us is just or virtuous enough to claim the right to govern. The way forward is to disperse power so widely and equitably that it ceases to be power and becomes love (since power can be defined only in inequality, is always a comparative relation involving *more* and *less*). He substitutes, thus, for the market's laws of supply and demand a specifically socialist ratio: consciousness 'That all have wants to satisfy/And each a power to supply'. The love and solidarity we need are possible precisely *because* we know we are not the free agents we imagine ourselves. The echo of the elegy for Toller in these closing paragraphs reaffirms an orthodox socialism: We –

> Can live since we are lived, the powers
> That we create with are not ours.

Freedom is still the recognition of necessity. And, in the original opening words of the sonnet sequence which immediately follows, 'Out of it steps the future of the poor'.

7   My Father's Prick:
The Long Poems

'Whether, as some psychologists believe,' Auden wrote in his commonplace book *A Certain World*, 'some women suffer from penis envy, I am not sure. I am quite certain, however, that all males without exception, whatever their age, suffer from penis rivalry, and that this trait has now become a threat to the future existence of the human race':

> Behind every quarrel between men, whether individually or collectively, one can hear the taunt of a little urchin: 'My prick (or my father's) is bigger than yours (or your father's), and can pee further.'
>
> Nearly all weapons, from the early spear and sword down to the modern revolver and rocket, are phallic symbols . . .
>
> Today our phallic toys have become too dangerous to be tolerated. I see little hope for a peaceful world until men are excluded from the realm of foreign policy altogether and all decisions concerning international relations are reserved for women, preferably married ones. (p. 299)

It is a commonplace enough thought. For an Auden so hostile to *kitsch* philosophizing to give it a separate entry among his *obiter dicta* means it is none the less genuine. In the long poems of the forties, confronted by the enormities of that war he had expected for a decade, Auden came to submit the whole phallic ethos of male power to a new and damning scrutiny. Naomi Mitchison had written of 'the curious, archaic maleness' of *Paid on Both Sides*, but had added, 'there is nothing anti-feminist about it, but something in one jumps out to welcome it.' Certainly the young men in that play are forced into a closed circle of killing in the name of their dead fathers by the urgings of their all-too-live mothers. But the alternative to the treadmill of vendetta is presented by that strange hermaphrodite figure the Man-Woman, who appears as a prisoner behind barbed wire to reproach a world where sexual differentiation itself seems to be the cause of violence.

'Letter to Lord Byron' had dismissed somewhat cavalierly the utopian 'dream...of being both the sexes'. In more serious vein a 1939 poem from *Another Time*, 'The Riddle', spoke of the fall into sexual duality, which had created 'the fallen man and wife', as the source of all contradiction and inequality. Only in the beloved's eyes can we learn at last to say:

> 'All our knowledge comes to this,
> That existence is enough,
> That in savage solitude
>   Or the play of love
> Every living creature is
>   Woman, Man, and Child.'

New Year Letter had been dedicated to a mother-figure, and was in one sense a confession of phallic incompetence in a world at war, dominated by the penis rivalries of a patriarchal order. *For the Time Being* is dedicated to the memory of his real mother, whose death in 1941 left Auden desolate. The personal crisis, compounded by a breakdown in the relation with Kallman, coincided with the global one. *For the Time Being* was written between October 1941 and July 1942 (in December 1941, after the bombing of Pearl Harbour, the United States entered the war); *The Sea and the Mirror* between August of 1942 and February 1944; *The Age of Anxiety* was begun in July 1944 and completed in November 1946. The world of these poems is like the 'politically powerless' and 'cynical' Panhellenic world which Auden found in C. P. Cavafy's poetry (*FA*, pp. 333–44).

The Sea and the Mirror is usually seen as a meditation on

art; but it is equally concerned with the idea of power. The Stage Manager's opening address to the Critics speaks of an 'authority' which can no longer give 'Existence its surprise' but multiplied to 'ghosts who haunt our lives' is still 'handy with mirrors and wires' at keeping us in our subject-positions, with a combination of habit, wonder and terror. This 'world of fact we love' may well be 'unsubstantial stuff'; but to face up to this is to take us into that realm of silence beyond even factitious meanings, 'On the other side of the wall'. It is this realm that the Narrator of *For the Time Being* fears, preferring even 'The nursery bogey or the winecellar ghost' and the 'violent howling of winter and war' to its unconditional challenge. All these, by comparison, offer a juke-box tune of consolation that fills out and denies that silence. It is the conviction of *The Sea and the Mirror*, however, that it is only in the silence outside discourse, beyond power, that meaning resides, for the silence is ripeness, 'And the ripeness all'.

The Sea and the Mirror is itself a postscript, imagining what might happen to the various characters of Shakespeare's *Tempest* after the play has ended. It opens with an address to departing critics. Prospero has broken his rod of power; Shakespeare has, in the play's final speech, craved our indulgence and departed. As Caliban explains to the Audience in the elaborate Jamesian prose which comprises the second half of the work, we may call for the author, 'the all-wise, all-explaining master' we believe in. But all we will get is the ugly brute Caliban himself, left behind on the island as the captains and the kings depart, the mere echo of 'our so good, so great, so dead author.'

Like Cavafy's Panhellenic world, Prospero's island is a place where the supposedly 'self-governing' kingdoms of the sovereign 'individual' stand revealed as satellites of a power which is always elsewhere, but which shows its hand in every tug of the puppet's wires. For Prospero language itself is a mere 'gift/In dealing with shadows':

But now all these heavy books are no use to me any
    more, for
Where I go, words carry no weight; it is best,
Then, I surrender their fascinating counsel
    To the silent dissolution of the sea
Which misuses nothing because it values nothing;
    Whereas man overvalues everything
Yet, when he learns the price is pegged to his valuation,
    Complains bitterly he is being ruined which, of
        course, he is.
So kings find it odd they should have a million
    subjects
    Yet share in thoughts of none, and seducers
Are sincerely puzzled at being unable to love
    What they are able to possess.

This reality beyond words is 'The lion's mouth whose
hunger/No metaphors can fill' of the Preface. We may, like
the clown, 'Double [our] meaning', but all the inflationary
doubles entendres of discourse cannot stuff this emptiness. We
are left with an inflationary spiral in which price is the mirror-
image of valuation, in a bitter parody of those laws of supply
and demand which play over the surface of reality, ignoring
questions of ultimate or intrinsic worth, and bankrupting us
in their endless play.

The implicit contrast here, between market price and
use-value, runs through the poem. Dealing in shadows as the
stockbroker deals in commodities, Prospero has cut himself
off from that 'Common warmth and touching substance' in
which alone a real world is touched. Prospero's power to
command has been that of the manager, valid only in so far
as his word can command his workers, the mental skills of
Ariel and the manual energy of Caliban. It is in *their* labour-
power that Prospero's expropriating magic is based. Kings
may hold power over their subjects but they cannot enter into
communion with their subjectivities, any more than the
seducer can ever really know the object he possesses and by
possessing turns into an exchangeable commodity. In the essay

'Balaam and His Ass' (*DH*, pp. 107–45), which contains a series of reflections on *The Tempest*, Auden offers a definition of the seducer Don Giovanni as one himself 'inconspicuous as a shadow' whose 'pleasure in seducing women is not sensual but arithmetical; his satisfaction lies in adding one more name to his list . . . [S]o far as any finite motive is concerned, he might just as well have chosen to collect stamps.' Prospero's motive, too, has been the accumulation of power for its own sake, turning a means into an end.

The language of finance subverts the most innocent words ('dear', for example) and puts a distance between event and interpretation. It is disenchantment with his *déraciné* magic that leads Prospero to ask, in one of his interspersed songs, '*Dare even Pope or Caesar know/The price of faith and honour?*' For Gonzalo too the gulf between signifiers and signifieds is where the subject falls into loss:

> Not in me the credit for
> Words I uttered long ago
> Whose glad meaning I betrayed;
> Truths today admitted, owe
> Nothing to the councillor
> In whose booming eloquence
> Honesty became untrue.

'Credit' and 'owe' add a new timbre to the idea of a 'booming eloquence'. By the same token, Gonzalo froze his assets, 'by speculation froze/Vision into an idea.'

Fact and value seem at odds in these fallen consciousnesses. When Ferdinand comes to address his love sonnet to Miranda, she is a 'Dear Other' who participates with him in the accumulation of capital, 'From moment to moment as you enrich them so/Inherit me', caught up in those inflationary spirals which Prospero fears may bring their own Wall Street Crash – 'Will Ferdinand be as fond of a Miranda/Familiar as a stocking?' But it is Trinculo who epitomizes most effectively this world of exchange values where relations between subjects have turned into relations between signs. Trinculo's detachment from the world of mechanic, merchant and king is profound:

There lies that solid world
These hands can never reach;
My history, my love,
Is but a choice of speech.

Everywhere signifiers have substituted for the things they
signify. When a terror shakes Trinculo's tree, 'A flock of words
fly out'. Trapped in language none of these characters can
evade the power relations imposed upon them by Prospero's
wand, that ultimate signifier and source of power. This
explains the key antithesis of the poem, indicated in the title.
For although as Caliban indicates in his address the mirror
is Shakespeare's metaphor for art, held up to the sea of nature,
there are more complex resonances. Alonso advises his son
to ascend his throne majestically while keeping in mind the
sea that dissolves all hierarchies of value dear to the subject:

> the waters where fish
> See sceptres descending with no wish
> To touch them...
>   ...the sands where a crown
> Has the status of a broken-down
> Sofa or mutilated statue:
>
>   . . .
>
> The cold deep that does not envy you,
> The sunburnt superficial kingdom
> Where a king is an object.

He warns against expecting sense from the words subjects
speak to princes. Such language is the 'prince's ornate mirror',
giving back only reflections of his own conscious wishes. It
is from the embarrassments of his own 'darkness' and dreams,
the sea of the unconscious, that revelation may instead come,
breaking the closed circle of reflections in which the mirrors
of language trap him. Otherwise he will disappear 'To join
all the unjust kings'. True power, Alonso proposes, lies not
in a cold detachment that seeks mastery. This will in the end
destroy. It lies instead in the 'dissolution of your pride'. In
the same way, waking from a dream 'Where Prudence flirted

with a naked sword,/Securely vicious', Sebastian finds proof of mercy in the fact that he wakes *without* a crown. The sestina works its changes upon the key words as if to remind of that closed circle from which only Failure and Exposure free him: 'Caught unawares, we prick ourselves alive', in a mirror inversion of the Sleeping Beauty story.[1] A break with the closed circuits of self-reflection offers true positionality: 'Just Now is what it might be every day,/Right here is absolute and needs no crown,/Ermine or trumpets, protocol or sword.' 'It is defeat gives proof we are alive.'

When the 'conjuror' artist comes to dismiss this Ariel 'whose obedience through all the enchanted years has never been less than perfect', he will be transfixed with horror to find reflected in Ariel's eyes not 'a conqueror smiling at a conqueror' but a 'gibbering fist-clenched creature with which you are all too unfamiliar...the only subject that you have, who is not a dream amenable to magic but the all too solid flesh you must acknowledge as your own'. He comes face to face, that is, with himself as Caliban, not the 'all-forgiving because all-understanding good nature' he had imagined himself. Like Caesar in *For the Time Being*, he finds power revealed to be trickery, the magic wand of Prospero a phallic toy:

> Can you wonder then, when... your spirits, because you are tired of giving orders, have ceased to obey, and you are left alone with me, the dark thing you could never abide to be with, if I do not yield you kind answer or admire you for the achievements I was never allowed to profit from...?

In 'Balaam and His Ass' Auden proposed that 'In a stage production, Caliban should be as monstrously conspicuous as possible, and, indeed, suggest, as far as decency permits, the phallic. Ariel, on the other hand...should, ideally, be invisible, a disembodied voice.' What the supposedly disinterested, spiritual voice of bourgeois art serves, in the end, is the principle of phallic power, Caliban pretending to be Prospero, the dog beneath the skin.

Auden's reading of *The Tempest* is not the traditional one.

It is, he says, 'a disquieting work', for whereas the other last plays 'end in a blaze of forgiveness and love' –

> in *The Tempest* both the repentance of the guilty and the pardon of the injured seem more formal than real . . . more the prudent promise of the punished and frightened, 'I won't do it again. It doesn't pay,' than any change of heart: and Prospero's forgiving is more the contemptuous pardon of a man who knows that he has his enemies completely at his mercy than a heartfelt reconciliation . . . He has the coldness of someone who has come to the conclusion that human nature is not worth much, that human relations are, at their best, pretty sorry affairs . . . One might excuse him if he included himself in his critical skepticism, but he never does; it never occurs to him that he, too, might have erred and be in need of pardon.

In Auden's text this blind spot is revealed in the easy assumption Prospero makes that, unlike Caliban, his brother Antonio can be brought back within the circle of reconciliation.

> All by myself I tempted Antonio into treason;
>   However that could be cleared up; both of us know
> That both were in the wrong, and neither need be sorry.

Antonio, however, feels himself the contemptuous victim of a theatrical imposture in which everybody has been cast into predetermined roles by the actor-manager Prospero. Now, he says sarcastically, 'As all the pigs have turned back into men/ . . . we can all go home again' and 'take life easily now as tales/Write ever-after'. But he declares himself different from the others, 'Your loyal subjects all, grateful enough/To know their place and believe what you say'. Power, Antonio says, is not so easily demitted:

> Break your wand in half,

> The fragments will join; burn your books or lose
> Them in the sea, they will soon reappear,
> Not even damaged: as long as I choose

> To wear my fashion, whatever you wear
> Is a magic robe; while I stand outside
> Your circle, the will to charm is still there.

Antonio's denial of his assigned place maintains Prospero in his position of pride and melancholy. The significance of this relation is suggested by the comments in 'Balaam and His Ass' on the role of dialogue in presenting 'a human personality in its full depth, its inner dialectic, its self-disclosure and self-concealment'. The soliloquy is inadequate for this because it is really 'a dialogue in the form of a monologue', addressed to the audience and so, we suspect, out to con us. A dialogue requires two voices, and, if it is to express 'the inner dialogue of human personality', must be of a specific kind. The pair must be similar, of the same sex, but also polar opposites, and inseparable. Only the master-servant relation satisfies all these conditions, and it defines all the relations of power that obtain under Prospero's auspices.

It extends, for example, to that between Miranda and Ferdinand, who, like all lovers – Auden notes in his essay – instinctively use the master-servant metaphor. Behind each relation lie the conflicting wishes of the divided 'volitional ego', wishes that, 'since the Fall, instead of being dialectically related, have become contradictory opposites': the wish to command, and the wish 'to have something to obey, to be the servant of'. This irresolvable contradiction often issues in the illusory solution represented by the myth of Narcissus, who 'falls in love with his reflection; he wishes to become its servant, but instead his reflection insists upon being his slave' (*DH*, pp. 113–15). This is why Miranda's Dear One is hers only 'as mirrors are lonely', and why so much of her language of love involves the same kind of shifting, flux-ridden transformations we find in Stephano's song. She and Ferdinand run the risk of the kind of narcissism represented by Tristan and Isolde, in Auden's description, 'Indifferent to each other as persons with unique bodies and characters', important to each other only as externalized icons of their own desire (*DH*, pp. 121–2).

For the Time Being is subtitled 'A Christmas Oratorio', the last word teasingly close to Auden's first work for several voices, *The Orators*. In the friction between oratorio and oratory lies the whole theme of the work. The voice of power in *For the Time Being* speaks with the same accents as the 'Address for a Prize Day' in the earlier work, and it follows the same trajectory. In both cases an apparently rational, authoritative and controlling sensibility breaks down towards its conclusion into incoherence, self-justification and contradiction, in a highly libidinized scenario of catastrophe and massacre, revealing, as Auden still believed, that liberalism could easily don a brown shirt, and was, indeed, the final authorizing voice of Fascism. 'Civilisation must be saved even if this means sending for the military, as I suppose it does', says Herod, in weary recognition of the inevitable, excusing his decision to massacre the innocents. Herod is strong on the Law. It is part of that litany of losses he rehearses that will follow from allowing the Christ child to live. Reason will be replaced by Revelation; instead of Rational Law, 'Knowledge will degenerate into a riot of subjective visions'; Justice will give way to 'Pity as the cardinal human virtue, and all fear of retribution will vanish'; 'Idealism will be replaced by Materialism.' 'Naturally', Herod adds, 'this cannot be allowed to happen.'

Herod's bad faith stands self-revealed when he stumbles into contradiction, evincing two equally powerful but unhappily contradictory arguments for going ahead with the massacre. If, he says, Christ is allowed to demonstrate that a sinless life is possible, 'God would expect every man, whatever his fortune, to lead a sinless life in the flesh and on earth. Then indeed would the human race be plunged into madness and despair.' That passing allusion to 'fortune' indicates how little this is a question about 'nature'. He has just argued quite the opposite, revealing his true attitude to the lower orders: if Christ lives, 'Every corner-boy will congratulate himself: "I'm such a sinner that God had to come down in person to save me. I must be a devil of a fellow." Every crook will argue: "I like committing crimes. God likes forgiving them. Really

ing the maintenance of a status quo of which he is a
major beneficiary, is revealed in his contemptuous references
to those 'materialistic Masses' whose need, 'Diverted from its
normal and wholesome outlet in patriotism and civic and
family pride...will be driven into totally unsocial channels
where no education can reach it'. Protecting 'this little civilized
patch' against 'the old barbaric note' means, in reality,
defending the power and privileges of an Empire. The
coherent, powerful figure of authority gives himself away in
the collapse from mealy-mouthed smugness to hysterical
plaintive whine which concludes this special pleading:

> Ask anyone you like. I read all the official dispatches
> without skipping. I've taken elocution lessons. I've hardly
> ever taken bribes. How dare He allow me to decide? I've
> tried to be good. I brush my teeth every night. I haven't
> had sex for a month. I object. I'm a liberal. I want
> everyone to be happy. I wish I had never been born.

Herod preserves the delusion that he is simply a liberal
private citizen with a job to do, instead of a wielder of power
and authority. That is, he passes the buck. It is only in the
contradictions of his rhetoric, self-loathing and self-pity, that
we can read another story. In the words of the opening
sequence, 'the miracle cannot occur' so long as his language
refuses its contradictions, insists on its correctness and clarity.
'Unless you exclaim – "There must be some mistake" – you
must be mistaken.' Only in the doubling back of discourse
of 'The Meditation of Simeon' can the Real be found, for 'The
Real is what will strike you as really absurd.' Instead of what
Simeon calls the 'flip cracks and sententious oratory' of official
discourse, the true Word is one in which power is diffused
so widely that it turns into the non-coercive, democratic
discourse of which the Angels sing:

> As the new-born Word
> Declares the old
> Authoritarian
> Constraint is replaced

By His Covenant,
And a city based
On love and consent
Suggested to men,
All, all, all of them.

The Narrator is himself revealed as a party to the discourse of power, when he invites us to remain formal believers while practically submitting to the power of Caesar, offering us the shallow confidence of a word that is 'ever legible', with a 'Meaning unequivocal', where even sin, in his specious logic, is valid as a 'sign' of Goodness. In *Modern Canterbury Pilgrims* Auden was to inveigh against 'an obscuring of the Word behind the splendors of the flesh, reduction of spiritual life to a mechanical and automatic routine of physical acts' (p. 42). This helps us to see why Auden deliberately chose the polyphonic form of the oratorio to present his vision. Throughout the poem revelation is multiplied and dispersed into many consciousnesses. There is no central controlling consciousness where truth resides. Only in the always undisclosed child is the Word one and unitary. All claims to unequivocal meaning must be false.

The repetition of words and phrases can give a gloomy air of eternal return to the poem, a sense that nothing will ever break out of these mechanical and automatic routines in which the flesh is trapped. But there is a different kind of repetition, like that use of ploche, anaphora and parison in Gabriel's address to Mary, where meaning overflows the words, and the paronomasic repetition of such key concepts as 'love', 'choose', 'know', 'flesh' spins a surplus of meaning like that of 'the Word/Who utters the world out of nothing', revealing 'The truth at the proper centre/ . . . Of language and distress'. In the same way, there is a distinction between the genuine polyphony of those who respond positively to the annunciation and birth – the shepherds and wise men – and the orchestrated uniformity of those who resist it, worshipping instead the old principle of power. The former sing with antiphonal voices, the latter in a monotonous co-ordinated chant, as in the Fugal-Chorus of 'The Summons', with its banally intoned repetition, 'Great is Caesar', full of lists and catalogues.

'The Temptation of St Joseph' is to succumb to this patriarchal discourse, seeing himself in the traditionally offered terms as a pathetic victim, cuckolded by the coming of the Lord, so that even in accepting meekly what has happened he ratifies the old oppressive order. But Joseph has to go beyond this, cauterize all those last reflexes of phallocratic power. He must answer all the questions himself, neither deferring to nor blaming the one of whom he asks 'Father, what have I done?' Joseph has to seek absolution for all those crimes in which the male principle has perpetually reinscribed itself in the discourse of power, a catalogue of which expresses everywhere the –

> gallantry that scrawls
> In idolatrous detail and size
> A symbol of aggression of toilet walls.

He has, that is, to atone for a history which is a series of campaigns in that 'Sex War' of which the soldiers sing after Herod's soliloquy. To avoid conscription to that war, Joseph must accept not only that 'Today the roles are altered; you must be/The Weaker Sex whose passion is passivity.' He must also undergo that symbolic emasculation of which Rachel speaks after the soldiers' ribaldry: 'Somewhere in these unending wastes of delirium is a lost child, speaking of Long Ago in the language of wounds.'

To redeem that lost child he must take the holy family back in a 'Flight into Egypt' which is also, in classically Freudian terms, a return through the mirror-phase in which the gendered subject is constructed, 'through the glass/No authority can pass', to a realm where placement under the sign of the father is abolished. The voices in the desert lament that once 'All Father's nightingales knew their place,/The gardens were loyal: look at them now'. The 'Temptation of St Joseph' had told us that 'Upon the nursery floor/We gradually explore/Our members till our jealous lives' discover 'A vague but massive feel/Of being individual'. At the same time, entry into individuality is entry into 'a long life of lies'. Only in dissolving the phallic core of selfhood, by contrast, can the collective truth be recovered in this flight. At the heart then of that revelation offered and refused every Christmas lies a 'future...freed from our past', a 'new life' in 'a great city that has expected your return for years'. The city remains a vision of an authentic socialism, beyond patriarchy, beyond the repressive and repressed selves of that prudent, incestuous bourgeoisie revealed to be bankrupt in the 'Temptation'.

Exile from the true city is the source of the restlessness, envy and self-contempt that afflicts all the four allegorical characters of *The Age of Anxiety*, wandering in search of their absconded selves when the real object of their quest should be another way of living. The narrator tells us that in wartime 'everybody is reduced to the anxious status of a shady character or a displaced person'. But this merely compounds a larger, onto-logical crisis for a creature with 'no one-to-one correspondence between his social or economic position and his private mental life'. The allegorical form itself – each of the characters is supposed to represent one of Jung's four faculties of the psyche, Intellect (Malin), Feeling (Rosetta), Intuition (Quant) and Sensations (Emble) – is a way of representing this self-belatedness, in which the characters live in perpetual arrears, not understanding what is happening to them until it is too late. At the beginning of Part Five, when they have returned exhausted from their journeyings, each would rather go home alone to bed, but refuses to say so out of deference to all the others. In this collective estrangement of their individual wishes no one is satisfied. This is a figure, in miniature, of the larger self-estrangement that afflicts a world at war, dividing peoples and driving them to mutual destruction, as in Malin's memory of one of his bombing-raids:

> Conscious in common of our closed Here
> And of Them out There, thinking of Us
> In a different dream, for we die in theirs
> Who kill in ours and become fathers.

This war, as Malin records at the opening of 'The Seven

Ages', begins in the primal Oedipal guilt of symbolic parricide and incest:

> already there is
> Dread in his dreams at the deed of which
> He knows nothing but knows he can do,
> The gulf before him with guilt beyond,
> Whatever that is, whatever why
> Forbids his bound; till that ban tempts him;
> He jumps and is judged: he joins mankind,
> The fallen families, freedom lost,
> Love become Law.

With *The Age of Anxiety*, Auden worked his way through that crisis of Oedipal revolt against the particular life that had animated all his early work. But it would be wrong to see this as a Prospero-like reconciliation, as acceptance and contentment. The subversive worms still niggle and wriggle in the gut of his world. In the Freudian terms appropriate to this poem, anxiety is always associated with the fear of castration. The response of the homosexual Malin, attracted to young Emble, is to decide not to enter into competition for him with Rosetta. Yet his sense of being on trial persists. In 1946, Auden concluded his essay on 'K's Quest' with a bleak view of a world where one is always on trial for a crime that cannot be named, but which bears all the hallmarks of the Oedipal insurrection. Kafka's K, he says, 'has a name consisting of only one letter and no position in the world'. The other characters have many-lettered names and occupations, or rather, they seem to have to K:

> For what Kafka seems to be saying is: 'What is generally called individuality is nothing of the kind, but only the *persona* or mask of action which is all we can know about others; individuality is something that can only be known subjectively, and subjectively individuality is the simplest brute fact that the "I" which feels and knows and acts can never be defined by what it feels and knows and acts; it can be reduced to the barest minimum of a single letter,

but to nothing, never.' Man, therefore, can never know the whole truth, because as the subject who knows, he has to remain outside the truth, and the truth is therefore incomplete.

From this follows the paradox that K's only guarantee that he is following the true way is that he fails to get anywhere. If he succeeded in getting his way, it would be proof that he had failed.

Lacking a full name and a position in the world, K is not inscribed under the name of the Father. A castrate subject, he cannot enter into the penis-rivalry of the urchin, for without a patronym how can he claim 'My prick (or my father's) is bigger than yours (or your father's)'? Yet, as for Ransom and the Airman, the wound can be the source of a more authentic identity; failure and weakness may be the only way to be Truly Strong. The subject who knows remains outside the truth, as Antonio and Prospero do in their different ways. Yet he has, nevertheless, a place in the world, even if it is only that gap between Ariel's 'one evaporating sigh' and the reiterated 'I' of the Prompter, no more than the preordained echo of a disembodied voice. It is here that, like Prospero, doubting or disputing all those particular meanings in which he might be fixed,

Trembling he takes
The silent passage
Into discomfort.

8 Caesar and Clio: Poetry under a Faffling Flag

Auden's attitude towards the social function of art is a problematic one in the three fifties collections, *Nones* (1951), *The Shield of Achilles* (1955) and *Homage to Clio* (1960), but it merely extends that fretting about its irresponsibility which began to emerge towards the end of the thirties, and found its first coherent expression in the poems about art and artists in *Another Time*. In *Secondary Worlds* Auden tried to resolve this by the traditional Christian trope of paradox: 'One might say that for Truth the word *silence* is the least adequate metaphor, and that words can only bear witness to silence as shadows bear witness to light' (p. 136).

This contradictoriness runs through all his observations on language, focused in his famous remark in 'Writing' (*DH*, p. 23) that 'it is both the glory and the shame of poetry that its medium is not its private property.' Repeatedly, the contradictions surface in the nexus of personal and public language, whether this latter is the language of the politician, the bureaucrat, the mass media, or the atomized, malleable public they have created for their own purposes. Auden's response is to assert in 'The Poet and the City' that:

> So long as artists exist, making what they please and think they ought to make, even if it is not terribly good, even if it appeals to only a handful of people, they remind the Management of something managers need to be

reminded of, namely, that the managed are people with faces, not anonymous numbers, that *Homo Laborans* is also *Homo Ludens*. (*DH*, p. 88)

The Management is the ruling elite East and West attacked in 'The Managers' (*Nones*), people it seems at first more to be pitied for their hard work and long hours, lacking the fun they had 'In the bad old days'. They may not 'manage/To behave like genuine Caesars' (or Lenins); but 'Reducing to figures/What is the matter, what is to be done', they still have 'The last word on how we may live or die'. For them, it is *we* who are the matter, and we who can be reduced to mere matter by their decisions. For all their tribulations, they still enjoy the bureaucratic pleasures of gambling with *our* lives. *They* will not have to pay for their mistakes, belonging 'To the very select indeed, to those/For whom.../...there will be places on the last/Plane out of disaster'. Their 'careworn/Look', for which we may be tempted to feel sorry, is still the look of power.

Against them, as the dedication in *Nones* to the Niebuhrs makes clear, the wise and witty tongue, the song from the resonant heart in the grand old manner no longer work. These forms have been hopelessly compromised by a mass society, where 'All words like peace and love,/All sane affirmative speech,/Had been soiled, profaned, debased/To a horrid mechanical screech.' In 1950–1, for veteran socialists like Auden and the Niebuhrs, such a profane language was not confined to the Eastern bloc, but was embodied in the United States by the horrid mechanical screech of McCarthyism, in a language 'Concocted by editors/Into spells to befuddle the crowd', 'pawed-at and gossiped over', leaving the only surviving civil style that of a marginalized 'suburb of dissent', wry, ironic, *sotto voce*. It is the quietness of Auden's dissenting style, in the fifties, which misleads the critic into believing he has renounced politics. 'Music is International' contrasts the premise of its title with the parochial demands for allegiance implied by the word 'unamerican'. 'Even the dinner waltz in/Its formal way is a voice that assaults/International wrong', he tells us, in an ironic recall of 'September 1, 1939'. This insistence on art's internationalism, a refusal of the petty solidarities of nation and power bloc, runs as a theme through all the poetry of the fifties, bringing upon its head the same indignation East and West, though, he says in 'The Dyer's Hand', 'their terms of disapproval may vary..."materialistic" ..."decadent cosmopolitan"..."communistic".'

In *Secondary Worlds* Auden was to write that: 'To write a play, that is to construct a secondary world, about Auschwitz, for example, is wicked: author and audience may try to pretend that they are morally horrified, but in fact they are passing an entertaining evening together, in the aesthetic enjoyment of horrors.' This has generally been taken, somewhat smugly, as a condemnation of politically motivated art, *à la* Brecht. But it is in fact a much larger indictment of the whole frivolous distraction of art in a historical world of suffering. This is why, in 'Homage to Clio', the arts have no icon for the Muse of History, 'who look[s] like any/Girl one has not noticed'. Clio inhabits that realm of silence Prospero had to confront, that historical world where everyone dies in particular and the innocent always have to suffer. Only the newspaper photograph, provisional, instant, unrepeatable, can represent a world of unique historical facts.

The pathos of a history which averts its gaze from Nanking, Dachau, Teruel, Vienna, is figured in the doubleness of this Clio who presides over all the later volumes, bringing us 'face to face/ By ones' with her silence. She is at once our absolute point of reference –

> you, who have never spoken up,
>   Madonna of silences, to whom we turn
> When we have lost control, your eyes, Clio, into which
>
>   We look for recognition after
> We have been found out –

and yet herself the bewildered victim of history, on whom we can turn our own extempory pity –

I have seen
Your photo, I think, in the papers, nursing
    A baby or mourning a corpse: each time
You had nothing to say and did not, one could see,
    Observe where you were, Muse of the unique
Historical fact, defending with silence
    Some world of your beholding.

'Homage to Clio' is composed of twenty-three four-line stanzas – like the version of *Spain 1937* Auden decided not to reprint in his 1965 *Collected Poems*. In some senses it is a response to *Spain*, its stanzas echoing in image and motif corresponding moments in that poem. Here, for example, in stanza 17, the corresponding passage in *Spain* speaks of how 'Our fever's menacing shapes are precise and alive', and in 13 and 14, where now history falls silent, *Spain* has it boisterously replying. The most significant echo, though, is stanza 21, which spells out that silence as one in which we may win reprieve for our crimes:

Muse of Time, but for whose merciful silence
    Only the first step would count and that
Would always be murder, whose kindness never
    Is taken in, forgive our noises

And teach us our recollections. . .

This is a direct recollection of the kind of 'brashness and noise' for which Auden sought forgiveness in his Foreword to the 1965 *Collected Poems*, in stanza 21 of *Spain*: 'Today the inevitable increase in the chances of death;/The conscious acceptance of guilt in the fact of murder.' Yet for all the sense that 'Homage to Clio' sets out to refute *Spain*'s 'inexcusable' rhetoric, what both poems share is an idea of history's doubleness as at once a pattern of unique events and the generalizing discourse within which those events are interpreted.

Whereas the opening stanzas of *Spain* tell us of the importunate world of history where it is 'Today the struggle', 'Homage' opens with the poet quietly reading in a spring garden, and reserves the language of combat for nature. Yet by the end that reading has become a more serious matter. *Spain* ends with the lines Auden regretted in 1965 as 'wicked doctrine':

> The stars are dead; the animals will not look:
> We are left alone with our day, and the time is short
> and
>   History to the defeated
> May say alas but cannot help or pardon.

In 'Homage', the poet on whom the animals 'Keep watch' finds himself, by the end, wondering just what opinion *History* might form of him. That 'pardon' or 'alas' are both in his mind is indicated by the remark that according to Aphrodite 'to throw away/The tiniest fault of someone we love/Is out of the question.' Nature gives up nothing. But History is a matter of what is preserved and what deleted from the scribal record, what is read or left unread. The urgencies of history return in the poem's closing lines in self-effacing anxiety about the poet's place:

>   Approachable as you seem,
>   I dare not ask you if you bless the poets,
> For you do not look as if you ever read them.
>   Nor can I see a reason why you should.

At issue in both poems is the sense of a history made up of changing and unrepeatable human subjects. Central to both is that concern about the writer's responsibility, as a citizen, for a world where people die in earnest. Each too envisages an imaginary dialogue its very assumptions deny. And the deepest distress they share, for all the po-faced earnestness of one and the louche playfulness of the other, issues from a sense of the essential frivolity of art, in a primary world where the first step would always be murder.

But whereas 'History' is invoked direct in *Spain*, *Clio* is not History but simply its *Muse*. It is the act of historical exegesis which the poem foregrounds, apparent in the various verbs of cognition which open up a space between perception and evaluation. As the poet sits reading his book he is 'read' by all those 'sharper senses' around him, which interpret him simply in terms of immediate utility ('inedible', 'unsatisfactory', 'unsafe'). 'To observation/My book is dead', he says, and these lives 'by observations. . .live/In space, as unaware of silence' as the twin goddesses of nature, Artemis and Aphrodite, 'Whose subjects they are'. Their subjectivity, however, is limited in this subjection, for they are excluded from that silence, Clio's own, in which meaning grows. A book is, after all, not dead, but a locus of meanings. If History *speaks* in *Spain*, Clio is the patroness of *writing* and *reading* in 'Homage'. She takes us beyond the sense-impressions of nature and the 'pictures' of dream, into a scriptural estrangement from event which is the ground of cognitive and hermeneutic freedom:

> your silence already is there
> Between us and any magical centre
> Where things are taken in hand.

Lives that obey her move like music, 'Becoming now what they only can be once,/Making of silence decisive sound'. And, in a characteristic play on words, Auden adds, 'it sounds/Easy, but one must find the time.' The casually idiomatic last phrase grows in significance, for living in history as a dimension of meaning in time means quite literally finding that time, grasping it in the movement of its formation.

In 'Homage' the power-brokers are relegated to the realm of nature, categorized as the Big who rarely listen, and listed only under the generic epithets that distinguish one species of despot from another, 'The Short, The Bald, The Pious, The Stammerer'. Imagining themselves world-historical individuals, they are reduced in fact to genotypes, in the realm of Clio registered only in their effects on that larger, processive and anonymous history, creating that 'great host/Of superfluous screams' she has to care for. Like Tamburlaine in the poem 'T the Great', whose name was once 'A synonym in a whole armful/Of languages for what is harmful', each despot in time recedes to a nursery-tale bogey-man, ousted from his eminence by successive challengers. He finds his final niche filling the merely verbal space provided by the secondary world of an absurd crossword anagram, 'A NUBILE TRAM'. Skulking in the corner of a newspaper where today's history and tyrants roar loudly, to be superseded in turn by tomorrow's, 'T cannot win Clio's cup again.'

The real 'Makers of History', the poem of that name insists, are not the commanders whose names and faces appear on the coinage, but the 'Serious historians' who interpret them, the clerks, even, who, in the absence of an actual historical instance, could and easily did 'compose a model/As manly as any of whom schoolmasters tell'. The 'reiterations of one self-importance' on the coins are discredited by each successive new coinage. The Emperors are as exchangeable as the coins on which they figure, and, in the melting-pot of legend, are turned into 'one/Composite demi-god', attributed with prodigious feats and achievements, but also the subject of moralistic exegesis, gossip, prurience, etc. Clio's real favourites, by contrast, are those anonymous benefactors who improved their horses, supplied answers to their questions, made their things, even the 'fulsome/Bards they boarded'. Great men, whether historical or legendary, depend upon the labours of others – labours which are both productive and fictive, making history by supplying both the raw materials and the ideological means by which it is embodied.

Auden's resort to classical models in these post-war volumes is a complicated one. 'The Horatians' for example are not poetic quislings like Virgil. Yet theirs is not a position outside the power-relations of the Augustan settlement, for they still entertain the 'worldly wish' for 'a genteel sufficiency of/land or lolly'. The demeaning last word undercuts the gentility of that 'sufficiency' by vulgarly naming what it's really based on. The English version of Horatianism has the air of an unreal, *literary* pastoralism, its adherents finding in the Anglican Church the well-heeled patron which allowed them to live as 'pastors adjective/to rustic flocks' or 'organists in trollopish/cathedral towns' – the lower case of that adjective suggesting that such a modest way of life is not totally free from prostitution. They live, after all, not outside the economy, but in its obscurer nooks, where 'Authority/never pokes a suspicious nose', and if in these *'embusqué* havens' they seem to be 'political idiots', there is method in their madness. Auden seems to be endorsing such unencumbered withdrawal, but the poem is curiously double-edged. If Flaccus, for example, thought well of his odes, he knew that compared to Pindar they were of small stature, and his life 'compared with authentic martyrs/...of no account'.

The Caesarism of thugs and bureaucracies which Auden saw as linking his own age with that of Augustine (*FA*, pp. 38–9), is the key to the politics of these later volumes, extending that critique of temporal power begun in *For the Time Being*. In the thirties, Marxism had seemed to offer a standpoint outside the totality, from which it might be dispassionately viewed. Spain and Stalin had shown that particular mode of knowing to be equally compromised by its position in the circuits of power. In 'Criticism in a Mass Society' in 1941 Auden had written that a free society is ruled out by the unholy alliance between the cynicism of the elite and the ignorant hedonism of the masses, which perpetuates a 'closed system of reflex responses', offering immediate gratification in place of knowledge. But 'the only check on authoritarian control by the few, whether in matters of aesthetic taste or political choice, is the knowledge of the many' (p. 134). Caesarism works as much by the unscrupulous manipulation of public opinion in a so-called democracy as by the operation of the secret police: 'in a modern society, whatever its form, the great majority prefer opinion to knowledge, and passively allow the former to be imposed upon them by a centralized few' (p. 127). Most people live, that is, in the political unconscious, that realm where ideology utters its subjects in every opinion they mouth: 'To be unconscious is to be neither an individual nor a person, but a mathematical integer in something called the Public which has no real existence' (p. 134). It remains desperately necessary, then, to take some purchase on this closed system that is not vulnerable to its recouping powers. Auden finds this in the fact of supersession itself. Our age is not alone he says, in being 'an age of transition', with the implication 'that if only we are patiently passive our faults will disappear of themselves when the new order has stabilized itself'. All ages are such. Our advantage is that we know it: 'This realization robs us of false hopes, of believing, if we are fortunate, that the Absolute Idea has been at last historically realized, or of expecting, if we are unfortunate, a millennium around the corner. At the same time it should keep us from despair; no error is final' (p. 135).

Auden's Christianity, then, is neither a quietist cult of waiting for the millennium, nor a recantation of his radical past. It is, rather, a translation into a new discourse of those impulses which lay behind his thirties writing, a resistance to temporal power in all its forms, whether it is exercised by the thugs and bureaucrats of Hitler and Stalin, or the managers and media manipulators of a supposedly democratic mass society 'soiled, profaned, debased' by McCarthyism.

'Criticism in a Mass Society' had ended with a plea for a radical Social Democracy. By it, he meant a non-coercive socialism, full-blooded but achieved through consent and education. This was no mere passing transitional philosophy. In 1965 he wrote of himself as 'sufficiently close to Mr Waugh theologically and to Mr Woolf politically to act as a moderator' (*FA*, p. 493), and the following year he spelt out what this improbable Catholic Fabianism took as its first premise:

> As an Episcopalian, I do not believe that Christianity did triumph or has triumphed...I consider the adoption of Christianity as the official state religion, backed by the coercive powers of the State, however desirable it may have seemed at the time, to have been a 'bad', that is to say, an un-Christian thing. (*FA*, p. 41)

'Constantinism' is the continuation of 'Caesarism' by other means, a strategy to close off all alternatives to its power. But the strategy cannot work, as the poem 'Ischia' in *Nones* makes clear. For dissent grows in the very suburbs of power.

'Ischia' speaks of that post-Augustan world in which politics has been dethroned, to be replaced by the private life. But power remains omnipresent, the invisible signature under-writing pleasure in all its forms. In 'Ischia', the *imperium* of

Tiberias had succeeded the militant Caesars, as the *Pax Americana* has replaced Hitler and Mussolini:

> There is a time to admit how much the sword decides,
>   with flourishing horns to salute the conqueror,
>   impassive, cloaked and great on
>   horseback under his faffling flag.

As on Tiberias' Capri, Pleasure can be 'a jealous, sometimes a cruel, god'. Vesuvius may appear homely in this beneficent light, 'looming across the bright bland bay/like a massive family pudding', but its omen can be read by those with a sense of history: cities suffocated under its lava. The 'happy stranger' is reminded on Ischia's quays 'that all is never well' by the braying of a donkey in 'utter protest at what is the case', or the sighing of his master 'for a Brooklyn/where shirts are silk and pants are new'. Ischia does not 'lie about pain or pretend that a time/of darkness and outcry will not come back'. The island may 'correct/our injured eyes', but, in a poem which abounds in shifting viewpoints, 'tall Restituta's all-too-watchful eye' still presides over all things, and her 'annual patronage, they say, is bought with blood.' Money still rules this world where, as the peasant knows, 'nothing is free' and 'whatever you charge shall be paid'. Such ostensibly idyllic places still look to the 'soiled productive cities' for their sustenance. The poem does not deny 'these days of exotic splendour' to which it alludes in closing; but 'exotic', taking up the 'happy stranger' earlier, turns them into touristic moments, 'mileposts in an alluvial land', not perpetual homes. There is even here a complicity between Pleasure and Power, of which money is the intermediary, and the alternative to both is represented by that St Francis evoked in the second stanza, whose way of rejection was also one of affirmation beyond the money economy, a renegade aristocrat seeking truth:

> Changes of heart should also occasion song, like his
> who, turning back from the crusaders' harbour, broke
>   with our aggressive habit
>   once and for all and was the first

>   to see all penniless creatures as our siblings.

The light ironies of 'Fleet Visit' (its very title a pun) in *Shield* hints at the political order which sustains this world. The sailors of the US Sixth Fleet come ashore in an innocently 'unamerican place'. But it is 1951: 'unamerican' is a highly charged adjective, synonymous with 'traitorous' on the lips of a McCarthy. They are ostensibly here to protect not repress, not 'because/But only just-in-case'; yet, like the Greek raiders at Troy, they come ashore from hollow ships. They are 'mild-looking middle-class boys'; but they are not as mild as they look, any more than the ships which 'Without a human will/To tell them whom to kill' *look* 'humane', 'as if they were meant/To be pure abstract design/By some master of pattern and line', worth every cent of the billions they cost. The boys 'look a bit lost' and the ships are 'hollow', in a moral sense, for they are both instruments of destruction. The order they sustain is in the end a predatory and imperial one, where the 'master of pattern and line' exploits the mass culture of boys who read the comic strips, not Homer, for whom 'One baseball game is more /. . . than fifty Troys', and who would be prepared to wipe out fifty Troys to defend those all-american games. The disparity between how things 'look' (used four times) and how they are is that between art and history too: Homer's poetry made the violence of history look good. The tone of all these poems is a profound ambivalence: the price we pay for an affluent society is our own collusion in repression elsewhere, banality at home.

The poems in *Nones* repeatedly return to those moments of late Imperial decline in which an order, crumbling from within, awaits, yearns for and fears its supersession. The most evocative of these is 'The Fall of Rome', where it is not external threat but internal disintegration which brings about collapse – an inflationary economy expressed in an inflated culture. Everywhere a crisis of legitimacy infects a world eyed by creatures 'Unendowed with wealth or pity'. The poem ends with a typical Auden decentring of the Imperial ideal by cutting to that elsewhere from which Rome's despatch will finally be delivered:

Altogether elsewhere, vast
Herds of reindeer move across
Miles and miles of golden moss,
Silently and very fast.

The same point is made in 'A Walk After Dark', which
concludes *Nones*:

It's cosier thinking of night
As more an Old People's Home
Than a shed for a faultless machine,
That the red pre-Cambrian light
Is gone like Imperial Rome
Or myself at seventeen.

Yet we still live in the vanishing afterglow of that light. This
is not a pacified world: 'For the present stalks abroad/Like
the past and its wronged again/Whimper and are ignored.'
The truth is 'Somebody chose their pain,/What needn't have
happened did', and, though the poet is no more specific than
this, it is the dream of supersession which fingers the culprit.
This very night, somewhere in the margins of the universe,
some small event may already have set in process that grand
refusal which will finally overthrow the laws by which we
regulate our world. Some 'judgment', though unspecified,
seems to await himself, his friends, 'And these United States'.
1948 was a year in which the post-war rivalries between US
and Soviet dominated blocs came to a head, but it is not
necessary to be specific to catch the generalized anxiety of this
whole volume. The immanence of supersession, at the height
of imperial middle-age, is what lurks behind all these poems,
but it's not the clash of one power-bloc with another which
animates them – rather it is the contrast between power and
an alternative way of defining human life which is at issue.
 Auden is not taking sides in the immediate political confrontation. In the 1954 'Ode to Gaea', viewed from an aeroplane,
the various 'sub-species of folly' specific to each national
territory below seem arbitrary and unreal, embarrassing the
tired old diplomat who cannot decide whether he should 'smile

for " our great good ally", scowl/at "that vast and detestable empire" or choose/the sneer reserved for certain Southern countries'. Here too, 'on this eve of whispers and tapped telephones/before the Ninth Catastrophe', the real distinction is between the systems of power, 'the Greater Engines... and the police/who go with them', 'the tormentor's/fondling finger' and the orators' lies, on the one hand, and a natural beneficence represented on the other by an Earth which in its plenitude can be equated with natural Justice. So, in 'Memorial for the City', Auden's real frontier cuts across the East – West divide, bisecting them laterally between what his 1948 essay on Yeats called 'the social person and the impersonal state'.

Augustine's two cities here are not an otherworldly and a worldly one, perpetually estranged. Rather they are two ways of viewing the same reality. The eye of the camera and the eye of the crow see the real in terms which record only its surface, 'a space where time has no place', reduced to one-dimensionality. The 'hard bright light composes/A meaningless moment into an eternal fact.' But such candour lies, for 'The crime of life is not time.' Time, on the contrary, is the dimension in which redemption becomes possible. Where we are now, after all, is 'Among the ruins of the Post-Vergilian City/Where our past is a chaos of graves and the barbed-wire stretches ahead/Into our future till it is lost to sight'. For it is precisely in being 'lost to sight' that such redemption lurks, that *beyond* which the eye confined to the present cannot encompass. The world has been divided before, between, for example, Church and State. The New City 'rose/Upon their opposition, the yes and no/Of a rival allegiance', and section II of the poem rehearses some of those changing divided cities in a familiar Audenish potted history.

Immediately after section III, with its vision of the barbed-wire running through all things, the appeal to ' *Let Our Weakness speak*' introduces that alternative voice to the discourse of Power, first enunciated by Auden in his doctrine of the Truly Strong, and now embodied in that second Adam who speaks of redemption amidst all acts of dereliction, from the first

Adam onwards through a whole gamut of mythical and historic archetypes.

Christ, this surplus, is the perpetual otherness of history, in which 'Metropolis, that too-great city' will be judged. To 'all who dwell on the public side of her mirrors' there will be no peace. 'Our grief is not Greek', the poem had said, the arbitrary change of phoneme opening up a world of difference and revealing the historical exchangeability of the signifier. Another play on words, 'The facts, the acts of the City bore a double meaning:/Limbs became hymns', embodies in the supersessions of language the model of a historic conversion. So, at the end of the poem, the suffering turns round on those who refuse to apportion or accept blame for suffering, turning the photographs into evidence and the photographers into culprits, their disinterestedness complicity:

> At the place of my passion her photographers are
>   gathered together;
> but I shall rise again to hear her judged.

In *A Certain World* Auden adds a small twist to the observation about art and Auschwitz in *Secondary Worlds*. 'Christmas and Easter', he observes, 'can be subjects for poetry, but Good Friday, like Auschwitz, cannot. The reality is so horrible it is not surprising that people should have found it a stumbling block to faith' (p. 168). Yet Auden not only made a poem about the hour of the crucifixion the title poem of *Nones*, and opened that volume with a poem about Good Friday, he also took both poems and made them part of a long sequence, 'Horae Canonicae', which is at the centre of his next volume, *The Shield of Achilles*. This fretful return to the scene of the primal crime has about it both the ambiguous penitence of the culprit and the obsessive compulsion to know of the detective in a Whodunit. 'Just as we were all, potentially, in Adam when he fell,' Auden says in *A Certain World*, 'so we were all, potentially, in Jerusalem on that first Good Friday before there was an Easter, a Pentecost, a Christian, or a Church.' This moment of supersession must have appeared to its participants as merely an everyday, minor episode in a marginal colony.

Imagining who he himself might have been, Auden suggests a Hellenized Jew from Alexandria, absorbed in intellectual argument and reacting with prim distaste to the all-too-familiar sight of the crucifixion, 'averting my eyes from the disagreeable spectacle'. This averting of the gaze links the Madonnas of 'Nones' with the Clio of 'Homage', and it implicates, too, that Thetis with whom we identify in 'The Shield of Achilles', binding together the three volumes into a meditation on the evasions and sudden revelations of history, those moments when we have lost control and turn for recognition and forgiveness.

In 'Compline', the sixth poem of 'Horae Canonicae', such an individual looks back to 'Nones', the hours between noon and three, only to admit to a total amnesia. Now, at this moment before sleep, it should be possible to find that 'instant of recollection/When the whole thing makes sense'. Instead, there is a gap, filled with noisy irrelevancies:

> Actions, words, that could fit any tale,
>   And I fail to see either plot
> Or meaning; I cannot remember
>   A thing between noon and three.

All that he is left with is a profound unease. The repressed event returns in every motion of body and soul. It is implicit in the idea of equity, of rhythm, in the hilarity of the stars and the motions of the heart, in the 'unknowable justice' and 'the name of a love/Whose name one's forgotten'. The amnesia is the site of both crime and redemption, the crucifixion of 'Nones'.

'Nones' had contained the same contradiction, between the certainties of our negative knowledge ('What we know to be not possible') and the unsettling intuitions that tell us the world is quite different, foretold time after time by wild hermits, shamans and sybils, or revealed in a child's chance rhyming, and now come to pass 'Before we realize it.' Whereas in 'Compline' everything seems to be posthumous, here it seems to be premature, over too soon, barely mid-afternoon yet 'already' the blood of the sacrifice dry on the grass:

                we are not prepared
For silence so sudden and so soon;
    The day is too hot, too bright, too still,
Too ever, the dead remains too nothing.
    What shall we do till nightfall?

In prospect, the deed had seemed impossibly remote; now, in retrospect, impossibly near, yet time and space alike are compacted, distorted, as the parts of speech themselves succumb to disorientation, in enallage and ploce. The crowd has departed, each one blaming all the others, blaming 'the crowd', a paradox which is turned on its head by the line which echoes *Spain* ('We are left alone with our day') as it affirms that complicity in crime that makes a community of us: 'We are left alone with our feat.' In this solitude, the three Madonnas 'Turn their kind faces from us/And our projects under construction,/Look only in one direction,/Fix their gaze on our completed work'. Just as the poem had opened with a retrospective prolepsis that compounds time, so now the gaze of the Madonnas reveals the culprits (us) to be simultaneously redundant (a 'Discarded artefact', 'Outliving our act') and predisposed – for behind every act 'We shall always now be aware/Of the deed into which they lead.' Knowledge comes belatedly, but it is always–already too late, and always will be.

This sense of a time out of sync is reinforced by the dis-placements of the rhymes, which follow no consistent pattern and crop up unexpectedly in the middle of lines, rather than in their proper places, just as 'this death' unpredictably makes its presence felt in the midst of the most innocent of activities. Thus each stanza repeats the perplexity which asks 'how can we repeat this?' Like 'our wronged flesh' it works undisturbed while we are away, distracted, dreaming, 'restoring/The order we try to destroy, the rhythm/We spoil out of spite'. As in 'Compline' an implicit rhythm and order underlie our dis-traught consciousness. As in 'Compline' too, the death returns with an obsessive reiteration, though, unlike 'Compline', con-sciousness has not yet learnt to repress it into euphemism, evasion or unease, still revolves on its enormity; but –

> we have time
> To misrepresent, excuse, deny,
>   Mythify, use this event
> While, under a hotel bed, in prison,
>   Down wrong turnings, its meaning
> Waits for our lives.

History is the site of a crime whose recollection is repeatedly repressed. In 'Prime' it seems that the self is freed of this burden, waking 'Without a name or history.../Between my body and the day'. But it is precisely in this interval that it must re-enter its fallen historical state. 'The memory has to name me, resume/Its routine of praise and blame.' The smiling instant in which the day is still intact, a sinless Adam 'still previous to any act', has to give way to that drawing of breath for which 'the cost,/No matter how, is Paradise/Lost of course and myself owing a death.' The careful enjambement which plunges Paradise into its Loss enacts just how much this Fall is a rite of passage into history, just as the text of 'Prime' takes its silent passage into textuality by naming the Miltonic inspiration on which it draws.

The waking self had emerged from a world of dream described in insistently political terms as a 'rebellious fronde'. Consciousness's reunion with body is, at the end, equally politically charged, flesh being 'No honest equal, but my accomplice now,/My assassin to be', while his name 'Stands for my historical share of care/For a lying self-made city,/Afraid of our living task'. It is as the subject of history, then, that the subjected self confronts the day's task, 'the dying/Which the coming day will ask'.

In 'Vespers', two paths cross at twilight, under the shadow of the crucifixion – that of the Arcadian and that of the Utopian. This passage has generally been interpreted as Auden's rejection of any socialist hopes for the future, since the Utopian's 'New Jerusalem' is described in uncongenial terms, as one where 'a person who dislikes work will be very sorry he was born', the secret police will be 'our boys' now, and 'even the chefs will be cucumber-cool machine minders';

whereas Eden is described in terms which recall all Auden's
declared preferences. But biography can deceive. The speaker
may be rightly alarmed that the Utopian dreams of the 'august
day of outrage' when vengeance is his, 'when the unrepen-
tant thieves (including me) are sequestered.' But this suggests
that, though these two meet at a crossroads and pass, they
are also figuratively the two thieves on the cross, one of whom
was saved. It was not, one might remember, the dream of
Eden, of an impossible return to innocence, that brought
salvation to one of the thieves in *Luke* (23, xxxix–xliii), but
a wish to enter into the Kingdom. 'Vespers' left-handedly
subverts the smugness of the Arcadian Auden, and it brings
a niggling suspicion of guilt:

> Was it (as it must look to any god of cross-roads)
> simply a fortuitous intersection of life-paths, loyal to
> different fibs?

> Or also a rendezvous between two accomplices who,
> in spite of themselves, cannot resist meeting

> to remind the other (do both, at bottom, desire
> truth?) of that half of their secret which he would most
> like to forget,

> forcing us both, for a fraction of a second, to
> remember our victim (but for him I could forget the
> blood, but for me he could forget the innocence),

> on whose immolation...arcadias, utopias, our dear
> old bag of a democracy are alike founded:

> For without a cement of blood (it must be human, it
> must be innocent) no secular wall will safely stand.

The poem endorses neither Arcadian nor Utopian. Their
'different fibs' are tricked into truth, revealing that they are
both accomplices at the crime, and each, by challenging the

half-lie of the other, gestures towards that truth which is their common secret, that third that completes their trinity.

'Horae Canonicae' then is not finally a blasphemous religious poem about 'Good Friday' but a secular poem about 'our dear old bag of democracy'. It uses the Christian fable as a vehicle, not because it does not credit it – it clearly does – but because the very meaning of that crucifixion, within Christian belief, is that Christ offered himself to be used, to become the sacrificial vehicle of meanings other than himself, incarnate in him. The poem itself, that is, shares in the guilty doubleness of which it speaks, proclaiming a secret it would half like to forget, that its innocence is founded in blood, and that under all the arcadias and utopias of art lies that historical share of care symbolized by the victim – '(call him Abel, Remus, whom you will, it is one Sin Offering)' – without whom 'no secular wall will safely stand.' 'Horae Canonicae' is one of the most insistently political of all Auden's poems, not just in its incidental imagery, but in its attempt to address that crisis on the site of modern history compacted into the contradictions of a single line in *Spain*: 'today the/Fumbled and unsatisfactory embrace before hurting.' What it calls for is in fact 'The conscious acceptance of guilt in the fact of murder.'

'Arcadian tales are hard-luck stories too', says the sonnet 'Words' in *Homage to Clio*. In 'Horae Canonicae' the site of the crime is always that place of the skull where the rose of self-punishment grows. In 'Bucolics', the other major sequence in *The Shield of Achilles*, the arcadian landscapes disclose, on examination, their own death's-head. 'Horae Canonicae' takes us through the seven stages of our crucifixion in time. The seven 'Bucolics' by contrast seem to present the landscapes of a timeless, spatial world, nature set against culture. History, however, infiltrates them all. The two sequences intersect at a crossroads which is also the place of the cross. Like the seven stages and seven ages of *The Age of Anxiety*, profane Pastoral and sacred Passion meet at the scene of the crime.

That this crime is as much to do with Oedipus as Christ is revealed by the opening of 'Winds', the first poem:

> Deep, deep below our violences,
> Quite still, lies our First Dad, his watch
>   And many little maids.

Throughout the sequence, the playful irresponsibility of the pastoral tradition, invoking the variety of art forms – poetry, painting, music – and figured repeatedly by the idea of language, of a discourse that cannot be held accountable, vies with the deadly earnest of these violences. Pastoral is revealed not simply as a game of words, but also as an enunciation of power, in all its forms. The landscape too offers opportunities and resistances to the power-brokers of politics. In 'Mountains', for example, we are told: 'Caesar does not rejoice when high ground/Makes a darker map', for a serious being cries out for a gap through which he can move his armies. In 'Plains', by contrast, the flat lands offer easy hegemony to 'Caesar with all his They':

> If a tax-collector disappear in the hills,
>   If, now and then, a keeper is shot in the forest,
> No thunder follows, but where roads run level,
>   How swift to the point of protest strides the crown.
> It hangs, it flogs, it fines, it goes. There is drink.
>   There are wives to beat. But Zeus is with the strong.

The strong are 'Born as a rule in some small place' but 'they chamber with Clio' on the plains where the big battles are fought. No more than language is the landscape free from its historical share of care. There is nothing here which belies Auden's 'Marxist' credo in 'I Believe':

> On the whole Marx seems to me correct in his view that physical conditions and the forms of economic production have dictated the forms of communities: e.g. the geographical peculiarities of the Aegean peninsula produced small democratic city-states, while the civilisations based on river irrigation like Egypt and Mesopotamia were centralised autocratic empires.

The plains breed the raw material of armies: the absence of frontiers beyond which 'the dreamer/Can place his land of

marvels' encourages a restlessness and resentment which
spawns fantasies of authoritarian vengeance:

> If I were a plainsman I should hate us all
>
>   . . .
>
> What could I smile at as I trudged behind my harrow
> But bloodshot images of rivers howling,
>   Marbles in panic, and Don't-Care made to care?

In such a place, 'What goal of unrest is there but the Navy?'
The oppressive 'First Dad' of 'Winds' is not some dawn homi-
nid or even that God as first cause 'proved' by Paley's argument
from evidences. As the noticeably baroque language of the
poem suggests, speaking of 'the boneless winds that blow/
Round law-court and temple', he is born again in every
generation, to be placated by 'every verbal rite' of the poet
and tamed into a figure of the Authentic City as the concerned
paterfamilias, hurrying to inspect his rain-gauge. In 'Woods',
the second poem of the sequence, we are taken through a
transformative history of aesthetic attitudes which chart
changing social and political assumptions. For Piero di Cosimo
'Sylvan meant savage in those primal woods.' Later 'Reduced
to patches, owned by hunting squires', the woods 'whispered
still of most unsocial fires', those witches and outlaws warned
against by Crown and Mitre, Church and State. Even now
they 'Reveal a lot about a country's soul':

> A small grove massacred to the last ash,
> An oak with heart-rot, gives away the show:
> This great society is going smash;
>
>   . . .
>
> A culture is no better than its woods.

Ecology too is a matter of power. The pastoral as a genre
is charged with political resonance. 'Mountains' may refuse
the idea that the Lake District is simply 'Another bourgeois
invention, like the piano', but it does insist on the mountain
as 'a fine refuge', where 'These farms can always see a panting
government coming.' 'Lakes' observes that Christendom only

got started when 'Her pensive chiefs converged on the Ascanian lake' for the Council of Nicaea; while, in the present, it recommends that 'Sly Foreign Ministers should always meet beside one.' 'Islands' once lay 'Beyond the long arm of the Law'. Runaway Saints and security-obsessed Sovereigns alike like islands. 'His Highness and The People both/Pick islands for their jails.' Here once, 'Exterminated species played/Who had not read their Hobbes'; but they soon discovered for real, taught by men, that life is nasty, brutish and short. This last point reinforces the drift of the whole sequence: it is culture that transforms nature, interpreting and transfiguring it. The poets Auden and Sappho are in there holding forth about themselves with the dictators Napoleon and Tiberias, revealing that shared selfishness which, as an island is a lake turned inside out, is the inversion of a true sense of community.

In a dramatic peripety, the poem enacts the movement of this false consciousness, incapable of grasping that its supposedly sovereign insularity is founded on that society from which it derives its being:

> What is cosier than the shore
>   Of a lake turned inside out?
> How do all these other people
>   Dare to be about?

It may be that, in their 'democratic nudity', you cannot tell 'The keeping from the kept'. Nevertheless, there is a common economic bond to these lives, which can be conjugated in their separateness but still share the same verb; and it is a bond they share with the farmer and fisherman, who may complain about each other and the tourists but are also linked by the global market in which they all pursue their livelihoods.

Lakes offer a 'lacustrine atmosphere' of health and sanity, humanizing, doctoring our sickness. However, even this carries with it a negative, selfish side: 'Liking one's Nature, as lake-lovers do, benign/Goes with a wish for savage dogs and man-traps', refusing to share 'Lake Eden' with 'every mortal Jack and Jill'. 'Lakes' too withdraws into a petty privacy, as it retreats into a self-indulgent playing with language which substitutes name for thing. Like those other poets he cites this one owns only by naming:

> But that's not going to stop me wondering what sort
>   Of lake I would decide on if I should.
> Moraine, pot, oxbow, glint, sink, crater, piedmont,
>   dimple...?
>   Just reeling off their names is ever so comfy.

Comfyness is a mimsy parody of real comfort, in that pentecostal sense, and just as it is in the shifting, unbounded, unpropertied air of the opening poem that 'holy insufflation' and the 'Goddess of winds and wisdom' are found, so it is in the fluid, uncontainable energies of 'Streams' that a true picture of comfort resides in the concluding poem.

All features of landscape are subject to those laws of property which demarcate and constrain, limit and dispossess. But air and running water represent an order beyond property (where ownership is always someone else's exclusion), a playfulness which is an image of 'pure being, perfect in music and movement'. Streams 'in their bearing are always immaculate' and 'well-spoken', talking to themselves in a language which precedes Babel. Streams connect. As carriers of culture and commerce they overcome those separations enforced by landscapes which 'exclud[e] as alien/the tales and diets of all other strata'. Streams correspond to an authentic language, contain the prospect of a true humanity, teach us to 'love the absent one' by continually 'coming from a distance' and, in the sentiments of 'The Poet and the City', offer a model to *Homo Ludens* by making 'fun of our feuds by opposing identical banks', transferring the loam from one side to the other in the transit downstream.

This quiet allusion to the Cold War is then quietly extended in a typical ellipsis. Even turned to labour – as 'toil at a turbine' – water keeps its innocence, speaking to the soiled heart of man 'raging at what it is',

> of a sort of world, quite other,
>   altogether different from this one

with its envies and passports, a polis like that
to which, in the name of scholars everywhere,
    Gaston Paris pledged his allegiance
    as Bismarck's siege-guns came within earshot.

The *en passant* obliquity of the reference does not seem to
have provoked scholars anywhere to comment, but it is as
significant for what it fails to say as for what it does. The allusion is to the lecture the French medievalist Gaston Paris
delivered at the Collège de France on 8 December 1870, a
text of which was privately published in New York in 1935
under the title 'Patriotism vs Science'.

Paris's lecture, delivered in a city under German siege,
surprised his audience by proclaiming loyalty to a '*grande patrie*'
of science like that of the City of God, transcending national
frontiers. In the less kindly words of Julien Benda, much
bandied around in the McCarthy era, he was advocating that
kind of *trahison des clercs* of which formerly left-wing intellectuals were accused during the Cold War. The obliquity of
this particular internationalist protest, however, part
arrogance, part evasiveness, conceals a louder silence, which
only Clio might unfold. That Auden moves on at once to a
dream vision which recalls both *Piers Plowman* – written in
the wake of the Peasants' Revolt – and his own echo of that
poem, 'The Malvern Hills', with its vision of an awakening
proletariat – suggests that even in his evasions Auden inscribes
an unconscious and confessional sub-text.

For if his vision of a dance of loved ones in a ring recalls
the 'perichoresis' of 'Compline', it recalls too the crime which
has been forgotten in that poem. 'Streams' ends with water
'wishing the least of men/their figures of splendor, their holy
places'. The holy place that now presides over the city of Paris,
the Cathedral of *Sacré Coeur*, was built as an act of triumph
and expiation by a returning French bourgeoisie which, in
1871, massacred something like seventy thousand working
men and women in a few days. It testifies, then, not to a sacred
but to the 'soiled heart raging at what it is' of an earlier stanza.
These massacres were carried out because, only three months

after Gaston Paris's rather marginal speech, 'the least of men' established, for two months, the first workers' state in history, proclaiming a *polis* without benefit of bourgeoisie to which internationalists everywhere could pledge themselves. For a scholar who had rallied to the Spanish Republic in this same internationalist tradition to speak of Paris's *polis* yet not acknowledge the Paris Commune seems not so much repression as displacement.

'Horae Canonicae' begins with an image of an aristocratic French rebellion, the Fronde, as a metaphor for that which is repressed into the unconscious, 'Disenfranchised, widowed and orphaned/By an historical mistake', to emerge again in dream. 'Bucolics' ends with a dream-vision which is simultaneously arcadian and utopian, which distracts us away from that Paris in which the ghost of a proletarian revolution stalks abroad, haunting Europe. It is as if, slipping off into dream here as at the same moment in 'Compline', Auden cannot remember a thing that happened between noon and three, cannot remember that 'cement of blood (it must be human, it must be innocent)' on which his and Gaston Paris's international community of scholars, 'arcadias, utopias, our dear old bag of democracy are alike founded'. In 'Sext', we recall, first manual and then intellectual labour are seen as the foundations of culture and crime alike. For *Homo Ludens*, the playing poet, still relies on *Homo Laborans*, the working man and woman, without whom 'no secular wall will safely stand.' Clio and Caesar alike rely on a third power, that worker, artificer, artisan figured, in the title poem of *The Shield of Achilles*, by the lame and sweating smith, Hephaestos, a heavenly proletarian who is as silent as Clio, and also turns away from what his hands have wrought.

The double stanza pattern of 'The Shield' would suggest that this poem juxtaposes Ariel and Prospero, beauty and truth. And indeed Thetis, looking over Hephaestos' shoulder as he makes the shield for Achilles, does expect to see pastoral scenes like those on Keats's Urn. Her wish to see idyllic images on an instrument of war suggests a contradiction. For her, the shield is also an instrument of propaganda, offering she hopes images of that *patria* for which it is sweet to die, as her son will.

Instead, the shield depicts not the simple antithesis of a world easily divided between order and violence, culture and nature – 'Marble well-governed cities/And ships upon untamed seas' – but one in which they are inextricably confounded, 'An artificial wilderness/And a sky like lead' – the oxymoron indicating not only the artifice of the smith's craft, but also the man-made nature of the desolation it depicts. Callan sees Hephaestos as 'the aesthetic god', depicting 'not the ideal Thetis envisioned...but the utopian reality', something Callan equates with 'Hitler's dream of a racially pure Nordic state...apartheid...and the Marxist dream of pure Communism' – which is rather unfair to Hephaestos and to Marx.[1] For what this sweaty armourer produces is a true picture of war and what it brings in its wake, as opposed to ennobling propaganda. When Callan quotes Auden's comment from *The Dyer's Hand* that 'A society which was really like a good poem, embodying the aesthetic virtues of beauty, order, economy and subordination of detail to the whole, would be a nightmare of horror' (p. 85), his quotation turns back upon the all-American Mom Thetis, for it is her wish that this describes, not Hephaestos' reality.

But Hephaestos himself cannot escape contradiction. For this work in heavy metal, exhaustingly produced by hard labour, and depicting an ugly and problematic world, manages to achieve the transformation of pain and disorder into art. Poem and shield both force open a division between the beauty of the representation and the ugliness it represents, translating 'shining metal' into 'a sky like lead' in a way which both affirms and conceals its artifice under the success of its illusion.

As Callan's comments reveal, the role of the reader is crucial in this poem, for what it sets up is a potentially infinite regress of perspectives in which the hermeneutic circle is never closed. You, gentle reader, look over my shoulder as I look over the speaker's shoulder as he looks over Thetis' shoulder as she looks over Hephaestos', who in turn looks at a world in which 'A crowd of ordinary decent folk' (like you, me and Mr Callan) look on as three pale figures are led forth and shot – which is where all looking ceases. The crowds do nothing, the officials are bored, the sentries sweat:

> The mass and majesty of this world, all
>   That carries weight and always weighs the same
> Lay in the hands of others; they were small
>   And could not hope for help and no help came:
>   What their foes liked to do was done...

But it is all all right. For these are only 'figures' on a shield. The hands we are in are Hephaestos' own, or Auden's; and we can here wash our own of complicity in that crime, just like the crowd, the sentries and the officials. Words have no weight. We are in fact 'passing an entertaining evening together, in the aesthetic enjoyment of horrors.' Richard Johnson, in *Man's Place*, even sees Thetis' pastoral stanzas offering a 'positive image of possibility' which refutes Hephaestos' ultimately insufficient realism with a vision of redemption.[2] There is no cause for alarm.

But there is cause for alarm. The last stanza should be one of Thetis' pastoral pieties. Instead, in a movement in which the three parties to the shield's making – commissioner, producer, user – are named for the first time, the figures and voices momentarily gathered here disperse, Hephaestos hobbling away in thin-lipped silence, Thetis crying out in dismay 'At what the god had wrought/To please her son', rather than at the fact he is a man-slayer or that he too will not live long. The representation has more effect than the reality. We too, poet and reader alike, go our separate ways, moved more by the rhetoric of suffering than the knowledge that such things are actually happening out there, at this moment as we read or write – today in El Salvador, yesterday in Teruel, Nanking, Dachau. Is it Achilles who is 'Iron-hearted, man-slaying', or is it us? The look we see reflected back from the shining metal is our own. What stares out of the mirror of the poem is still –

> Imperialism's face
> And the international wrong.

The essay 'The Dyer's Hand' concludes:

> We hear a lot about the gulf between the intellectual and the masses but not enough about the ways in which they are alike. If I meet an illiterate peasant we may not be able to say much to each other, but if we both meet a public official, we share the same feeling of suspicion; neither of us will trust him further than we can throw a grand piano. If we enter a public building together, we share the same apprehension that perhaps we shall never get out. Whatever the cultural differences between us, we both sniff in an official world the smell of the unreality in which persons are treated as statistics. The peasant may play cards in the evening while I write poetry, but there is one political principle to which we both subscribe, namely, that among the half dozen or so things for which a man of honor must be prepared, if necessary, to die, the right to play, the right to frivolity, is not the least.
>
> Highbrows and Lowbrows of the World, unite!

This is the same gospel proclaimed in the 'Hermetic Decalogue' of 'Under Which Lyre', Auden's Phi Beta Kappa poem at Harvard in 1946. The poem has been misread partly because of its institutionalized status and its sub-title, 'A Reactionary Tract for The Times', for what Auden is in reaction against is precisely that institutionalization of learning and culture which is apparent everywhere, from Yale to Princeton and Broadway to the Book Reviews. Lest Harvard should feel itself smugly excluded from this, Auden's 'occasional' poem rises impishly to the occasion with its own Ten Commandments, beginning:

> Thou shalt not do as the dean pleases,
> Thou shalt not write thy doctor's thesis
>   On education,
> Thou shalt not worship projects nor
> Shalt thou or thine bow down before
>   Administration.

Hermes has always led an undercover existence in Auden's poetry. He appears, without being named, in *New Year Letter* as the 'candid psychopompos' who conducts the souls of the dead to the underworld, and again in the airport lounge of 'In Transit' (1950), as the 'professional friend' who 'smiling leads us indoors' and the tannoy voice 'that from time to time calls/Some class of souls to foregather at the gate'. Here, too, he presides as that god of boundaries, crossroads and thresholds who rules over the gates of dream and vision, as in 'Prime', 'Compline', 'Streams' and 'Vespers'. In 'Atlantis' in 1941 Hermes appeared by name as the 'master of roads', patron of all who are 'Travelling and tormented,/Dialectic and bizarre'. In a 1968 poem, 'Forty Years On' from *City Without Walls*, he again makes a covert appearance. The poem, we discover in the last line, is spoken by the thief, pickpocket and balladeer Autolycus, returning forty years later to that Bohemia which, for the biographical author, is the Oxford of his youth and his decline. Here 'orators no more speak/of primogeniture, prerogatives of age and sceptre.'

Hermes might seem a merely speculative presence here but for that remark. For Autolycus was the son of Hermes, from whom he acquired the thief's gift of making things invisible. Hermes puts in invisible appearances throughout Auden's poetry, as that god of secrets and hidden things – of spies even – who himself has to be deduced from a riddling text. For he is also the patron of hermeneutics, of messages that

have to be teased out, of those codes and crossword puzzles
and *doubles entendres* which are Auden's verbal forte. In 'Under
Which Lyre', he is named the representative of a 'dialectic'
which subverts all the fixed convictions of a system of social
control which believes it has got the world taped. But the title
indicates a further riddle of primogeniture which wriggles
backwards and forwards in the poetry.

One war is over, the battle-weary young are being
shepherded – for Hermes also presided over Arcadia – through
basic college courses. But already another has commenced,
between the disciples of 'Pompous Apollo' (the 'official' god
of poetry and learning) and 'Precocious Hermes' – the god
of the provisional, who knows that to find Truth 'Thou shalt
not live within thy means'. The two sides in this 'dialectic strife'
are clearly demarcated:

> The sons of Hermes love to play,
> And only do their best when they
>   Are told they oughtn't;
> Apollo's children never shrink
> From boring jobs but have to think
>   Their work important.

Apollo is not satisfied with 'the throne,/Fasces and falcons'
of public power:

> But jealous of our god of dreams,
> His common-sense in secret schemes
>   To rule the heart;
> Unable to invent the lyre,
> Creates with simulated fire
>   Official art.

According to the Homeric Hymns it was not Apollo but
Hermes who invented the lyre, which he then gave to his
brother to assuage his anger at a theft. Hermes, the principle
of Arcadian play, is also, as Jung observed in *The Spirit
Mercurius* in 1943, the 'mediating, ambivalent principle in
alchemy', representing that 'final synthesis of male and female'
– like the Man-Woman of *Paid* – which transcends sexual

differentiation. But if Hermes is the 'genetic' father of the lyre, he is also its 'social' uncle, recalling that homosexual Uncle Henry of *The Orators* the Airman speculated might be his 'real ancestor'. (Hermes, the winged patron of con-men, may also cast a new light on the 'Flying Trickster' of that book, though, in his public role as god of eloquence, he belongs to the Enemy.)

Auden's whole poem engages in this displacing ambivalence, sidestepping the campus confrontations with a mock-heroic rhetoric which undermines the formal occasion it responds to. Nowhere is this clearer than in the unexpected invasion of the classical *mis-en-scène* by the problematic figure of a stoutly English Falstaff, the fool, who 'confronts forever/The prig Prince Hal'.

Falstaff is an uncle 'old enough to be his father' (*DH*, p. 183), and, in Auden's interpretation, a figure of bisexual narcissism, 'combining mother and child in his own person ...emotionally self-sufficient' (*DH*, p. 196). Falstaff is a double man in another sense, 'Overtly...a Lord of Misrule; parabolically...a comic symbol for the supernatural order of Charity as contrasted with the temporal order of Justice' symbolized by Prince Hal's actual father (*DH*, p. 198). If Falstaff then leads Hal to consort with low types, he is following in the footsteps of that Hermes who offers the precedent of a divine art consorting with rough trade. It is in such class terms that Auden defines comedy in the essay which precedes this in 'The Shakespearian City' (*DH*, p. 177):

[C]lassical comedy is based upon the division of mankind into two classes, those who have *arete* and those who do not, and only the second class, fools, shameless rascals, slaves, are fit subject for comedy. But Christian comedy is based upon the belief that all men are sinners; no one, therefore, whatever his rank or talents, can claim immunity from the comic exposure and, indeed, the more virtuous, in the Greek sense, a man is, the more he realises that he deserves to be exposed.

In all great drama, the essay concludes, 'we can feel the

tension of this ambivalent attitude, torn between reverence and contempt, of the maker towards the doer' (p. 181). This is the tone of Auden's late poetry. That radically estranging look, which in the thirties had led him to despise a venal society, is now transformed into the comic perspective of the anthropologist who knows that all cultures are historical artefacts but who can nevertheless admire, respect or forgive the diversity of forms they take.

In these late poems, the defamiliarizing gaze serves only to endear. In 'Whitsunday in Kirchstetten' (*AH*), for example, the poem bounces various idioms off each other in a way which relativizes them all, translating them into the new polyglot English of the 'metic' (an alien resident in a Greek city with some of the privileges of citizens). But while Babel still rules in this world, such 'tribal formulae' are merely local dialects of a single, levelling truth. Sacred and profane rituals can, to the anthropologizing outsider, share the same comical patterns: while the church 'quietly gets on with the Sacrifice/as Rome does it', outside the 'car-worshippers enact/the ritual exodus from Vienna/their successful cult demands.'

Economic change has translated this culture into new modes. The 'sons of the menalty' no longer have to choose their careers only from Army, Navy, Law or Church. If this culture is a product of military or fiscal contingencies, not manifest destiny ('if the Allies had not/conquered the Ost-Mark, if the dollar fell,/ the *Gemütlichkeit* would be less'), it is none the less real and tangible for that. Yet ninety kilometres away as the crow flies is the Iron Curtain where 'our habits end,/where minefield and watchtower say NO EXIT/from peace-loving Crimtartary, except for crows'. This is a complex and comic deposition of absolutes – the archaic name for Russia, the crow's-eye view, the deadpan slogans, reinforced by the wide sweep of the next remark, which reflects adversely on the values of both blocs: 'from Loipersbach/to the Bering Sea not a living stockbroker'. Is the Cold War, then, really simply a matter of making the world safe for stockbrokers?

Even here, the stranger's look can suddenly turn withering. In 'The Poet and the City' Auden wrote that 'Today, there is only one genuine world-wide revolutionary issue, racial equality. The debate between capitalism, socialism and communism is really a party issue' about how best to distribute the grub. In the poem the priest's elevation of the host leads him to put East and West in their place in the name of a Third World which turns the lunch tables on them both:

> But to most people
> I'm the wrong colour: it could be the looter's turn
> for latrine duty and the flogging block,
> my kin who trousered Africa, carried our smell
> to germless poles.

With a little aftershock, we realize that it is the poet's kin who are the looters, that 'civilising' Africa meant introducing the flogging block. Yet it is all said with such old-world charm that it cannot offend. The very ease with which he gets away with such wicked innuendoes means we can easily miss the link between this image of imperialism, in its strangely affectionate dismissiveness, and 'the Body of the Second Adam/ . . . shown to some of his torturers' just before. These evasions are those of a language which lacks certain resonances: 'There is no Queen's English/in any context for *Geist* or *Esprit*.' And this encourages a larger evasion, that of the final lines: 'about catastrophe or how to behave in one/what do I know, except what everyone knows –/if there when Grace dances, I should dance.'

That catastrophe lurks everywhere in this last decade. If translation is a recurrent theme of the poems, it is not simply translation from one language or idiom into another. For over all presides that death which is the ultimate translation: 'What is Death?' asks a 'Short', 'A life/disintegrating into/smaller simpler ones'. In this secular, death-defined world Godhead challenges all temporal powers:

> He appears in this world, not as Apollo or Aphrodite might appear, disguised as a man so that no mortal should recognize his divinity, but as a real man who openly claims to be God. And the consequence is

inevitable. The highest religious and temporal authorities condemn Him as a blasphemer and a Lord of Misrule, as a Bad Companion for mankind. Inevitable because, as Richelieu said, 'The salvation of States is in this world,' and history has not yet provided us with any evidence that the prince of this world has changed his character. (*DH*, pp. 207–8)

Auden takes the human beyond anthropology into the physiological and biological in many of these last poems. In 'Lines to Dr Walter Birk' (*CWW*) for example he 'admits how easy it is to misconster/what our bodies are trying to say, for each one/talks in a local/dialect of its own that can alter during/its lifetime' – children run high fevers on the least provocation, the organs of old men suffer in silence. 'A New Year Greeting' (*EG*) speaks of all those little local catastrophes that happen to the yeasts, bacteria and viruses of the body every time it takes a bath, ending with a vision of a microcosmic Apocalypse 'when my mantle suddenly turns/too cold, too rancid, for you, /...and I/am stripped of excuse and nimbus,/a Past, subject to Judgment'. The conscious subject, deposed from its sovereignty, stands revealed as a subject of the material order which reclaims it, and the semiotic systems within which it lived as no more than 'excuse and nimbus'. The secret is at last out of the bag. As in 'Rois Fainéants' (*CWW*) the feigned sovereigns of consciousness are paraded through the streets, reflexes of a power which lies elsewhere:

> Everyone knew, of course, it was a staged play,
> Everyone knew where the real power lay,
> That it was the Mayor of the Palace who had the say.

'Epithalamium' (*CWW*) likewise starts as a marriage hymn in the realms of culture, speaking of folk-tales and ritual, moves from culture back to 'Mrs Nature' – the title coyly retaining culture's upper hand – before plunging us into a strange evolutionary saga which speaks of the human simply as organized matter, emerging from those 'inhuman purges'

in the dark backward of evolution of which all living stock
today is the lineal descendant:

> Wherefore, as Mudfords, Audens
> Seth-Smiths, Bonnergees,
> with civic spear and distaff
> we hail a gangrel
> Paleocene pseudo-rat,
> the Ur-Papa of princes
> and crossing-sweepers.

When Auden draws an analogy between Falstaff and Christ,
when he reverts to the idea of the Incarnation in these later
poems, he is making a radical correlation. The named historical subject is not a transcendent being, any more than the
Christian God. Rather Auden's God is that material ground
of being from which the particular creature emerges, deriving
its local powers from a source which remains inscribed in all
its manifestations. The place of the Incarnation is also that
of Carnival, that farewell to the Flesh which is the repeated
loving, affectionate and regretful tone of all the last volumes.
As he wrote in 'Concerning the Unpredictable' in 1970,
discussing the evolutionary view of a universe of choice and
chance depicted by Loren Eiseley, in a study which is a
pervasive influence on these poems:

> Carnival celebrates the unity of our human race as mortal
> creatures, who come into this world and depart from it
> without our consent, who must eat, drink, defecate,
> belch, and break wind in order to live, and procreate
> if our species is to survive. Our feelings about this are
> ambiguous. To us as individuals, it is a cause for
> rejoicing to know that we are not alone, that all of us,
> irrespective of age or sex or rank or talent, are in the
> same boat. As unique persons, on the other hand, all
> of us are resentful that an exception cannot be made in
> our own case. We oscillate between wishing we were
> unreflective animals and wishing we were disembodied
> spirits, for in either case we should not be problematic

to ourselves. The Carnival solution of this ambiguity is
to laugh, for laughter is simultaneously a protest and
an acceptance. During Carnival, all social distinctions
are suspended, even that of sex. (*FA*, p. 471)

This emphasis lies behind the ecological concern of Auden's
later poems. In 'Ode to Terminus' (*CWW*), Hermes takes the
form of that 'God of walls, doors and reticence, nemesis/
[which] overtakes the sacrilegious technocrat'. He 'can teach
us how to alter our gestures', supreme 'translator':

> In this world our colossal immodesty
> has plundered and poisoned, it is possible
>   You still might save us, who by now have
>   learned this: that scientists, to be truthful,
>
> must remind us to take all they say as a
> tall story, that abhorred in the Heav'ns are all
>   self-proclaimed poets who, to wow an
>   audience, utter some resonant lie.

The poem had opened with a reference to those scientific
pronouncements about telescopic or microscopic events which
in the 'elegant euphemisms of algebra' seem harmless enough,
but 'translated/into the vulgar anthropomorphic tongue' are
used as illicit analogues for human behaviour, 'symbolic of/the
crimes and strikes and demonstrations/we are supposed to
gloat on at breakfast'. In the same way, 'Bestiaries Are Out'
had seen the model of the hive used as an ideological defence
of the 'Princes of this world' against revolt (*AH*). Terminus
by contrast tells us that even the most objective of scientific
facts is only an interpretative model. For Terminus, our conviction that 'all visibles do have a definite/outline they stick
to' is only a pragmatic inference. Fog, in the title poem of
Auden's last volume, *Thank You, Fog*, becomes itself a
Christmas Lord of Misrule, reducing outdoors to 'a shapeless
silence' and insulating a 'restful' and 'festive' holiday from 'the
world of work and money'.

There is an interesting corrective to the image of Auden

as a grouchy conservative in his old age in those remarks on Carnival. A satisfactory human life requires paying respect to Prayer, Work and Laughter, he says. Those who try to live by prayer alone become pharisaic, those by work alone, 'insane lovers of power, tyrants who would enslave Nature to their immediate desires – an attempt which can only end in utter catastrophe' (p. 473) – a catastrophe which in several of these poems Auden equates with nuclear war. Against them, Auden gestures positively to those who lack only one of the triad: 'The hippies, it appears to me, are trying to recover the sense of Carnival which is so conspicuously absent in this age, but so long as they reject Work they are unlikely to succeed.' The qualified approval is reiterated in 'Prologue at Sixty' where Auden throws in his lot with a younger genera-tion against the 'Cosmocrats' jumbo-jetting through time-zones, heads of state 'who are not all there' signing secret treaties, a world of 'bugged phones, sophisticated/weapon-systems and sick jokes'.

The accidents of evolution and history have deposited him by 'chance and my own choice' in 'this unenglish tract' of Austria which has seen many successive violations, Turks, Boney's legions, Germans, Russians. No more than the place can the subject rest assured in a fixed, continuous identity: 'Who am I now?' he asks, 'An American?' No, a New Yorker,/who opens his *Times* at the obit. page,/whose dream images date him already, whose day turned out torturers/who read Rilke in their rest periods'.

In 'Joseph Weinheber' (*CWW*) he had written of this same Austria that 'the Shadow/[has] lifted, or rather/moved elsewhere', for 'never as yet/has Earth been without/her bad patch, some unplace with/jobs for torturers'; and had gone on to link this negative utopia with those 'good family men' who now keep a religious watch 'on apparatus/inside which harmless matter/turns homicidal', casting nuclear scientists as bad stewards in the service of a false Prince. Here by contrast Auden disowns the past and present crimes of his own generation, opting instead for the spirit of Carnival which, overthrows differences of age:

Can Sixty make sense to Sixteen-Plus?
What has my camp in common with theirs,
with buttons and beards and Be-Ins?
Much, I hope. In *Acts* it is written
Taste was no problem at Pentecost.

Pentecost for Auden means that speaking with tongues in which a single truth is variously proclaimed.

It is thus that, in the title poem of *Epistle to a Godson*, he delights in the accolade of 'boozy godfather', making connections between his generation and that of the sixties. Asking who he is to 'offer ghostly platitudes/to a young man' he distinguishes between now and 'yester times' when the old 'could nicely envisage the future/as a named and settled landscape their children/would make the same sense of as they did,/laughing and weeping at the same stories'. There is a double-take here, for if it is no longer possible to do this it is only because that earlier generation has been proved wrong in such confidence. Such stories were always lying pastorals, cast in bourgeois terms as tales of honest cobblers and evil counts, actually presuming a world where 'the poor were what they were used to being,/the creators of wealth not, as now they are,/an expensive nuisance.' That this is Auden's sly parody of middle-class selfishness and not his own opinion is confirmed by the parenthesis that follows: 'Nobody/has dared suggest gassing them, but someone/surely will.' It is not the mob, but the 'ochlocratic media' which, as in the age of Stagmantle and Beethameer, rule the roost.

The paradox which opens an ironic gap between 'poor' and 'creators of wealth' is the key. The future which has us 'gallowed shitless' still has its origins in the disparities of political power: 'global Archons' would be 'figures of fun, if/very clever little boys had not found it amusing to build devices for them more/apt at disassembly than any/old fire-spewing theogonic monster'. These nuclear devices can disassemble all political assemblies and their fables of democratic involvement. If what is to happen 'occurs according to what Thucydides/defined as "human", we've had it'. But

Thucydides, describing the degenerations of Greek society brought about by the Peloponnesian War, wrote as an aristocratic pessimist whose culture's fables assumed the unchangingness of human nature. As 'The Greeks and Us' reveals and his contrasts between classical and Christian drama take for granted, Auden assumed no such thing. He starts from an assumption of the transformative character of 'human nature', which has converted a paleocene pseudo-rat into the named and bourgeois creatures at a wedding, flakers of flint into Homer's heroes and then into spacemen. The tongue-in-cheek Jeremiads of this poem are counterbalanced by the witty parentheses which disown them. But power remains a serious business, and 'To be responsible for the happiness/of the Universe is not a sinecure.' On the contrary, the future for the 'elite lands' of the First World may hold a Way of poverty.

It is 'only/the unscarred overfed enjoy Calvary/as a verbal event'. The well-fed pride themselves on their aesthetic refinement, like those torturers who read Rilke in their rest periods. Neither satire nor shoddy workmanship will shame them. The only way to challenge them is to show that we, who care about hunger, also have the best tunes. The impish invocation of his godson's own father's revolutionary past, in the allusion to *The Destructive Element*, suggests that Uncle Wiz is here more subversive than he appears. The utopian dimension of art still holds out the possibility of a reclaimed world, where freedom and order are consonant, not at odds:

> to give a stunning
>
> display of concinnity and elegance
> is the least we can do, and its dominant
> mood should be that of Carnival.
> Let us hymn the small but journal wonders
>
> of Nature and of households, and then finish
> on a serio-comic note with legends
> of ultimate eucatastrophe,
> regeneration beyond the waters.

The poem plays with a paradox only half redeemed by Marx's remark that history repeats itself as farce. Auden had begun by saying that, unlike previous generations, he neither can nor will offer paradigms or advice for the future. He warns against listening to fairy tales – and then tells one. But history is not simply endless novelty. If it were, no tale could outlive its generation. His godson's generation are now repeating the serio-comic follies of Auden's own. Auden's contemporaries are complaining about them in the way Auden's parents did, and this only echoes the patrician grumbling of Thucydides two millennia ago. If all pleasures come from God, Auden goes on, then no individual life is necessary, all are expendable. Nobody owns himself. But in this case, in a happy pun, the expendable is also the spender. Accidentally interpellated to his patronym, young Philip Spender, like all of us, experiences nevertheless that flavour of uniqueness that goes with particular being. Living is a matter of repeatedly reinscribing ourselves in the discourse which names and gives roles. As Auden has to remind himself 'I *am* your godfather', so Philip is advised:

> Be glad your being is unnecessary,
> then turn your toes out as you walk, dear,
> and remember who you are, a Spender.

Throughout these last poems, commitment to the carnal body means insisting, as in *The Dyer's Hand* (p. 87) and the title of section VIII of 'Thanksgiving for a Habitat', on the centrality of Brecht's axiom, 'Grub First, Then Ethics'. Grub feeds the body, the individual. Until it does, there can be no feeding of the soul, the person. The unnecessary genetic accident and the named particular being, both parts of the double man, are equally in need of sustenance; but the order of priority is clear.

If the pleasures of the flesh are celebrated in the centrepiece of *About the House*, 'Thanksgiving for a Habitat', what endows them with value is the certainty that we must lose them. From the very first poem, 'The Birth of Architecture', we are within that shadow: the birth being, ironically, the prehistoric 'gallery grave' which records too the birth of a culture-making species. Every poem is an epitaph – in this one, quite literally, 'The Cave of Making', which records an imaginary conversation 'with the shade of Louis MacNeice. The transit between then and now is 'hardly a tick by the carbon clock, but I/don't count that way nor do you'. The ambiguous colloquialism links human time-scales to humane scales of importance.

For the experiencing individual, there is only the 'still prehistoric *Once*' before experience, and the historical '*After*' which creates its own myths of origin and destination. In that *Once*, all the once-actual moments of living time are condensed into a single compact stratum of pastness, like coal under the immense pressure of the present, the product of a collective patriarch whose whole historical function, it seems to those two foregrounded pronouns, was to produce them:

> to you, to me,
> Stonehenge and Chartres Cathedral,
> the Acropolis, Blenheim, the Albert Memorial
> are works by the same Old Man
> under different names: we know what He did,
> what, even, He thought He thought,
> but we don't see why.

The 'Immortal Commonwealth' of the natural world is a conditioned one; by contrast, the human world is a conditional realm, constituted in discourse, taking umbrage at death and constructing a 'second nature of tomb and temple' only possible to lives that 'know the meaning of *If*'. In the second poem of the sequence that conditional imagining brings the anthropologist's gaze to bear in a double deconstruction. For if the burial rites and codes of honour of the past are disclosed in all their puzzling difference, our own preoccupations are equally estranged:

> Nobody I know would like to be buried
> with a silver cocktail shaker,
> a transistor radio and a strangled
> daily help, or keep his word because
>
> of a great-great-grandmother who got laid
> by a sacred beast.

The irreverent demotic devalues the once authoritative myths and ritual. All ages live on the assumption that they are keeping their word, and all alike break it. For it is in the very nature of the human to act askew to its self-definitions, to be other than it claims, constantly betraying the very words it uses to justify itself. A world 'has still to be built', the first poem had said. This second poem raises doubts about the status of the concept of building itself, for if 'Only a press lord/could have built San Simeon', we need to ask in what sense that building can be attributed to Randolph Hearst rather than to those unnamed workers who actually put bricks to mortar. Class as a discourse of exclusions runs through the sequence. In the first poem, masons and carpenters – the actual makers – were seen as belonging to nature, but architects, the conceivers and commissioners, to the realm of the human. Yet 'no unearned income', the poem says, subverting its own privilege, 'can buy us back. . ./. . . the art/of believing footmen don't hear/human speech.' The language, shifting, labile, in turn betrays all our hierarchies of rank and meaning into a common fallibility.

'The Cave of Making' recalls how Auden and MacNiece 'once collaborated, once at a weird Symposium/exchanged winks as a juggins/went on about Alienation'. Turning an objective process into a subjective one enacts the very alienation of which it speaks. A fact about exploitation in a class society – the alienation of labour into capital, 'unearned income' – becomes a vogue word with which intellectuals make their careers and conceptualize their fashionable despair. But if the poet as 'maker' seems outside this money economy, there is a residual guilt, surfacing in the reproachful unintended ambiguity of the word 'collaborated'. For this is not an innocent context. Auden has just spoken of how 'we shan't, not since Stalin and Hitler, /trust ourselves ever again: we know that, subjectively,/all is possible.' The 'subjective' is constituted only as the reflex of a discourse which carries power in every instance of its utterance, subjecting them to its meanings: their 'ancestors probably/were among those plentiful subjects/it cost less money to murder.' Auden and MacNeice themselves, in a poem which plays off 'good mongrel barbarian English' and 'Roman rhetoric' as systems of power, became self-conscious at a moment when the idiom of chivalry, by Tennyson out of Malory, still held power, and 'the Manor was still politically numinous.' Both experienced those social transformations which emptied the churches, made the cavalry redundant, and offered a new language for interpreting the 'real' ('the Cosmic Model/became German'). In an earlier age, both would have filled a different slot in the social formation, bards to some tribal chief or Baroque Prince. Even now, it would be an illusion to imagine themselves outside the money economy. It may be a 'privilege' to 'serve this unpopular art which cannot be.../...hung as a status trophy by rising executives', but as the connotations of 'privilege' and 'serve' both indicate, autonomy is merely relative. Even here such affluence and privilege as they have is built upon exploitation coyly evoked, to be ostensibly dismissed, in a parenthesis: '(It's heartless to forget about/the underdeveloped countries,/but a starving ear is as deaf as a suburban optimist's...)'. The starving are not good 'clients'.

That other form of subjection returns to haunt the feast in 'Grub First, Then Ethics'. The poet may be able to point to the latest democratic American cooker, blue-printed for a world 'where royalty would be incognito' and all cooks are equal. It may no longer be possible to tell 'who is to give the orders' from a person's hands; now only the host at a dinner-party, not some objective hierarchy of precedent, decides who is to be 'put below the salt'. Such democratic dining is still a privilege, however, 'for the subject of the verb/to-hunger is never a name' but an animal creature excluded from the discourse of subjects. 'Where the/power lies remains to be seen,/the force, though, is clearly with them' – that is, with those tyrants whose language rides the most apparently innocuous words, even 'chefs' and 'master-dish'. The Third World realm upon which this thoroughly modern, 'polite' and 'liberal' kitchen depends for its privileges is still repressed, the theme only of well-fed fantasies about starvation. Everywhere, Auden's poem subverts its own satisfactions. This is the meaning of that ghostly intrusion that repeatedly disturbs the feast, even when, like MacNeice or Plato (the enquirer here), it is welcome.

If death is outside the language, it infiltrates everywhere in this sequence as the sign of a larger guilt, revealed in those fantasies of global extermination for which the speaking subject in some way feels responsible while he casts himself as mere victim. For in whatever language he inscribes himself, he persists hubristically in seeing himself as 'Adam's sovereign clone', a self-sufficient individual, deludedly believing himself 'dominant/over three acres of a blooming/conurbation of country lives'. That this is the hubris of usurpation is disclosed by a wider web of relations. The poem is full of the language of consanguinity, from 'great-great-grandmother', through 'the flesh/Mum formulated', to the 'water-brethren' with whom he recognizes affinity. To wipe away a spider's web is a denial of creatureliness which reveals another aspect of kinship: 'fools/who deface their emblem of guilt/are germane to Hitler.' There is a scale of genocide, in a world whose very vitality is founded in death and, the voice of carnival proclaims, there is no way of quitting the feast.

A culture 'in whose creed/God is edible' must acknowledge its foundation in guilt, as 'Tonight at Seven-Thirty' admits. So, in section II, the food chain is only another aspect of the Chain of Being, where extinction (euphemistically translated as 'translation') is the name of everybody's game:

> I ought
> to outlast the limber dragonflies
>
> as the muscle-bound firs are certainly
>   going to outlast me: I shall not end
> down any esophagus, though I may succumb
>   to a filter-passing predator,
>
> shall, anyhow, stop eating, surrender my smidge
>   of nitrogen to the World Fund
> with a drawn-out *Oh* (unless at the nod
>   of some jittery commander

    I be translated in a nano-second
       to a c.c. of poisonous nothing
  in a giga-death).

As so frequently in these late poems, the apparently casual parenthesis contains the real anxiety, complicity in a world of power that is the obverse of all that festive eating. Chronos who devours his children still presides over these poems, displaced, repressed, evaded in all those euphemisms with which death is denied in the elegy for MacNeice, or translated into the icy evasions of military verbal overkill.

'Geography of the House' reminds of our common fleshiness with a euphemistic joke: the lavatory is what 'Arabs call *the House where/Everybody goes*'. Its primal pleasures again recall the common fact of mortality, figured by the morning visit in which 'we/Leave the dead concerns of/Yesterday behind us.' Far from being a whimsical moment out of the general argument, this poem reminds us, like the bedroom in 'The Cave of Nakedness', that we are 'corporal contraptions'; and that our 'verbal contraptions', whether of poetry or politics, emerge from and dissemble this material base. The prayer in the bog to 'Keep us in our station:/When we get pound-noteish' is thus an apposite one.

The last poem in the sequence spells out that creaturely communism at the bottom of all Auden's late verse, the 'Common Life' which, in spite of murder, makes us inhabitants of 'a common world'. Chronos still presides over history:

        It's a wonder that neither
has been butchered by accident,

or, as lots have, silently vanished into
    History's criminal noise
unmourned for. . .

It is Hermes who is set against Chronos. For 'the sacred spells are secret to the kind', 'and if power is what we wish/they won't work'. Nevertheless, '*The ogre will come in any case*:/so Joyce has warned us.' If this final Hermetic secret were acknowledged,

those jittery commanders, gallowed shitless with their phallic
missiles, might think twice before pulling the chain of being
while sitting in their station.

Throughout his poetry, Auden had been preoccupied with
that process by which, as subjects of language, we are constantly misrepresented to ourselves. The Arcadian function
of poetry lies in its ability to turn language self-reflexively back
upon itself in order to undo the folded lie of ideology. In the
words of 'In Praise of Limestone':

> It has a worldly duty which in spite of itself
> It does not neglect, but calls into question
> All the Great Powers assume: it disturbs our rights...

for it is not a site 'Where something was settled once and for
all', but one where everything has to begin all over again. In
1953 'The Truest Poetry is the Most Feigning' postulated
poetry's origins in the comic tradition, among the sons of
Hermes. 'Good poets have a weakness for bad puns', because
they know that language has to be tricked into meaning. There
is no 'natural man'. The most primitive candidate for the title
is already a construct of culture, a self-made creature whose
very identity lies in self-forgetting, in those repressions out
of which a coherent subject is formed, which lurk, waiting
their chance, in the interstices of every sentence, the corners
of every forthright utterance, as pun, ambivalence, innuendo,
waiting to trip us up in our pomposity and faking. But, then,
the very excess of language, slipping elusively between our
fingers, tripping off the tongue, testifies to its origins in a public
world, refuses to be pinned down to our authorial and authoritative statements, for every statement is made while standing
in some station or other, though it posits its own position as
absolute, outside the language:

> For given Man, by birth, by education,
> Imago Dei who forgot his station,
> The self-made creature who himself unmakes,
> The only creature ever made who fakes,

> With no more nature in his loving smile
> Than in his theories of a natural style,
> What but tall tales, the luck of verbal playing,
> Can trick his lying nature into saying
> That love, or truth in any serious sense,
> Like orthodoxy, is a reticence?

The poem too turns back on itself, to swallow its own tall tale.

Auden's commonplace book, *A Certain World*, was published in 1971. It is thus a fairly authoritative expression of the late Auden's viewpoint. Its last entry is an account of the way language construes the material world as it articulates the verbalizing I. Writing, he says, originates not in the writer but in an already constituted dialogue, the trace of 'encounters, in the primary world, with sacred beings or events':

> Even the purest poem, in the French sense, is made of words, which are not the poet's private property but the communal creation of the linguistic group to which he belongs, so that their meaning can be looked up in a dictionary. (p. 424)

The dictionary is not the final resort of textuality, but the place where textuality opens into history, where words can be held down to their commitments. If we have no 'nature' in ourselves, we should beware of those 'natural styles' which attempt to recruit us to their absolute 'truth'. Yet at the same time, the idea of a 'personal' truth set against the public lies is the most deceptive illusion of all, the romantic lie in the brain of the sensual man in the street, the delusion of personal autonomy. The self-made creature who himself unmakes is made and unmade again and again in the infoldings and unfoldings of language. Language can be turned back on itself in a deconstructive movement that reads its stutterings and falterings, the point where its polished antitheses break down, those moments of self-forgetting where the creases show.

Auden's notorious intellectual eclecticism is not a weakness. Like his macaronic style, his deliberate collisions of idiom and image, his frequent metonymies and puns, it points to the artifice of language, reminds us of what is left out, left over, in every utterance. Comprehensiveness and coherence can, as he proposed in *New Year Letter*, be the clearest sign of that absolutist fore-closure which is the enemy of truth. It is in the provisional and speculative, the play of signifiers that constantly subvert their own tendency to settle into platitude, that the unicorn of meaning, that mythical beast on which we found all our projects, may flash whitely among the cedars. The very disparity and incongruity of Auden's 'influences' have this function. For it is where Marx and Freud, Christianity and Nietzsche do not fit, where the congruence slides under the smoothing hand and the soothing tongue of language, that an insight hides. The punning correspondences between overlaid systems of thought only expose more clearly the residual differences where meaning loiters. The uncontainable surplus always runs ahead of any movement to closure, inviting us to begin again, read of our losses.

'Truth' is not the absolute possession of a privileged subject. Rather it secretes itself in the gaps between one subject and another, one sign and the next, in a common and divided world. Auden's terms in *A Certain World* are Christian, but their tenor is socialist:

> What the poet has to convey is not 'self-expression', but a view of reality common to all, seen from a unique perspective, which it is his duty as well as his pleasure to share with others. To small truths as well as great, St Augustine's words apply.
>
> 'The truth is neither mine nor his nor another's; but belongs to us all whom Thou callest to partake of it, warning us terribly, not to account it private to ourselves, lest we be deprived of it'. (p. 425)

In 1936, in 'Letter to Lord Byron', he wrote scathingly of that Home Counties vision of the future, all plate-glass, chromium-plating and Aertex underwear, as no more than the ideology of the well-to-do, their worries too personal and their cars too fast 'To look too closely at the wheeling view'. In the north, 'the old historic battlefield', he suggested, 'The scars of struggle are as yet unhealed.' The scars are the traces of a struggle that continues, where there is no easy healing into wholeness. The unitary subject and the unitary nation are alike mythical beasts, traversed by a class struggle that may abate from time to time, but never ceases. I write at the beginning of the ninth month of the Miners' Strike, on a day when a British state apparatus unequivocally committed to the victory of *its* ruling class has brought the full weight of the law to bear on that struggle, through its courts appointing an official receiver to take over the assets of the NUM. Fifty years after Auden the Yorkshireman wrote those lines, that 'old heroic battlefield' is still the front line. Whatever the outcome of this dispute, one thing is sure: there can be no 'final solution' for the ruling class, as long as it continues to rule. For as long as there is power there will be resistance. No unitary 'truth' can hold undisputed sway –

> Well, you might think so if you went to Surrey
> And stayed for week-ends with the well-to-do
> · · ·
>
> But in the north it simply isn't true.
> To those who live in Warrington or Wigan,
> It's not a white lie, it's a whacking big 'un.

Notes

Chapter 1　The Folded Lie: Auden and Ideology

1 *Thought*, September 1950.
2 Joseph Warren Beach, *The Making of the Auden Canon* (Minneapolis, University of Minnesota, 1957).
3 Ibid., pp. 92, 96, 250.
4 Ibid., p. 253.
5 John G. Blair, *The Poetic Art of W. H. Auden* (Princeton, N.J., Princeton University Press, 1965).
6 Ibid., pp. 1–9.
7 Herbert Greenberg, *Quest for the Necessary: W. H. Auden and the Dilemma of the Divided Consciousness* (Cambridge, Mass., Harvard University Press, 1968), pp. 2, 6–7, 196.
8 Gerald Nelson, *Changes of Heart* (Berkeley and Los Angeles, University of California Press, 1969), p. 145.
9 George W. Bahlke, *The Later Auden* (New Brunswick, Rutgers University Press, 1970), pp. 22, 26, 147, 150.
10 Frederick Buell, *W. H. Auden as a Social Poet* (Ithaca, N.Y., Cornell University Press, 1973), pp. 73, 1, 19–20.
11 François Duchêne, *The Case of the Helmeted Airman* (London, Chatto and Windus, 1972), pp. 200ff., 24, 106, 181, 156.
12 Richard Johnson, *Man's Place* (Ithaca, N.Y., Cornell University Press, 1973), pp. ix, xii.
13 Ibid., p. 246.
14 Edward Callan, *Carnival of Intellect* (Oxford and New York, Oxford University Press, 1983), p. 20.
15 Blair, *The Poetic Art*, pp. 65–74.
16 Edward Mendelson, *Early Auden* (London, Faber and Faber, 1981), pp. 361, 364, 365.

17 Lack of space precludes a fuller discussion of Auden's critical reception here. Part of this has already appeared in Stan Smith, 'Auditing Auden', in *Literature and History*, autumn 1984.

18 Monroe K. Spears, *The Poetry of W. H. Auden: The Disenchanted Island* (New York, Oxford University Press, 1963), pp. 45, 102.

19 Ibid., pp. 144–5.

20 Beach, *The Making of the Auden Canon*, p. 226.

21 Dennis Davison, *W. H. Auden* (London, Evans Bros, 1970), pp. 17–19.

22 W. H. Auden, 'The Group Movement and the Middle Classes', in R. H. S. Crossman, *Oxford and the Groups* (Oxford, Basil Blackwell, 1934), p. 90.

23 See the essay on 'Ideology and Ideological State Apparatuses', in his book *Lenin and Philosophy* (London, New Left Books, 1971).

Chapter 2   Dissolving the Mask: The Early Poems

1 'Criticism in a Mass Society', in Donald A. Stauffer ed. *The Intent of the Critic* (Princeton, N.J., Princeton University Press, 1941), pp. 131–5.

2 Edward Mendelson, *Early Auden* (London, Faber and Faber, 1981), pp. 65–80.

3 J. K. Galbraith, *The Great Crash 1929* (London, Penguin, 1961), p. 25.

4 Christopher Caudwell, *Illusion and Reality* (London, Macmillan 1937; new edn London, Laurence & Wishart, 1946, p. 257ff).

Chapter 3   Read of Your Losses: *The Orators*

1 Richard Johnson, *Man's Place* (Ithaca, N.Y., Cornell University Press, 1973), p. 72.

2 Justin Replogle, *Auden's Poetry* (Seattle, University of Washington Press, 1969), pp. 110–12.

Chapter 4   The Look of the Stranger

1 Charles Osborne, *W. H. Auden: The Life of a Poet* (London, Methuen, 1980), p. 129.

2 Edward Mendelson, *Early Auden* (London, Faber and Faber, 1981), p. 167.

Chapter 5   No Favourite Suburb: Letters from Iceland, Sonnets from China

1 Edward Callan, *Carnival of Intellect* (Oxford and New York, Oxford University Press, 1983), pp. 133–4.
2 Ibid., pp. 131–5.
3 Edward Mendelson, *Early Auden* (London, Faber and Faber, 1981), pp. 357–8.
4 Charles Osborne, *W. H. Auden: The Life of a Poet* (London, Methuen, 1980), pp. 206–7.

Chapter 6   Conscripts to Our Age: *New Year Letter*

1 Humphrey Carpenter, *W. H. Auden: A Biography* (London, Allen and Unwin, 1981), pp. 306–9.
2 John Fuller, *A Reader's Guide to W. H. Auden* (London, Thames and Hudson, 1970), pp. 138–9.
3 Ibid., p. 143.
4 Ibid., p. 139.
5 Ibid., p. 138.
6 Edward Callan, *Carnival of Intellect* (Oxford and New York, Oxford University Press, 1983), p. 176.

Chapter 7   My Father's Prick: The Long Poems

1 The pun is pointed, and to the point. In *A Certain World*, under the heading 'Double-Entendre, Unconscious', Auden observes 'It must have been sheer inattention. . .that permitted Laurence Binyon to write: 'Why hurt so hard by little pricks?' (p. 122). Auden's attention is standing to it, here.

Chapter 8   Caesar and Clio: Poetry under a Faffling Flag

1 Edward Callan, *Carnival of Intellect*, (Oxford and New York, Oxford University Press, 1983), p. 16.
2 Richard Johnson, *Man's Place* (Ithaca, N.Y., Cornell University Press, 1973), pp. 169–71.

Select Bibliography

Because of his many revisions and excisions, Auden's work presents particular difficulties for the bibliographer. Some of these are discussed in Joseph Warren Beach, *The Making of the Auden Canon* (Minneapolis, University of Minnesota Press, 1957). The standard bibliographies are B. C. Bloomfield, *W. H. Auden: A Bibliography: The Early Years Through 1955*, and B. C. Bloomfield and Edward Mendelson, *W. H. Auden: A Bibliography 1924–1969* (Charlottesville, University Press of Virginia, 1964 and 1972). This is supplemented by Addenda in *The Library*, 6th series, vol. 4, 1 March 1982. See also Joseph P. Clancy, 'A W. H. Auden Bibliography 1924–1955', in *Thought* (Fordham University), xxx (Summer 1955). The major biographies are Humphrey Carpenter, *W. H. Auden: A Biography* (London, Allen and Unwin, 1981) and Charles Osborne, *W. H. Auden: The Life of a Poet* (London, Methuen, 1980), but important biographical material is also contained in Edward Mendelson, *Early Auden* (London, Faber and Faber, 1981). Carpenter lists manuscript collections.

Reasons of space preclude a fuller bibliography here. The list below confines itself to separate single volumes of Auden's work which contain substantially new or revised material. All of the poems and some of the 1930s prose discussed here can be found in either W. H. Auden, *Collected Poems*, edited by Edward Mendelson (London, Faber and Faber, 1976), or *The English Auden: Poems, Essays and Dramatic Writings 1927–1939*, edited by Edward Mendelson (London, Faber and Faber, 1977), to whose scrupulous scholarship all Auden critics are indebted.

Critical studies of Auden are not included here. A guide to this work can be found in Martin E. Gingerich: *W. H. Auden: A Reference Guide* (Boston, Mass., G. K. Hall; London, Prior, 1977) and can be supplemented by the checklists in *W. H. Auden: The Critical Heritage*, edited by John Haffenden (London, Routledge & Kegan Paul, 1983), which is a substantial collection of original reviews of Auden's work as published. Bibliographical information on critics discussed here has been provided in the end notes to the text.

Poems have usually been quoted from the first text in which they appeared in that form. The initials after the various titles below are the abbreviations used throughout the text. Fuller bibliographical information on Auden and his contemporaries can be found in my *20th Century Poetry* (London, Macmillan, 1983). Except where otherwise stated all volumes are published by Faber and Faber, London, and Random House, New York. Where the date of American publication precedes that of the English, the American date has been added in brackets.

Poems, privately printed by Stephen Spender, 1928; reprinted by University Microfilms, Michigan, Ann Arbor, 1966.

Poems, 1930; 2nd edn, with changes, 1933.

Poems, 1934; N.Y., Random House (contains *Poems*, 1933, *Orators*, *Dance of Death*).

The Orators: An English Study 1932; 2nd edn 1934; 3rd edn 1966.

The Dance of Death 1933.

The Poet's Tongue (ed., with John Garrett), London, G. Bell & Sons, 1935.

The Dog Beneath the Skin (with Christopher Isherwood), 1936; revised text, N.Y., Random House, 1937.

Look, Stranger!, 1936; as *On This Island*, N.Y., Random House, 1937.

Spain, 1937.

Letters from Iceland (with Louis MacNeice), 1937; 2nd edn 1969.

The Oxford Book of Light Verse (ed.), Oxford, Oxford University Press, 1938.

On the Frontier (with Christopher Isherwood), 1938.

Education Today – and Tomorrow (with T. C. Worsley), London, Hogarth Press, 1939.

Journey to a War (*JW*) (with Christopher Isherwood), 1939; 2nd edn, with changes, 1973.

Another Time, 1940.

New Year Letter, 1940; as *The Double Man*, with textual differences, N.Y., Random House 1941.

For the Time Being, 1945 (1944).

The Collected Poetry, N.Y., Random House, 1945.

The Age of Anxiety, 1948 (1947).

Collected Shorter Poems, 1930–1944, 1950.

The Enchafèd Flood, 1951 (1950).

Nones, 1952 (1951).

The Rake's Progress (with Chester Kallman), London, Boosey and Hawkes, 1951.

The Shield of Achilles 1955.

The Magic Flute (with Chester Kallman), N.Y., Random House, 1956.

W. H. Auden: A Selection By the Author, London, Penguin Books, 1958.

Homage to Clio, 1960.

Elegy for Young Lovers (with Chester Kallman), N.Y., Schott, 1966.

The Dyer's Hand (*DH*), 1963 (1962).

About the House (*AH*), 1966 (1965).

The Bassarids (with Chester Kallman), N.Y., Schott, 1966.
Collected Shorter Poems, 1927–1957, 1966.
Collected Longer Poems, 1968.
Secondary Worlds (*SW*), 1969.
City Without Walls (*CWW*), 1969.
A Certain World: A Commonplace Book (*CW*), 1971 (1970).
Academic Graffiti, 1971.
Epistle to a Godson (*EG*), 1972.
Love's Labours Lost (with Chester Kallman), Berlin, Bote and Bock, 1972.
Forewords and Afterwords (*FA*), 1973.
Thank You, Fog, 1974.
Collected Poems, ed. Edward Mendelson, 1976.
The English Auden (*EA*), ed. Edward Mendelson, 1977.
Selected Poems, new edn, ed. Edward Mendelson, 1979.

Books with a Contribution by Auden

An Outline for Boys and Girls and Their Parents, ed. Naomi Mitchison, 'Writing, or The Pattern Between People', London, Gollancz, 1932.
Oxford and the Groups, ed. R. H. S. Crossman, 'The Group Movement and the Middle Classes', Oxford, Basil Blackwell, 1934.
The Old School, ed. Graham Greene, 'Honour', London, Jonathan Cape, 1934.
The Arts To-day, ed. Geoffrey Grigson, 'Psychology and Art To-day', London, John Lane: The Bodley Head, 1935.
Christianity and the Social Revolution, ed. John Lewis, 'The Good Life', London, Gollancz, 1935.
Poems of Freedom, ed. John Mulgan, 'Introduction', London, The Left Book Club, 1938.
I Believe, ed. Clifton Fadiman, untitled essay, London, Allen and Unwin, 1939.
The Intent of the Critic, ed. Donald A. Stauffer, 'Criticism in a Mass Society', Princeton, Princeton University Press, 1941.
Poets at Work (*PAW*), ed. Charles D. Abbott, 'Squares and Oblongs', N.Y., Harcourt, Brace, 1948.
Modern Canterbury Pilgrims, ed. the Dean of New York, Oxford, A. R. Mowbray & Co., 1956.
The Kafka Problem, ed. Angel Flores, 'K's Quest', N.Y., Gordian Press, 1975.

Index

All texts by Auden (volumes, individual poems, essays and reviews) are indexed separately, except for the two definitive collections of poetry and the two volumes of collected essays, forewords and afterwords cited as sources throughout the text.